Rules Get Broken

John Herbert

Oakley Publishing Company, Inc.

Printed in the United States of America.

For information address:

Oakley Publishing, Inc.
140 Broadway, 46th Floor
New York, NY 10005

Library of Congress Cataloging-in-Publication Data

Herbert, John

Rules Get Broken/John Herbert

Library of Congress Control Number: 2009921703

p. cm.

ISBN: 978-0-9818400-4-8

First Edition

10 9 8 7 6 5 4 3 2 1

Visit our Web site at
http://www.oakleypublishingcompany.com

To Jerry

Bob Wieland

To Nancy—

Who first saved my life

And then taught me how to live it.

Prologue

One

I've come here today to be with my wife.

The January wind whips at my pants and bites at my exposed cheeks. The ground under my feet is frozen, hard as stone, and the grass crunches like gravel when I step on it. The late afternoon light is fading rapidly, and a flat gray sky promises that the snow the forecasters are predicting will materialize shortly.

I look around me. As far as I can see, there is not another soul in sight. I look down at my feet and shiver, and I remember a telephone call on a Sunday morning two summers ago.

The telephone had rung that morning at ten minutes after seven, and I wondered who could be calling at that hour as I ran to the phone. I picked up the receiver on the third ring, and the voice at the other end asked for Mr. Herbert.

"Which one?" I replied automatically, knowing that I recognized the voice.

"Mr. John Herbert," the caller answered.

"Is this Dr. Werner?" I asked.

"Yes, it is," the caller replied.

But that's really the middle of my story. So much happened before that phone call. And after.

I should start at the beginning. Thanksgiving Day, 1968.

Two

I was 22 in 1968—single, Protestant, college graduate as of June, my parents' only child, philosophically conservative, not bad-looking.

I spent Thanksgiving Day that year at my grandparents' home with my parents, my aunt and uncle and their four daughters—just as I had every year since I was born.

Thanksgiving Day was always the same. Every year after dinner the women and children would clear the table while my father and uncle retired to the living room. Then, as soon as everything had been brought into the kitchen, my grandfather would invite his five grandchildren to join him in his Thanksgiving Day walk around the block to make room for dessert.

When we were little my cousins and I always argued about who got to walk next to Grandpa and hold his hand. My grandfather wisely settled this annual disagreement by dividing the walk into thirds, with two of us getting to walk next to him for the first third, two of us the second third and, best of all, one of us the last third on the final leg back to the house. To this day I think that was his way of rewarding patience.

As we got older we voluntarily broke into two groups of three, the first group consisting of the two youngest grandchildren on either side of my grandfather and the second group consisting of the three older grandchildren bringing up the rear. Year after year our walk, like Thanksgiving, was the same.

But in 1968, our Thanksgiving walk was different. Different because, although I didn't know it at the time, our Thanksgiving walk that year would set into motion a series of events that would shape my life forever.

My grandfather was walking up ahead with my two youngest cousins, Kimberly, 13, and Meredith, 11, while my two older cousins, Christine and Sarah, were walking behind with me. Christine was 23. Sarah was 22.

The three of us had always been close, and young adulthood had not yet changed that. The girls walked on either side of me, and each had an arm through mine as we either took part in or disengaged from the conversation that my grandfather was having in front of us with the two younger girls. During one of the moments of disengagement Sarah asked me what I was doing for New Year's Eve.

"I don't know," I answered with a shrug. "I'll probably stay home. Or go out with my folks."

"How come?" Sarah asked. "That doesn't sound like you."

"Well, to tell the truth, I don't know anybody around here to ask out. All the familiar faces have disappeared since I went away to college, so… I think it's gonna be a quiet night."

"I'm going to be in the same position, I guess," Sarah admitted sadly. "I mean, not that I would have expected anyone to ask me out this far in advance, but I don't know of anyone out there who might even ask."

We walked for the next minute or so without saying anything, listening instead to Meredith tell Grandpa about some boy in her class.

Suddenly Sarah squeezed my arm and gave me a coquettish look. "You know, I just might have an idea that would work for both of us. For New Year's Eve, I mean."

"Oh yeah? What?" I asked, less than enthusiastically.

"Well," Sarah began, "there's this girl I know at work. Her name is Peggy. Peggy Reilly. She's nice, really nice, and I think you'd like her. And if you could get me a date with Ted Norris, I'll get you a date with Peggy, and we can go out for New Year's Eve together."

Ted had been my roommate at college, and Sarah had met him over the summer at a family barbecue. He had been a starting halfback on the university's football team and was now in his second year of medical school at Seton Hall University. He was big, good looking, a lot of fun to be with, and like me, had recently broken up with the girl he had dated through college. He was any girl's dream date, so this was a great idea for Sarah, but not one that particularly excited me.

"A blind date for New Year's Eve? Sarah, you gotta be kidding me. You are kidding me, right?"

"No," she replied without a second's hesitation. "I'm dead serious. I would love to go out with Ted, and I know you'd really like Peggy."

I shook my head. "Peggy Reilly, is it?"

"That's right."

"She's Irish, I presume?"

"Yes, she's Irish. So what? What difference does that make?"

"Sarah, you know me. I'm not Irish, and I'm sure as hell not Catholic. What would ever make you think that a good Irish Catholic girl and I would get along?"

"Well, I'd like to think you wouldn't get into a heated discussion about sex or religion," Sarah shot back. "This is supposed to be a date, stupid. A fun evening. Nothing else."

"And tell me again why you think I'd really like this Peggy Reilly," I asked, ignoring the look of exasperation on Sarah's face.

"Well, for one thing, she has a great sense of humor and…"

"Oh God, Sarah. I don't believe you just said that."

"Said what?"

"That she has a great sense of humor. That's what every girl says about every girl that she's trying to get a date for. 'She's got a great sense of humor.' No, I don't think I like this idea."

I could see that I had offended her. She withdrew her arm from mine and wrapped both her arms around herself as we rounded the last corner of the block and started to head back to the house.

"Well, all I can say is, she does have a great sense of humor. And she's not ugly, if that's what you're thinking."

"Is she good looking?" I asked as gently as I could.

"Yes," Sarah answered, again without a second's hesitation. "She's very good looking. Some people might even say she's beautiful."

The sensible part of my brain told me to change the subject, or better yet, to say nothing at all, but the other part of my brain, the part that always got me in trouble, told me to find out more about this Peggy Reilly. As was all too often the case, I listened to the other part.

"Describe her to me."

"Why?" Sarah asked, obviously annoyed. "She's Irish, and she's Catholic."

"Okay. I shouldn't have said that. I shouldn't have even thought it. Now describe her for me."

Sarah took my arm again. "Let's see. She's about maybe five eight. She's slim, not skinny or anything like that, but definitely not heavy. And she has black hair, really thick black hair, down to her shoulders, and she has blue eyes. Beautiful, brilliant blue eyes. I think she's beautiful."

"You do?"

"I do."

"And you wouldn't lie to me just to get a date with Ted for New Year's Eve?"

"Yes, I would," Sarah replied with a teasing look in her eyes, "but this time I don't have to."

I shook my head again. "You're too much, Sarah," I said with a sigh. "Tell you what I'll do. I'll call Ted tomorrow and see if he's free for New Year's Eve and if he'd like to take you out. If he says yes, then you can see what this Peggy says when you see her Monday morning. How's that?"

"That's great!" Sarah exclaimed as she gave my arm an excited squeeze. "And I know you're going to love her."

"I better, Sarah, or your name is mud."

Sarah just giggled and gave my arm another squeeze as my grandfather and the two girls on either side of him slowed down and turned onto the walk leading up to my grandparents' house and my grandmother's pies.

Three

I was about to hang up when Ted answered his telephone on what must have been the tenth or eleventh ring.

"Ted, where the hell were you?"

"Who's this?"

"John. John Herbert."

"John. Long time, no hear. What d'ya mean, where the hell was I? I'm here. In my apartment. In New Jersey."

"I know that, Ted. But you took so long to answer the phone, I ...never mind."

"So now that we got that out of the way," Ted said lightly, "what's up?"

"Well, first a question. What are you doing New Year's Eve?"

"That's the name of a song, isn't it?" Ted asked.

"I think so, but answer the question, will you?"

"Why? You want to take me out? I'm an expensive date, pal. I eat a lot, and I drink a lot."

"Yeah, but at least you're easy."

"That's true. I'm easy."

"Seriously though," I continued, "what are you doing New Year's Eve?"

Ted let out a sigh loud enough for me to hear, and the tone of his voice became serious. "Nothing, probably. Not a goddamn thing. What about you?"

"Well, that kind of depends. On you. Do you by any chance remember my cousin Sarah? Sarah O'Connell? You met her at the barbecue at my parents' house in July?"

"The blond?" Ted asked after a moment's thought. "The skinny blond?"

"Well, I would have said the slender blond, but yes, the skinny blond."

"Yeah, I remember her. Skinny but funny. Seemed like a nice kid. Why?"

"Well, I was with Sarah yesterday while I was at my grandparents' house for Thanksgiving, and she made it pretty clear she'd like to go out with you sometime."

"She's got good taste, that Sarah. That's another thing I liked about her."

"Let me finish, will you?"

"Sorry."

"So, inasmuch as she doesn't have a date for New Year's Eve yet and you and I don't have dates for New Year's Eve yet, I thought that maybe..."

"You want to tag along with Sarah and me on our big night out? I don't think so, John."

"Ted," I moaned in exasperation.

"Sorry."

"Anyway, she has a friend. A very attractive friend, she says, and if you want to go out with Sarah, she'll fix me up with her friend, and the four of us can go out together for New Year's Eve. What do you think?"

"Why don't you take Sarah, and I'll take the very attractive friend?" Ted asked without any hint he was kidding. He must have heard me slap my palm against my forehead. "Sorry. Just kidding," he assured me.

"Well, what do you say?" I asked.

Several seconds passed before Ted replied. "Yeah. Sure," he said finally. "What the hell. Sounds like fun. I think Sarah and I could have a good time."

"Great. So I can tell Sarah you'll take her out New Year's Eve?"

"Isn't that what we've been talking about?"

"Yes, Ted. That's what we've been talking about. But I just wanted to make sure we were on the same track before I told Sarah you'd be taking her out."

"We're on the same track, little buddy. Just let me know the time and place."

"I will, Ted. Hey. It just might be a fun evening."

"For you maybe. You got the good-looking one."

"Yeah, well, we'll see about that, won't we?"

"You sure will, little buddy," Ted replied with a drawn-out emphasis on the "sure."

I ignored his implication of impending disaster. "Take care, Ted. I'll call you in a couple of weeks, and we can sort out the details. Figure out where we want to go and all that. Okay?"

"You got it, pal. See you around."

Four

It rained all day on New Year's Eve 1968. The weather forecasters had said the rain would start to taper off around five-thirty that evening and the skies would be clear by eight—good news for the hundreds of thousands of people planning to gather in Times Square to watch the ball come down and welcome in 1969.

Unfortunately, the weather forecasters were wrong. When Ted and I arrived at Sarah's house at seven-thirty that night, a cold and penetrating rain was falling in sheets and showed no sign whatsoever of abating. In addition to the rain, fog was beginning to form, making the conditions just about as unpleasant as possible.

"This really rots," Ted complained as we struggled to put on our raincoats before getting out of the car, me in the driver's seat, Ted in the passenger seat.

"What rots?" I asked, wondering for a moment if Ted was having second thoughts about the evening.

"The rain," Ted replied. "By the time we get to the front door, we'll look like drowned rats."

"Don't worry about it, Ted," I said with a grunt, finally succeeding in getting my left arm in the raincoat sleeve. "Sarah'll love you no matter what you look like."

"Yeah, right," Ted grumbled. "You ready?"

"I'm set if you are."

As if on cue, we threw open our respective car doors, sprang from the car simultaneously and ran up the brick walk to Sarah's front door. We reached her front steps in a matter of seconds, but not before we were both soaked, so we stood on her front porch for a moment, out of the rain, wiping the water from our faces and shaking it off our raincoats.

"Shit," Ted muttered.

"What now?" I asked as I rang the doorbell.

"Nothing. Other than that I'm soaked."

I was about to tell him to stop complaining when I heard the lock turn on the inside of the front door. A second later and the door opened, bathing both of us in the bright light from Sarah's front foyer.

"Hi," Sarah said cheerfully. "I thought maybe you'd be late, what with the rain and all."

"Naw, it's not that bad," I replied, giving Ted a gentle push forward to signal him to enter first.

He took one step forward into the foyer and then stopped just inside the front door. In an instant, he transformed himself from grouch to charmer and, ever the shy one, wrapped a wet arm around Sarah's shoulders, pulled her into his side and gave her a quick but firm kiss.

"Happy New Year, Sarah," he boomed.

"Happy New Year to you too, Ted," Sarah giggled, turning away and out of his grasp, "even if it is four and half hours too early."

"And who do we have here?" he asked, still blocking the front door and oblivious to the fact that I was still standing outside on the front porch.

"Hey, Ted, any chance we can all meet one another after I get inside?" I interrupted, starting to push him further into the foyer so I could come in too.

"Oh, yeah," he replied. "Sorry."

"Hi, John," Sarah said, still giggling at Ted and his boldness. She took my hand, pulled me inside and gave me a little peck on the cheek. "How are you?" she asked.

"Wet. How about you?"

11

"I'm fine," she answered. She closed the front door, then turned around and looked at me.

"And now," she announced dramatically, "I'd like you to meet my very best friend, Peggy Reilly."

It was only then that I saw the woman who until now had been blocked from my view by Ted's bulk. She stepped partly around Ted and toward me and extended her hand.

"Hi," Peggy Reilly said. That was all. Just "Hi."

She gave me a quick smile that faded as quickly as it had appeared. A smile that immediately made me wonder what kind of first impression I had made on her. *Apparently not great,* I thought as I shook hands with her.

But Sarah was right. This Peggy Reilly was beautiful. Truly a striking woman. She was tall, like Sarah had said. Tall and slender. She had thick, black shining hair that hung in gentle waves down to her shoulders, and the contrast of the black hair against her white skin only made her more striking. She was wearing a simple tailored black dress with a small string of white pearls around her neck. Again the contrast of the black dress against her white skin was wonderful. But the thing that impressed me most in the few seconds that her hand was in mine was her eyes. Her incredible eyes. They were brilliant, brilliant blue. Bluer than any eyes I had ever seen, and so clear and sparkling I felt like I could look into them forever.

"Hi. Nice to meet you," I stammered.

"Nice to meet you," Peggy replied.

"Let me have your coats," Sarah interjected. "Then we can go downstairs, and you guys can make us a drink before we leave. What time are our reservations?"

"Eight-thirty," I said, struggling to get out of the wet raincoat. "So we have a little time."

The raincoat over my sport jacket was not an easy combination to undo. Ted had had time to get out of his raincoat while I was being introduced to Peggy, and he immediately handed it to Sarah. For some reason that put me under pressure to get rid of mine equally quickly, and I started to hurry. Seeing me struggle, Sarah tried to help me by grabbing the back of my raincoat while I tried to get my arms out of its sleeves without pulling my jacket off at the same time. Thanks to our combined efforts the raincoat suddenly came off, but when it did, it came off in a wide sweeping arc, hitting an umbrella stand to the right of the front door, knocking it over and sending four or five umbrellas skittering across the foyer floor.

The umbrellas hadn't come to a complete stop before Ted added to my embarrassment. "Nice move, John," he boomed again. "Why don't you wreck Sarah's house while you have a minute?"

But more notably, Peggy, who by now was standing a little apart from Sarah and me with her arms folded across her chest, also chimed in.

"Gee, Sarah, he's not even cool."

"You got that right," I reluctantly agreed with a laugh.

I looked over at Peggy as I picked up the umbrellas one by one and put them back in the now upright stand and tried to estimate how much damage I had done to myself. She stood perfectly still, her arms still folded across her chest, taking in everything I was doing. Our eyes met, and she gave me a wink and a smile. And in the split second we stood there looking at one another, I realized her "Gee, Sarah, he's not even cool" comment had been a test, and I had passed.

I looked at her for another second or two, smiled and turned towards Sarah. "You were right, Sarah," I said.

"About what?" asked Sarah, as she finished hanging up my raincoat and closed the foyer closet door.

"About Peggy Reilly. She is beautiful."

Five

Peggy Reilly and I dated for twenty-one months. On Friday night, October 3rd, 1970, I took Peggy to Harry's New York Bar in Manhattan and asked her to marry me. She said yes.

We were married on October 10th, 1971, at Saint Cecilia's Roman Catholic Church in Englewood, New Jersey, the church where Peggy had been baptized, had received her First Communion, and had been confirmed. The ceremony was to have been presided over by Peggy's parish priest, who was, of course, Roman Catholic, and by my parish priest, who was Episcopal. But my parish priest never showed up. The ceremony was beautiful anyway.

Our wedding reception was at Tamcrest, an exclusive and expensive country club north of Englewood. Peggy's mother had suggested the Knights of Columbus hall because that was all she could afford, but Peggy had a vision of her wedding day, and the Knights of Columbus hall wasn't in it. So with her mother's permission, she paid for the reception herself. Coming up with that kind of money wasn't easy, and she almost came up short, but almost doesn't count.

For two and a half years we lived in a two-bedroom apartment in Freeport on the south shore of Long Island. The apartment was only a two-block walk to the Long Island Railroad station, which was great for Peg's commute into Manhattan and only a twenty-five minute drive to where I worked in Westbury, which was great for me.

In 1974 we bought our first house, in Huntington on the north shore of Long Island. A delightful old center-hall Dutch colonial with four bedrooms, a bath and a half, a small but adequate kitchen, a living room, a dining room, a beautiful sunroom, and a spacious addition to the original house that became our family room. We worked on our house constantly. We scraped, spackled, sanded, painted and papered. Together, we made our house our own.

In 1977 we had our first child, a daughter named Jennie, and in 1979 our second, a son named John.

Life was good. Together we built a life that made our families proud, and the Irish girl with the thick, black shining hair and the brilliant blue eyes became the center of my world.

Book
One

Six

Monday morning, July 28th, 1980, twenty minutes after nine.

"Good morning. North Shore Medical Group. How may I direct your call?"

Peg sat at the kitchen table, her third cup of coffee in front of her. John sat in his high chair next to her, happily sucking away at his bottle, Jennie across from her trying very hard to keep her crayon inside the lines on this her fourth picture of the day. Unwashed dishes were stacked in the sink, and a basket full of dirty laundry stood in front of the cellar door waiting to be taken down to the laundry room.

"Uh, yes. Dr. Edwards' office, please."

"One moment please," the operator replied.

Peg was put on hold for several seconds and then heard another line start to ring. Once, twice, three times, five times.

She looked absentmindedly at Jennie, then at John. *What beautiful kids,* she thought as the telephone on the other end of the line rang for the tenth time.

Jennie with her light brown hair. Wavy. Wispy. Her chipmunk cheeks. Her excited little smile. Those beautiful big blue eyes. A china doll, her grandfather called her.

And John. The happiest little guy you could imagine. Big, square head. Super fine, pale brown baby hair lying flat on his scalp. Big grin. Big dimples. The perfect little Irishman. Ready to tackle the world and everything in it.

19

"God, I'm beat," she said out loud. She picked up her coffee cup only to realize it was empty. She shook her head in exasperation and wondered how someone could listen to a telephone ring this many times without picking it up.

Finally, a voice came on the other end of the line. "Dr. Edwards' office."

"Hi. Good morning. This is Peggy Herbert. I'm a patient of Dr. Edwards."

"Yes, Mrs. Herbert. How are you?"

"Well not too good, I guess. Which is why I'm calling. I spent most of the weekend on our couch, too tired to do anything. I'm not in pain or sick to my stomach or anything like that. I'm just exhausted. More tired than I've ever been in my life. Anyway, I was wondering if Dr. Edwards could see me today?"

"Oh, I don't think today will be possible," said the voice on the other end of the line. "But let me check."

Peg could hear the woman sigh and "tsk" and "hmmm" as she scanned an already overbooked appointment book.

"No, I'm sorry, Mrs. Herbert. Unless this is an emergency, there's no way Dr. Edwards could see you today. I can fit you in tomorrow morning, however. Say around eleven o'clock? Can you come in then?"

"Sure. If that's the best you can do. Eleven o'clock? Is that what you said?"

"That's right, Mrs. Herbert. Eleven o'clock tomorrow."

"Fine. I'll see you then."

"All right, Mrs. Herbert. Bye-bye now."

Peg got up from the kitchen table and hung up the receiver. "Damn," she said to herself, suddenly feeling despondent. "I've got things I wanted to do today, but I feel like I'm slogging through quicksand."

"What's the matter, Mommy?" Jennie asked, looking up from her crayoning for the first time in several minutes.

"Nothing, sweetheart," Peg said, rubbing her forehead with her fingertips, trying to push away the fatigue that threatened to overcome her. "Mommy's just a little tired. That's all. Nothing to worry about."

Seven

She was trying to be patient, she told herself. She really was trying.
I mean, it's not like I was supposed to be here today, she thought. She looked around the waiting room Tuesday morning at the twenty or so other people waiting with her. *I'm the one who's being squeezed in, not the rest of these people. And it's only been what?* She looked at her watch. *Thirty-five minutes. So there's no reason to be upset.*

She was sitting in a leather wingchair in the far right corner of the North Shore Medical Group waiting room next to a small end table piled high with year-old, dog-eared magazines. She looked down at the magazine in her hands and continued to flip through it as she had been doing since she arrived, going through the motions of reading without seeing a single word.

Somewhere a telephone rang. No one answered it.

She took a deep breath and tried to regain her composure. She knew she wasn't herself, that fatigue was making her uncharacteristically short-tempered.

I have to stay calm, she admonished herself. *There was nothing that important I had to do today anyway. No reason to get upset.*

"Mrs. Herbert?" a nurse half called, half announced. "Mrs. Herbert?"

"I'm here," Peg answered, feeling for a moment like attendance was being taken. "I'm right here."

She closed her magazine quickly, carefully placed it atop the pile and walked across the waiting room to where the nurse was standing.

"Right this way, Mrs. Herbert," the nurse said, and she held open the door leading to the examining rooms and the doctors' offices.

Peg followed the nurse down the hall until they reached an examination room with an open door. The nurse stopped, turned and indicated that Peg should enter the room. "Dr. Edwards will be with you in a few minutes," she said, and she closed the door.

Peg stood in the middle of the little room and debated whether she should stand, sit on the one chair in the room, or climb up on the examining table. She decided to stand.

Two minutes later Dr. Edwards knocked on the door. He was a tall man, over six feet, and in his early forties. He always looked collegiate, almost preppy, with his over-the-collar, wavy brown hair, his round tortoise-shell glasses, brightly colored sport slacks and penny loafers. The slacks and the loafers were his attempt at informality, but were more than offset by a white button-down shirt, a tie and a crisply starched white knee-length lab coat. The nicest thing about him was that he always gave the impression of warmth and genuine concern whenever he spoke.

"Good morning," he said cheerfully as he lifted Peg's file from the Plexiglas rack on the outside of the door and entered the examination room.

"Good morning," Peg answered.

"Why don't you have a seat up there?" he said. He gestured towards the examining table and took the chair.

He waited until Peg had climbed up on the table before saying anything else. "So, I gather you're not feeling too well today."

"I feel like hell," Peg replied, "but I don't feel sick. At least not what I call sick. But all weekend and all day yesterday and today, I've been more tired than I've ever been in my life. A weird kind of tired. Not the kind you can push through. My husband and I were supposed to go sailing Saturday night with the couple across the street, but I bailed out a few hours before we were supposed to leave because I was exhausted. So tired I could barely move. And since then I haven't been able to make myself do anything that requires the slightest bit of exertion. No matter how hard I try, I just can't push through it."

Dr. Edwards looked at Peg for a few seconds before he spoke again. "Any other symptoms? Any pain anywhere? Nausea? Diarrhea? Anything other than the fatigue?"

"No, nothing. Just this overwhelming tiredness."

"I see," Dr. Edwards said thoughtfully. "Have you been out much this summer? Out in the sun, I mean?"

"Yes. All the time," Peg replied, surprised at the question. "Why?"

"Well, you look very pale to me..." Dr. Edwards' voice trailed off as he leafed through her file looking for something. When he didn't find it, he looked at her again, deep in thought.

"Why don't you get undressed," he said, "and slip into that gown next to you? I'll come back in a few minutes."

When Dr. Edwards returned several minutes later, Peg was sitting on the examination table just as he had left her, but clad now only in a thin pale blue open-backed gown, her arms wrapped around herself in an attempt to stay warm in the air-conditioned room.

He walked over to her, gave her a quick smile and took her hands in his. He looked at the top side of each of them, then turned them over and looked at her palms and wrists. He felt her neck under each side of her jaw and down her neck on either side of her throat. He slid the gown off of her shoulders, allowing it to fall to her waist, lifted each of her arms and ran his fingers under her armpits and around and under her breasts. He placed his stethoscope on her chest and back and listened to her breathe and tapped on her back in several spots. He asked her to lie down, and he pushed and prodded her stomach and abdomen and ran his fingers up and down the inside of her thighs. He told her she could slide her arms back into the gown, and when she had and was once again covered, he took her pulse and looked in her ears and her mouth. His manner was unhurried but efficient, without wasted motion or effort, and his skilled hands gave him the information he sought.

When he was done, he sat down on the chair at the foot of the examining table, folded his arms across his chest and looked directly at Peg for several seconds, as if he were reviewing in his mind one more time everything his examination had revealed to him.

"Well, two things are very apparent. First, judging from your color and your fatigue, I think you're suffering from anemia, so I want you to make an appointment with the lab for a blood test. Second, a number of the lymph nodes in your neck and under your arms are swollen. We need to find out why. But we'll start with the blood test. Okay?"

"Of course," Peg replied, as Dr. Edwards began to fill out a form for the lab detailing the tests he wanted done. "Then what?"

"That's going to depend on the results of your blood test," he said when he was finished, and he handed the form to her.

Peg gave a little shrug and looked down at the form in her hand, not overly comfortable with his answer.

"I suggest you go to the lab when you leave here," he continued. "If you do, we'll have the results by tomorrow morning. Then give us a call some time after ten o'clock, and my nurse will let you know what we need to do next. Okay?"

"I guess so," Peg replied.

Dr. Edwards gave her a warm smile and stood up. Then he wished her a good day, shook her hand and left the examination room on his way to his next patient.

Eight

Wednesday morning, July 30th, eight minutes after ten.

I've been here before, Peg thought. The phone in Dr. Edwards' office rang for what had to be the twenty-fifth time. Finally a voice on the other end of the line. "Good morning. Dr. Edwards' office."

"Yes. Good morning. My name is Peggy Herbert, and I had a blood test taken yesterday afternoon at Dr. Edwards' request. He told me to call you this morning and said you'd be able to let me know what I'm supposed to do next. Based on the results of the blood test."

"Let me check, Mrs. Herbert. I'll be right back to you."

A minute passed, then another.

"Yes, Mrs. Herbert," the voice on the other end of the line suddenly said. "We have the report from the lab, Dr. Edwards has looked at it, and he does want to see you today. Can you make a three-thirty appointment?"

"Yes, I can do that," Peg replied without hesitation. "Did Dr. Edwards say anything else? About the report, I mean?"

"No, I'm sorry, he didn't."

There was silence on both ends of the line for several seconds.

"Is there anything else I can do for you, Mrs. Herbert?" the voice asked.

"No. Nothing at all. I'll see Dr. Edwards this afternoon at three-thirty."

"Have a nice day, Mrs. Herbert."

"You too."

The voice hung up, and Peg stood in the kitchen looking at the receiver in her hand.

Nine

She arrived early for her Wednesday afternoon appointment, at three-twenty to be exact, to be absolutely certain that when her name was called, she'd be there. But that was almost an hour ago. It was now four-fifteen, and for the last fifty-five minutes all she had done was chew on the sides of her fingers, first one hand, then the other. And each time she realized what she was doing, she very consciously clasped both hands together and placed them in her lap before starting to nibble on her lower lip. And when she realized she was biting her lip, she brought a finger to her mouth and repeated the process, over and over again.

Finally, at eighteen minutes after four, she heard her name being called. "Mrs. Herbert?" yesterday's nurse again half called, half announced. "Mrs. Herbert?"

"I'm here," Peg answered, louder than she had intended to. "I'm here."

"I'm sorry you had to wait so long," yesterday's nurse said as she led Peg down Internal Medicine's hall for the second time in as many days. "Dr. Edwards had an emergency over at the hospital this morning, and we still haven't recovered. Here we are."

She stopped at a closed door halfway down the hall, knocked softly, waited a second, then opened the door and stepped just inside. From where she was standing out in the hall, Peg could see she was being ushered into Dr. Edwards' office and not an examination room. The nurse indicated with a small wave that Peg should come into the office and pointed to the leather armchair next to Dr. Edwards' desk.

"Please. Have a seat. Dr. Edwards will be right with you."

Peg did as she was told, and as soon as she was seated, the nurse left and closed the door behind her. She was just starting to take in the clutter of patients' files, medical journals, lab reports, X-ray envelopes and "While You Were Out" messages that covered the desk, part of the floor and the top of a bookcase that ran along the wall, when the door opened and Dr. Edwards came in.

"Good afternoon," he said, extending his hand to Peg for a gentle handshake. "I'm sorry I'm so late, but it's been a difficult day."

"So I gathered," Peg replied with a small smile.

Dr. Edwards returned her smile, looked at her for a second or two longer than she would have expected, and sat down behind his desk. He rummaged through the pile of patient files stacked in the center of the desk, and when he found Peg's, he removed the lab report clipped to the inside of the maroon folder. He looked at the report for several moments, then looked up and across the desk at Peg.

"Based on the results of your blood test," he began slowly, "I'd like you to see another doctor. I have someone in mind, and I think I can arrange for him to see you this afternoon."

Peg swallowed hard. "Today?"

Dr. Edwards nodded.

"What kind of doctor?"

"An oncologist," Dr. Edwards replied, looking directly into her eyes, measuring the impact of his answer.

He waited a moment before continuing. "I think you have some form of blood cancer. I'm not an expert in this area, and I could be wrong, but your white cell count is very high, and your red cells are very small and underdeveloped. Which would explain why you've been so tired."

Peg tried to swallow again, but she couldn't. She said nothing. Questions at that moment seemed superfluous. She just sat quietly looking down at her hands in her lap, one placed flat on top of the other, and bit her lower lip. Finally, she raised her head and met Dr. Edwards' gaze. "Okay," she said with a weak and frightened smile.

Dr. Edwards turned to the Rolodex file on his desk and found the telephone number of a Dr. Goldstein, an out-of-group oncologist to whom he had referred patients before. He dialed the number and gave Peg a reassuring smile. She could hear the phone ringing at the other end of the line. Then it stopped.

"Yes, good afternoon. This is Dr. Edwards with North Shore Medical Group."

A pause.

"I'm fine, thank you. I have a patient sitting here with me, a Peggy Herbert, and I'd like to make an appointment for her to see Dr. Goldstein as soon as possible. When do you think that might be?"

There was silence on the other end as someone scanned another already overbooked appointment schedule.

"No, two weeks from today is not what I had in mind. Actually, I was hoping Dr. Goldstein could see Mrs. Herbert this afternoon."

The person on the other end asked a question that Peg couldn't hear.

"That's right," Dr. Edwards replied.

Another pause.

"I think that'll be fine, but let me check."

Dr. Edwards turned the mouthpiece of the receiver into his shoulder and looked across the desk at Peg. "Can you make an appointment at five-thirty tonight?"

"Yes," Peg answered quietly.

"Yes, that'll be fine. Mrs. Herbert will see you tonight at five-thirty."

Another pause.

"Thank you very much for your help. I appreciate it."

He hung up the receiver and began to write something on a prescription form. "Here's Dr. Goldstein's address and phone number. He'll see you at five-thirty," he repeated, and he handed the slip of paper to Peg. "I'll fax your lab report over to him now so he has a chance to look at it before you get there."

He stopped, seemingly in mid-thought.

"Call me tomorrow if you can, and let me know how you made out and if there's anything I can do to help."

"I will," Peg replied, and she rose to leave. A quiet "Thank you."

An equally quiet "Good-bye."

And she was gone.

Ten

Peg pushed open the front lobby door of the North Shore Medical Group building. She started to go down the walk leading to the parking lot, but stopped after only a few steps as if she had hit an invisible wall. She brought her hands up to her mouth, clasped almost as in prayer, and looked up at the blue summer sky winking at her through the leaves of an overhanging dogwood tree.

"Cancer," she whispered to herself as she stared upward, blinking back tears. "I have cancer," she continued, allowing the terror that the word generated to well up from inside and wash over her.

"Cancer," she repeated incredulously. "I can't believe it. I have cancer, and this is how I'm going to die. My God!"

"Are you all right?" a voice next to her asked suddenly.

She turned quickly to her left and saw an elderly man and his wife on the walk, looking at her with obvious concern. "Is there anything I can do?" he asked before she could answer his first question.

Peg shook her head while brushing away her tears with both hands. "No. No, thank you," she replied trying to smile, without success. "I'm fine. But thank you anyway. Thank you very much."

Unconvinced, the elderly man looked at her for a moment longer and then took his wife's arm and guided her towards the front lobby door.

Peg remained where she was standing, breathing deeply, trying to regain control of her emotions, and with each breath, she felt herself retreat from the precipice of panic.

When she had finally succeeded in calming herself, she looked at her watch. It was four forty-five.

What do I do now? she thought. *Should I call John?*

She began to nibble on the side of her thumb. *No,* she said to herself. *I won't do that. I won't call John until I see Dr. Goldstein. Until I know for sure this whole thing isn't just a false alarm.*

She sighed and looked at her watch again. It was still four forty-five. *So what do I do? By the time I get home, it'll almost be time for me to leave for my appointment. But if I go now, I'll be more than a half hour early.*

A few seconds of deliberation.

But there's no way I can go home now and face the children, and God knows what else. I can't do that. So… I'll go over to Dr. Goldstein's office and just sit and wait for him.

The decision made, Peg turned around, went back inside and walked across the lobby to the main registration desk. "Is there a pay phone somewhere I can use?" she asked the receptionist.

"Yes, there is," the woman behind the counter replied. "Down the hall to the end, on the left."

Peg thanked the woman and proceeded down the hall, finding a bank of pay phones on the wall next to the doors leading to the rear parking lot. She rummaged through her pocketbook for change, and after finding the coins she needed and dropping them into the phone one by one, dialed her home number.

Linda Taylor, the neighbor who was watching the children for the afternoon, answered the phone on the second ring. "Hello?"

"Hi, Linda. It's me."

"Hi. How're you doing?"

Peg hesitated for a second before responding. "Not too well. I'll fill you in when I get home. But I've got a different problem now. While I was with Dr. Edwards, he made an appointment for me to see another doctor this afternoon. At five-thirty."

"Why's that a problem?" Linda asked.

"Well, if I see this other doctor, I won't be home by five like I promised. So I was wondering if maybe you could stay a little longer? Maybe until six-thirty? I'm sorry for asking, Linda, but Dr. Edwards really wanted me to see this other doctor today."

Linda was more than just a neighbor; she was a close friend of Peg's and a good person. "Don't worry about it," was her immediate response. "Paul can have his dinner a little later than usual tonight. It won't kill him, and he'll understand. And don't worry about the kids either. They're fine. Go. I hope everything turns out okay."

Peg said thanks, smiled sadly to herself at Linda's last words, and hung up.

Eleven

When Peg arrived at Dr. Goldstein's office, the waiting room was almost full in spite of the late hour. She identified herself to the nurse at the reception window and took one of the last two remaining seats. She immediately picked up a six-month-old issue of *Better Homes and Gardens* out of reflex, but before opening it, she looked around the waiting room at the other patients.

They were all ages. Some in their seventies, some in their mid to late fifties, some within a year or two of her, and one probably not yet twenty. Most were women. Some were extremely frail-looking, pale and thin. One or two looked downright emaciated. But others seemed to be in perfect health. Several women suffered from hair loss. One woman in her late fifties apparently had no hair at all and wore a brightly colored floral turban. Another woman, only a few years older, also had no hair but no longer cared and left her bald pate exposed for all to see. Each patient was different from the next in terms of age or state of health or general demeanor, but they all shared a look of quiet fear and deep concern. No one smiled. No one talked. Not even to the person sitting next to them who had brought them here. Not a word. The waiting room was absolutely quiet except for the sound of magazine pages being turned.

For a split second, Peg had the thought that these people were not waiting to see the doctor, but instead were waiting for their turn to die. She shuddered and could feel panic start to rise again from deep inside.

I can't let myself think like this, she thought. *I mustn't panic. This is probably just a false alarm. A complete waste of time. There's probably nothing at all wrong with me other than maybe I'm a little anemic. I don't smoke. I don't drink. Well, a little, but not much. I take care of myself. And for God's sake, I'm only thirty-four. Cancer doesn't happen to thirty-four-year-olds.*

She looked across the waiting room at the rail thin eighteen or nineteen-year-old girl she had seen when she first walked in.

Well, maybe it can, but still… that's the exception, not the rule. Besides, I've got too much to live for, and two little kids that can't be without me. Dear God, you know that's true. You know how much I love my babies and my husband, and you know how much they love me and need me. You know that. Please don't let me be sick. Please don't let me have cancer. Don't let me die. Please. Not now. Not of this. Please let me see my babies grow up. I don't know what I've done to deserve this, but please don't punish them for whatever it is. Please, God, don't. Please.

She started to think about what she might have done to make this happen to her, but stopped as soon as she began. She knew thinking like that wasn't going to help. She also knew that although she wasn't perfect, she was a good person. A good mother. A good wife.

I've got to calm down. This is silly. There's nothing wrong with me. Nothing. That's all there is to it. Nothing! I just have to get a hold of myself. Got to be tough. Strong. Everything's going to be fine. There's nothing to worry about!

As if to lend form to her resolution, she forced herself to stop looking around the waiting room, snapped open the *Better Homes and Gardens* on her lap, more or less to the middle of the magazine, and struggled to immerse herself in an article describing the preferred way to plant boxed rose bushes.

By five forty-five, the waiting room was empty except for Peg. She was still sitting in the seat she had selected when she first arrived, in the corner next to the magazine table, her *Better Homes and Gardens* still on her lap and still opened to the article on boxed rose bushes, when the nurse came to the reception window and slid open one of the sliding glass panels.

"Mrs. Herbert?" she called out too loudly given there was no one else in the waiting room. "The doctor will see you now."

35

Peg closed her magazine and tried to appear calm as she walked across the waiting room to the door that the nurse was holding open. As she entered what appeared to be an administrative area, a young man to her left got up from behind one of the desks and came over to her, his hand extended.

"Mrs. Herbert? I'm Dr. Goldstein. Nice to meet you."

Peg shook his hand, managed a quiet "Hi" and a wan smile, and tried to hide her surprise and disappointment.

Unlike Dr. Edwards, Dr. Goldstein was young, in his early thirties at most, and unlike Dr. Edwards, his appearance was totally unimpressive. He was about five-six and soft looking. Almost pudgy. He wore wire-framed glasses, and his dark brown curly hair, which came well over his collar, looked as if it had not been combed for days. He wore wrinkled chinos and an equally wrinkled checkered button-down shirt. And although his greeting was polite, his demeanor was abrupt. In short, he wasn't another Dr. Edwards, and somehow at this moment, another Dr. Edwards was precisely what she needed.

He picked up a file from the reception nurse's desk, glanced at it to confirm it was the one he wanted, and started to walk down a short hall. With his free hand and without saying anything more, he gestured to her that she should follow him.

"Audrey, join us in a minute, will you?" he called over his shoulder to the nurse who had ushered her in from the waiting room. Then without turning around and still a step or two in front of her, he addressed Peg. "Dr. Edwards faxed me a copy of his examination report and your lab report, but I'd still like to examine you before we talk."

He stopped, turned to face her and indicated an open door on the left that led into one of his examination rooms. "Right here," he said with a weak smile.

Peg entered and stopped in the center of the room, awaiting further instructions.

"There's a gown on the examination table there," he said from the doorway, pointing to a carefully folded square of pale yellow material at the foot of the table. "Get undressed, and I'll be back in a minute." Without waiting for a reply, he pulled the door closed.

Peg did as she was told, carefully laying first her blouse, then her brassiere, then her slacks on one of the two chairs, and pulled on the pale yellow gown. She had just finished securing the gown's ties behind her neck when she heard several sharp knocks on the door, followed almost immediately by the door opening an inch or two and Dr. Goldstein's voice. "All set?" he asked.

Peg muttered yes, and Dr. Goldstein and the nurse stepped into the room.

"I'm going to take some blood first so we can take a look at it while you're here," he announced, and he walked over to a cabinet on the far side of the room. "Have a seat up on the table, would you?"

Again Peg did as she was told, and within moments Dr. Goldstein had taken a small vial of blood.

"I'll look at that when I'm finished here," he said to the nurse, handing the vial to her. "But before I do," he added, turning back to Peg, "I'd like to take a quick look at you."

Peg sat straight up and perfectly still as Dr. Goldstein undid the gown's ties and quickly folded it down to her waist. He ran his fingers under each side of her jaw, down each side of her neck and under each armpit. He ran his fingers over and under one breast and then the other. He examined her in silence and said nothing after he had finished. Instead, he picked up her file from the other chair and rapidly entered his observations.

"Why don't you get dressed and meet me in my office?" he said when he was done. "It's just across the hall. I'm going to take a peek at your blood sample, and I'll meet you there in a few minutes." A second later and he was gone.

Peg reached for her clothes. She tried not to feel violated, but somehow she did. Less than five minutes ago she had been sitting in the waiting room. Now five minutes later she was sitting alone in a cold examination room, half naked, blood taken, examination over. She shook off the feeling and hooked her bra.

When she was dressed, she opened the door and stepped out into the hall. Directly across from her was an office, its door open, which she assumed was Dr. Goldstein's. She crossed the hall and looked in somewhat tentatively to confirm it was empty. When she saw that it was, she entered, sat in one of the leather wing chairs in front of the large mahogany desk, folded her hands in her lap and waited.

The minutes passed slowly. The only sounds were the hum of the air conditioner in the window and occasionally the muted ring of the telephone in the outer office. For some reason, she didn't think about what Dr. Goldstein might say. Her mind for the moment was blank.

Footsteps coming down the hall signaled Dr. Goldstein's arrival. He came into the office holding a mug of coffee in one hand and a file folder in the other. He walked behind his desk, placed both the mug and the folder in front of him, and sat down. He swiveled his chair to his left, hit a key on his telephone console, picked up the receiver and waited.

"Audrey? Hold my calls for a few minutes, will you? Thanks."

He hung up the receiver and turned to face the silent woman sitting in front of him. He looked at her only long enough to make eye contact before picking up the folder he had just laid on the desk. He started to open the file, then stopped, closed it slowly and again looked at Peg.

"Mrs. Herbert, I wish I had better news for you, but unfortunately I don't." He paused. "My review of the lab report Dr. Edwards forwarded to me... in combination with my own examination of you and your blood sample... confirms that you have leukemia, which is a form of blood cancer. And given the rapid onset of your symptoms—for example, the extreme fatigue you told Dr. Edwards about—my guess is it's probably what we call acute myelogenous leukemia. We'll be able to confirm that after we've examined your blood sample more thoroughly, but for now let's just say you have a very aggressive type of leukemia."

He paused again and seemed to hesitate before he resumed speaking. "My examination also confirms that the disease has progressed considerably."

He gave Peg a moment to absorb what he had said.

"You need to know that this type of leukemia is definitely life threatening, although not necessarily terminal. In other words, although it's a very serious illness, if we attack it now, immediately and aggressively, we've got a reasonable chance of at least getting you into long-term remission. Hopefully, we can even cure you."

Peg blinked her eyes several times as she tried to absorb the words she had just heard. She knew she understood the words, but for several seconds she had difficulty believing they had been directed at her.

"What do we do?" she whispered.

"We're having the most success against this type of leukemia with chemotherapy," Dr. Goldstein replied. "Do you know what chemotherapy is?"

"I think so. Maybe. I don't know."

"Chemotherapy is a treatment regimen involving the introduction of chemicals into the body. Chemicals which kill the cancer cells, in your case the cancer cells in your bone marrow, while not affecting the healthy cells in the rest of your body. I have to be honest with you and tell you this isn't the most pleasant form of therapy, but it gets the job done. Usually, treatment continues for two to four weeks. Ideally, at the end of that two- to four-week period, the cancerous blood cells have been killed, leaving only healthy non-cancerous cells in your body. At that point, you're in what we call remission. We then discontinue the chemotherapy, and your body begins to repair itself, hopefully free of cancer."

Peg stared at him, her eyes wide with terror. *I'm not hearing this*, she thought, feeling the terror start to engulf her again. *This cannot be happening to me. It can't be. It just can't be.*

She struggled to find her voice. "What do I do now?" she asked, her voice hoarse from fright.

"Well, first, if you want me to treat you, I need you to consent to my being your attending physician. Is that what you want?"

He waited for Peg to answer. "In other words, do you want me to be responsible for your treatment?"

"Yes," Peg replied.

"Okay. Consider that done. Now the next thing we have to do is get you admitted to Huntington Hospital as soon as possible. Can you check in tonight?"

"Yes."

"I'm sorry for the urgency, but given your condition, time is not exactly our friend."

"I understand."

"I'd also like you to ask your husband to come to my office tonight so I can bring him up to speed on what we've found and how we're going to treat you. I'll be here for at least another hour and a half. Do you think he can get here in that time frame?"

"I think so."

"Good. I'm going to call the hospital now while you go home and pick up whatever you need." He looked at his watch. "It's five after six now. Can you be at the hospital by seven?"

"Yes," Peg answered quietly, tears rolling unchecked down her cheeks.

Dr. Goldstein pushed his chair back, stood up and started to come from behind the desk to escort her back to the outer office. The consultation was over.

"We can beat this," he assured her. "Believe me when I say that. There are a lot of things we can do today that were unheard of ten, even five, years ago. We can beat it. Believe me."

By the time he had finished saying this, he had come around to the front of his desk and now stood barely three feet from Peg's chair. But she made no move to rise. Instead, she sat totally still, staring at her hands, still carefully folded in her lap, one on top of the other. Tears ran down her cheeks and fell onto the back of her hand. She tried to wipe the tears away with her fingers, first from one eye, then from the other.

Finally she spoke. "I have a little girl who's almost three and a little boy who's only eight months old. They both love me very much. They both need me very much. What's going to happen to them if something happens to me? What will they do without me? What will they do without their mommy?"

Dr. Goldstein took a step closer to her chair. "I'll see you at the hospital later tonight," he said, placing his hand on her shoulder.

Peg nodded quickly, wiped the last of her tears away with the heel of her hand, and rose from the chair. And without so much as a glance at Dr. Goldstein, she turned and left the office.

Twelve

Peg stood on the back porch staring at the screen door. She knew she had been standing there too long. She knew she had to open the back door soon or Linda would open it for her, having seen her pull into the driveway several minutes ago. But she wasn't ready. Not yet. She had to make certain she was okay. She couldn't risk coming apart in front of Jennie.

I have to be calm, she told herself, her hand on the screen door handle. *I have to be relaxed. Have to look like everything's all right. I have to be strong for Jennie. Can't let her know how scared I am.*

How am I going to do that?

Never mind how. You have to.

She pulled the screen door open, and the screech of its spring announced her entry. She stepped into the pantry hall, letting the screen door slam behind her, and came around the corner into the kitchen. Linda was sitting at the kitchen table watching the children eat their dinners, Jennie across from her in her booster seat and John next to her in his high chair. Jennie had finished her chicken and most of her mashed potatoes and was busily chasing peas around her plate with a spoon. John was slumped diagonally in the highchair, eyes half closed, as he sleepily sucked at his almost empty bottle.

"Hi, Mommy," Jennie called out happily, upraised spoon in hand, when she saw Peg.

"Hi, sweetheart," Peg replied as she walked to the kitchen counter to put down her pocketbook and keys.

"How'd you make out?" Linda asked.

"Not well," Peg answered, trying to decide how much she could say in Jennie's presence. "I have to go to the hospital tonight."

"Tonight? Why tonight? What's the rush?"

Peg turned away from the counter. She started to walk towards the table, but she stopped after the second step, suddenly realizing her knees were shaking so badly they threatened to collapse under her. She put her hand on the counter to steady herself.

"I have leukemia," she answered, slowly and deliberately, her voice quivering in spite of her best efforts to sound in control. She inhaled deeply in an attempt to calm herself and then exhaled slowly. "So I have to go upstairs and pack. Right after I call John."

"God, Peg, I am so sorry," Linda said, staring at her in disbelief.

"Me too."

The two women remained silent and motionless for several seconds, looking across the kitchen at one another, across the gulf that exists between the sick and the healthy, tears in their eyes, not knowing what to say or do next.

Suddenly a three-year-old voice broke the silence. "What's wrong, Mommy?" Jennie asked, frightened at seeing her mother crying. "Are you sick, Mommy?"

In an instant Peg was at the kitchen table, lifting her daughter out of the booster seat for hugs and kisses. "Nothing's wrong, sweetheart," she said with complete assurance as she kissed Jennie on the cheek, the nose, the forehead, the cheek again. "Nothing serious, anyway. I just have to go to the hospital for a few days so the doctor can fix me up."

She looked into those huge eyes only inches away and felt her heart breaking. Breaking because she knew she was lying, and because the little girl in her arms would believe every word she said.

"Then I'll come home and be good as new."

"Then why are you crying, Mommy?" Jennie asked, as yet unconvinced.

"Well, I guess I'm crying because I'm not as brave as I should be, sweetheart. That's all. But there's no reason for you to be afraid. Mommies cry sometimes too, you know."

"Can I have ice cream for dessert?" Jennie asked, her fear erased by these last words and her attention now on other matters.

"Of course you can, sweetheart. Linda will get it for you while Mommy's upstairs. Okay?"

Peg put Jennie back into the booster seat and walked over to John, who was now wide awake. She ran her fingers through his hair and watched them glide across his head as he twisted and turned in his high chair. Then she looked up at Linda.

"I don't have much time. It's almost twenty of seven, and I need to call John before he leaves the office. If he hasn't already. After that, while I'm packing, could you call the Claytons for me, explain the situation, and see if they can come over to watch the kids until John gets home? So you're not tied up here anymore? Is that okay?"

"Sure," Linda replied. "Not a problem. Go."

Peg nodded in thanks, then lifted John out of the high chair and held him close to her chest. She closed her eyes and gave him a lingering kiss on the top of his head, feeling the warmth of his skin and the softness of his hair with her lips. She held him for perhaps half a minute and then slowly, reluctantly, bent down to slide him back into the high chair. Once she was certain he was secure, she straightened up and stood next to the high chair for a few more seconds, one hand on his shoulder, looking first at his upturned face and then at Jennie.

Suddenly, she leaned across the table, kissed Jennie on the forehead and left the kitchen. John squirmed in his high chair, trying to find his mother, wondering where she had gone. Jennie silently watched her disappear around the corner.

Thirteen

I should've been out of here a half hour ago, I thought as I surveyed the mountain of paperwork strewn from one end of my desk to the other, exasperated that I was still nowhere near an acceptable breaking-off point. *And why hasn't Peg called?* I asked myself, looking at my watch for what must have been the twentieth time. It was now almost six forty. *She should have called two hours ago. She said she'd call as soon as she got home.*

"So why the hell hasn't she called?" I said out loud without meaning to.

As I was having this conversation with myself, I heard the receptionist's telephone ring in the outer office and looked at my phone console to see what line was flashing. A call on any one of the first four outside lines at this hour was probably a customer who didn't know we were on Eastern Time. A call on the fifth line, "04" as we called it, at this time of night was personal, either my parents or Peg.

It was "04" that was flashing, but just in case, I answered it officially. "Good evening. Herbert Products."

"John, it's me."

"Hey, kid. Where you been? I've been worried about you."

"I just got in."

"I thought your appointment was at three-thirty."

"It was. I just got back from seeing Dr. Goldstein."

"Who's he?"

Peg started to answer me, but before she was able to she began to cry, and within a second or two she was sobbing uncontrollably and unable to speak.

"Peg? Who's Dr. Goldstein?"

No answer.

"Peg. Talk to me. Who's Dr. Goldstein?"

Again Peg tried to speak, but again she failed and continued to sob.

"Sweetheart, you've gotta calm down. I can't help you if I don't know what's wrong. Who's Dr. Goldstein?"

Still no answer. Hysteria and panic were now in control.

"Peg," I shouted into the receiver. "Stop it! Calm down! Take deep breaths and calm down! You have to calm down!"

My voice must have reached her because almost immediately I heard her breathing into the phone, rapid shallow breaths at first, and then as the seconds passed, deeper, more regular breaths. I could sense she was regaining control.

"Are you all right?" I asked hesitantly, hoping I was not going to trigger another panic attack by asking questions too soon after she had calmed down.

"Yes," was the muted reply after several more breaths. "I'm sorry for behaving like this," she continued, "but I'm so scared, John. I'm so scared."

"I can see that, sweetheart. But I don't know why yet. So now, without getting upset, tell me who Dr. Goldstein is."

"He's an oncologist," she said with a whimper, almost as if she were ashamed.

"An oncologist? Isn't that a cancer specialist?"

"Yes," she answered, and she started to cry again.

"Jesus, Peg," I exclaimed, feeling my head start to spin and momentarily forgetting how terrified she was. "You gotta be kidding me. What happened? What'd Dr. Edwards say?"

"He said he thought I had some kind of blood cancer. And he wanted me to see another doctor. Today. So while I was in his office, he made an appointment for me to see Dr. Goldstein."

"And what'd Dr. Goldstein say?" I asked, dreading the answer.

"He said I have leukemia," Peg cried out loudly, on the verge of losing control again. "He wants me in the hospital tonight," she continued in between sobs. "I'm supposed to be there in fifteen minutes. And he wants to see you tonight at his office. He's going to wait there for you."

I leaned back in my chair while she blew her nose. I looked up at my office ceiling, seeing nothing, at a complete loss for words.

This isn't happening, I thought stupidly. *Can't be happening. She was just a little tired. She wasn't sick. She was tired. Leukemia? My God!*

"Leukemia, John. People die from leukemia. And that's what I've got. Leukemia!"

What do I say to her? I asked myself, closing my eyes in the face of the enormity of what she had just said. *What can I possibly say to this?*

"Are you still there?" Peg asked.

"Yeah, honey," I answered, leaning forward again, the receiver in one hand, my head in the other. "I'm still here."

My mind was racing. I had to say something. Something encouraging, comforting, reassuring.

"We've obviously got a major problem here," I began, struggling to find the right words, the right tone. "But just because you have leukemia doesn't mean you're going to die. It just means you're sick, and we've got to make you well. The one thing you can't do, though, is panic. You can't let that happen. Because if you do, then you've really got a problem. So let's both try to stay calm until we have all the facts and know what our options are. Okay?"

"Okay," Peg murmured weakly.

"Have you got Dr. Goldstein's address and telephone number?" I asked, trying desperately to focus on something other than the word "leukemia," which was by now streaming non-stop through my brain.

"He's on East Main Street. 220 East Main. And his telephone number is 271-5349."

"I got it. How are you getting to the hospital?" I asked, focusing on the details, the logistics for the next few hours. *The details I can handle,* I thought. *It's leukemia I'm having a problem with. Gotta stick to the details for now.*

"I'll ask Amy Bennett to take me. I know she's home."

"Good. I'll come to the hospital right after I meet with Dr. Goldstein. You'll be admitted and in a room by then?"

"I guess."

Her voice was flat, mechanical, totally devoid of emotion, and her demeanor now was completely different from what it had been just minutes ago. I wondered if she had truly calmed down or gone into shock. I had no way to know. I was in my office; she was in our bedroom at home. I considered asking her to put Linda on the phone, but decided I would be overreacting. So instead I reverted back to the details, to that which I could control.

"How long can Linda stay?"

"She's going to call the Claytons as soon as I get off the phone with you and ask them to stay here until you get home from the hospital."

"I've got a better idea. Why don't I ask my folks to come over and take the kids back to their house tonight? I mean, we have no idea what time I'll be getting out of the hospital, and this way the Claytons can go home as soon as my folks arrive. What do you say?"

"That probably makes more sense."

"Are you okay, Peg?" I asked, hoping for some sort of response that would reduce the fear inside me, which was increasing with every passing second.

She didn't answer.

I could feel my throat start to close and became conscious of my heart pumping in my chest and my pulse pounding in my ears as I waited.

Finally she spoke. "Can you do something for me?"

"Anything."

"Can you pick up Jennie after you've seen Dr. Goldstein and bring her to the hospital with you? I'd really like to see her tonight. I'd ask you to bring John too, but it'll be too late for him, and they probably wouldn't let him in anyway."

"No, I'm sure they wouldn't, but I can bring Jennie if you'd like me to," I assured her.

Again, silence.

Our conversation was over. The news had been delivered, the plans for the next three hours made. We had nothing else to say.

"I love you, Peg," I said, blinking back tears and trying not to let the lump in my throat show in my voice.

"I love you too," she said softly, and then she hung up.

Fourteen

Tell me I'm too late, I thought, as I opened the door to Dr. Goldstein's office suite and stepped into an empty waiting room. I looked at my watch. *Seven-twenty. Peg said he'd wait for me, but this sure doesn't look good.*

I walked up to the reception window and saw that the inner office, although still illuminated, was also empty and closed down for the night. I looked around the waiting room to see if there was another door or another reception window. There wasn't. I glanced at my watch a second time to make certain I had read the time correctly and then slid open one of the window's sliding glass panels. I leaned through it far enough to make certain my voice would be heard in the farthest corners of the office suite.

"Hello?" I called, feeling simultaneously anxious and foolish. "Is anybody here?"

A voice came from somewhere inside the suite. "Mr. Herbert? Is that you?"

"Yes, it is," I replied.

A disheveled young man appeared at the end of the hall. "Come right in, Mr. Herbert," he called. "The door's open."

I withdrew my head and opened the door. He beckoned me towards him with a wave. "Join me down here in my office, will you?" he asked.

When I reached him, he extended his hand, introduced himself and immediately turned to go back into his office. "Nice to meet you," I muttered to his back.

He asked me to have a seat in one of the wing chairs facing his desk. I did as he asked and watched him sit down and pull a file that was presumably Peg's from the pile of folders covering his desk.

He's young, I thought as I looked at him. *Damn young. Probably a year or two younger than me.* A frightening thought, and yet I realized as I sat watching him that, young as he was, he was the man in charge. He was the boss. Not Peg. Not me.

He flipped open the file, looked at it briefly, and then without wasting time on any additional exchange of pleasantries, went right to the point of my being there. "I assume your wife has told you about our conversation this afternoon?"

"She has."

"There's no easy way to do this, Mr. Herbert," he continued, "so I'm going to be direct and very much to the point. First, your wife is a very sick lady. As she's already told you, she has leukemia, which is a form of blood cancer. Basically what happens is the white cells in the blood multiply out of control… so fast they never reach maturity, and in such great numbers they literally crowd out the red blood cells. That's why the first symptom your wife experienced was fatigue. Her blood doesn't have enough red cells anymore to carry the oxygen she needs to function normally.

"There are several types of leukemia. Some take years to develop and run their course. Others are far more aggressive. Unfortunately, your wife has what is called acute myelogenous leukemia, which is one of the most aggressive forms. Simply put, it's life threatening. However, with aggressive treatment… I'm talking about chemotherapy here… we're seeing more and more impressive remission rates every year."

He stopped for a moment to let what he had said sink in.

"Is my wife going to die?" I asked, deciding at that instant to jump to the end of this unfolding horror story.

"She might," he replied without hesitation, "but I don't think she will. Not if we start treatment right away. She's young, and she's strong."

"What are her chances?" I asked, searching his face for signs of doubt or lack of confidence.

This time he waited a moment before answering. "I would say she has a good chance of survival. Probably as high as 60%."

" 'As high as 60%'?" I shot back without thinking. "My God! You call that a 'good chance'?" Without realizing it, I had raised my voice considerably and was now leaning forward in my chair with one arm on the edge of Dr. Goldstein's desk. "I see that as a 40% chance of dying," I continued, shaking my head in disbelief.

Dr. Goldstein was unaffected by my outburst. He sat perfectly still, his hands clasped on top of Peg's file, and looked impassively across the desk at me. "As I said, Mr. Herbert, your wife is very sick, and her form of leukemia is very aggressive. But in answer to your question, yes, I think a 60% chance of survival is a good chance of survival. I would even say it's something to be thankful for."

I looked at him, hard, hating him at that moment for what he had said and for how he had said it.

A 60% chance of survival might sound good to you, pal, I thought as I stared at his expressionless face, *but we're not talking about your wife here, are we? We're talking about mine.*

But as quickly as my anger had flared, it began to disappear as I realized Dr. Goldstein wasn't the enemy. He was only the messenger, and maybe, just maybe, the rescuer.

I leaned back in my chair and looked at the framed diplomas and certificates on the wall next to me, and started to pick at a fingernail. Neither of us spoke for almost a minute.

"For what it's worth," I said finally, "I understand what you're saying, and I guess I agree with you. A 60% chance of survival is better than nothing. So what do we do now?"

"Well, your wife's probably being admitted to Huntington Hospital as we speak. My plan is to see her tonight and put in the orders for tests that need to be done before we can begin her chemotherapy. And then tomorrow, probably in the afternoon, I'll install what we call a central line. It's similar to an intravenous fitting, but larger and inserted into the subclavian vein just above the clavicle. Here at the base of the neck." He placed his middle finger and index finger in a hollow at the base of his neck to show me where this central line would be positioned. "This lets us deliver large doses of medication without having to worry about blood vessel collapse. Then Saturday morning, probably," he continued, "Monday morning at the absolute latest, we'll begin her chemotherapy."

He waited for me to say something.

"I told your wife we can beat this, Mr. Herbert, and I think we will."

I looked at him for as long as I dared, reflecting again on how young he was, before answering. "I hope so, doctor... because this is my wife we're talking about here... and I love her... very, very much."

I looked down at my hands, now clasped between my knees, and then up at him again. "She's my life. And I have to tell you... the thought of anything happening to her... is... impossible to even think about..." My voice trailed off involuntarily.

"I understand," Dr. Goldstein replied as he rose from his seat. "Believe me, I do. And be assured, Mr. Herbert, we'll do everything possible for your wife."

He extended his hand. Our meeting was over.

Fifteen

At seven forty-two I was walking back to my car from Dr. Goldstein's office. *The whole thing took less than twenty minutes,* I said to myself as I backed out of my parking spot and headed for the exit. *It took less than twenty minutes for him to tell me my wife has a 40% chance of dying.*

I waited for a break in the westbound traffic and turned west on Main Street, blinking back tears, heading for home to pick up Jennie before going to the hospital. I tried to think logically, but I couldn't. Instead, my mind was overwhelmed by disjointed questions and thoughts. More questions than thoughts, and mostly questions without answers. Some of the thoughts were practical thoughts, some terrible, some simply inane—one tumbling over another chaotically like waves on a beach in a powerful storm, each one demanding immediate recognition over the prior one.

I wonder how long Peg'll be in the hospital?

Have to remember to call the bank tomorrow morning and let them know what's happening. They're not gonna be happy campers. She was supposed to come off maternity leave in what? Two weeks? And now this. Gotta call 'em first thing in the morning.

The hell with the bank. Have to remember to call Peg's mom tonight when I get home and let her know what's happening. Maybe Peg's already called her. No. She couldn't have. No time. That'll be a tough call.

Wonder if Goldstein is the right guy? If he knows what he's doing?

God, who's gonna take care of the kids while Peg's in the hospital?

What if she dies?

She's not going to die.

But what if she does? Who'll take care of the kids then? How can I take care of a three-year-old and an eight-month-old and go to work?

What would life be like without Peg? Impossible to imagine.

Stop it, John. Stop thinking like that. Can't think like that. Peg's not going to die. Can't happen.

But the rest of this is happening.

What's Peg done to deserve this? Why her? Of all people, why her?

Leukemia! Shit!

Maybe Goldstein is wrong. He could be, you know.

Yeah, right. Who are you kidding? He isn't wrong, and you know it.

This is too terrible to be real. Can't be happening. Not to her. Not to us...

Sixteen

I pulled into my driveway a few minutes before eight and found Dave and Beth Clayton, the couple we were supposed to go sailing with Saturday night, sitting at the picnic table with my kids. Dave was on the far side watching Jennie color; Beth was on the side closest to me with John on her lap, entertaining him with a stuffed animal she was moving with her free hand.

Beth worked at the same bank as Peg in the personnel department and had become Peg's best friend during the seven years they had worked together. She was a little waspish in terms of dress and mannerisms, very refined and very precise, but she was also quick to laugh, not afraid to be the butt of a joke and a lot of fun to be with. Thirty-three years old, five-seven, with light brown hair that came just below her ears and framed her face with a single wave on each side, she was quite attractive, even though she rarely wore makeup.

Dave, on the other hand, was anything but refined and precise. Not that he was coarse, because he wasn't. He was just down-to-earth and direct, totally without pretense, equally quick to laugh and quicker to see the funny side in anything. Very much a "what you see is what you get" kind of guy. He too was thirty-three and about the same height as Beth, but had a physique that always reminded me of a fireplug. Short, solid and really tough to move. He was an ex-Marine and moved with the powerful grace of a man who knew how to take care of himself.

I'd first met Beth and Dave when they invited Peg and me to their apartment in Hastings-on-Hudson for a Christmas party in 1975. I liked them both instantly. A month or two later, Peg and I invited them for dinner at our house in Huntington. We had a delightful evening, but over dessert Beth admitted that seeing our house and the lifestyle it afforded convinced her they really needed to get out of their apartment and buy a home. Half in jest, I mentioned that the house diagonally across the street from us had just been put on the market. They returned to Huntington the next day, visited the house with a local realtor, and put down a deposit that afternoon. Six weeks later they moved in, and as they say, the rest is history. The four of us became best friends.

"Hi guys," I called as I got out of the car.

I walked over to the picnic table, gave Beth a quick kiss on the cheek and bent down to give John a kiss on the top of his head. I rumpled his hair and then walked around to the other side of the table to give Jennie a hug and a kiss.

"Hi, Daddy," she said without looking up and without interrupting her crayoning.

Dave got up from the picnic bench, and we shook hands.

"Sorry I'm so late," I apologized, looking first at him and then at Beth. Beth didn't answer, but instead quickly wiped away a tear before Jennie could see it.

"That's okay," Dave replied, squinting hard in an attempt not to cry. "How are you doing?"

"I don't know, Dave. I'm in shock, I guess." I put my briefcase down on the table. "When did you guys get here?"

"A little after seven," Dave answered. "So what's the story?"

"The story," I began, "is Peg has leukemia. But I guess Linda told you that."

"Yeah, but not a lot else."

"Well, the kind Peg's got is called acute myelogenous leukemia. Which is one of the most aggressive types. And it's life-threatening unless she gets treated right away."

"What do they do?" Beth asked as she brushed away another escaping tear.

"Chemotherapy. They'll start Saturday morning or Monday morning latest."

"What's the prognosis?" Dave asked. "Is this something they can cure?"

I looked across the table at Jennie, crayoning intently.

"Sixty percent," I said as quietly as I could.

"Sixty percent chance of cure?" Dave replied, not believing he had heard correctly.

"Of survival," I whispered. "The word the doctor used was 'survival.'"

"Jesus," he exclaimed softly, and he turned away from Jennie and me while Beth resumed wiggling the stuffed animal in front of John, now ignoring the tears running down her cheeks.

When Dave turned to face me again, he was dry-eyed, but his face was contorted with the effort of keeping his emotions in check. "Tell me about Dr. Goldstein," he said. "How did you hear about him? What do you know about him?"

"I never knew he existed until today. Dr. Edwards referred Peg to him this afternoon."

"What's he like?"

"What's he like?" I said, repeating the question. "He's brusque. Not warm and friendly. Not a great personality. And he's young. Probably a year or two younger than me. But he gives the impression of being confident. Of knowing his stuff."

"Where'll Peg be treated if he's her doctor?"

"First of all, he is her doctor as of this afternoon. Peg's already agreed to that. And he'll be treating her here at Huntington Hospital."

"How do you feel about that?" Dave asked.

"About what?" I asked, confused by the question.

"About him being Peg's doctor. About her being treated at Huntington Hospital."

"What do you mean, 'How do I feel about it'?" I answered, knowing a trace of annoyance was evident in my voice in spite of my effort to conceal it. "Peg's sick. She needs treatment. He can treat her. What else is there to say?"

"I guess what I meant to ask," Dave said, "was how do you feel about Peg being treated here in Huntington as opposed to Manhattan, let's say?"

"Haven't given that a thought. Haven't had a chance to. Why?"

Dave hesitated before answering. "Look, it's none of my business," he finally said, slowly, cautiously, "but if Beth were sick, I'd want her treated in Manhattan—not in a small-town hospital like Huntington Hospital."

"You may have a point," I replied, "but if I believe what Goldstein says, we don't have time to start looking for a cancer specialist in New York City. Peg needs treatment, and she needs it now—not next week or next month. Plus the fact that we've already agreed to her being his patient."

"Just listen to me for a minute," Dave urged. "Just for a minute. When I first came to New York," he began, "I worked for a research lab, and one of the doctors I worked with was a Steven Werner, who was doing some pretty advanced cancer research and was really well respected. Anyway, he left after I did and went to New York Hospital in Manhattan to do clinical research. Far as I know, he's still there, and I think he'll remember me. And if he does, maybe he'd agree to take Peg on as a patient. What do you think?"

"Jesus, Dave, I don't know," I said as I watched the crayon protruding from Jennie's balled-up little hand go back and forth. "I don't know how much experience Goldstein has, and Huntington Hospital sure as hell isn't New York Hospital, but still..."

"Let me at least call him," Dave pressed. "Let me see what he says. If it's yes, you make the decision then, not now. What d'ya say?"

The crayon continued to go back and forth, back and forth.

"Okay," I agreed, turning away from Jennie to face him. "Let's see what happens."

"Where can I reach you tomorrow morning?" Dave asked.

"My folks' house, I guess. By the time I get Jennie there tonight, I might as well spend the night there too. You got their number?"

"I've got it," Dave assured me.

We stood looking at one another for a moment or two, saying more without a single word than we ever could have in hours of talk. Suddenly, Dave reached out and gave me a powerful hug, holding me for several seconds. When we separated, he was crying, and his face was filled with pain. He wiped his eyes with the back of his hand.

"Take Jen to the hospital to see Peg," he said, his voice breaking. "We'll stay here with John until your folks get here."

I patted him on the arm and nodded in silent acknowledgement of my gratitude.

Beth shifted John from her lap to her hip and got up from the picnic bench. She gave my cheek a gentle stroke with her hand and looked at me sadly.

"Tell Peg we love her," Beth said, her words punctuated by swallowed sobs, "and that we'll be praying for her and for you... and tell her I'm sorry... that she's sick... and that I hope she gets better quickly... and comes home soon."

"I will, Beth."

I looked over at Jennie and held out my hand for her to take. "You ready, sweetheart? It's time to go see Mommy."

Seventeen

The hospital was only a mile and a half from our house, so there wasn't a lot of time for Jennie to ask questions. But the questions came anyway, as I knew they would, and I gave her the standard answers to the expected questions, one by one, almost as if I had taken a course on what to tell a three-year-old whose mommy is in the hospital. But some of Jennie's questions weren't expected and took me very much by surprise.

"Daddy, where's Mommy?"

I glanced up into the rearview mirror and saw her, perched in her car seat, looking at me.

"Mommy's sick today, and she had to go to the hospital so she can get better."

"Why is she sick, Daddy?"

"I don't know, honey, but the doctor will find out why."

"Is he a good doctor?"

"Yes, sweetheart, he's a very good doctor." *Funny how a three-year-old can zero in on the very same question the adults are asking,* I thought to myself.

"Is Mommy going to be all right, Daddy?"

"Yup. She'll be fine."

"Is she going to die?"

Jesus, I said to myself. *Where did that come from? What made her ask that?* A deep breath. "Of course not. She's just a little sick."

"Will she come home tonight?"

Another deep breath. *She's going to catch me if I'm not careful,* I thought.

"I don't think so, honey."

"Tomorrow night?"

"Maybe. We'll see."

Well done. Well deflected.

"I'm glad we're going to see her."

"Mommy's going to be glad to see you too, sweetheart. I'll bet she misses you a whole lot already."

"Who's going to tuck me in tonight and hear my prayers?"

"Well, either Grandma or Grandpa or I will. How about that? Will that be okay?"

When Jennie didn't answer for several seconds, I looked into the rearview mirror again and saw her staring pensively out the side window next to her car seat.

"Well, what do you say? Will that be okay?" I asked.

"I guess so," she answered in a small, sad voice.

Not a great endorsement for Grandma, Grandpa or Dad, I thought, *but then that's why they invented mommies, isn't it?*

"I miss Mommy," Jennie said a few seconds later, still staring out the side window.

"Me too, honey. Me too."

Eighteen

Visiting hours had long since started by the time we arrived at Huntington Hospital, so I had to park in the lot farthest from the main entrance. As we walked from the car to the sidewalk leading to the front doors of the hospital, Jennie's chatter stopped, and she became quiet. Perhaps she was frightened by the size of the building looming in front of us, or perhaps she was thinking about my answers to her questions. But whatever the reason, she walked next to me in silence, taking four steps to every one of mine, her hand buried in my hand.

When we reached the hospital lobby, we went to the visitor registration desk and checked in with one of the receptionists, an elderly lady in the red and white striped uniform that earned her and volunteers like her the nickname "candy stripers." She informed us Peg was on the fifth floor, East Wing, Room 512, and directed us to the elevators.

I pressed the up button, and the doors of the middle elevator quietly slid open. We stepped inside, and Jennie, never having been in an elevator before, immediately started to look around her, trying to understand what we were going to do in this tiny room without furniture. I pressed the fifth floor button, and as the elevator began to rise, Jennie first looked down at her feet and the floor in response to the pressure she felt from the elevator's rapid rise, and then up at me with the wide, happy grin of discovery. At another time, in another place, the look would have struck me as priceless. Tonight, it only served to underscore the sadness of what was happening.

When the doors opened on the fifth floor, we were met with all the sights, sounds and smells that characterize any hospital. It was still early in the evening, so all of the hall lights were ablaze, the paging system asked doctor after doctor to pick up line so-and-so or report to room such-and-such, and the air was heavy with the smell of cleaning solvents and disinfectant and, to my nose, sickness.

We followed the signs pointing the way to the East Wing, Jennie's hand still buried in mine, her sandals going slap, slap, slap on the polished vinyl tile floor. Within moments we were outside of Peg's room. The door was ajar, but before we had a chance to knock, Peg called out to Jennie.

"Is that you, sweetheart?"

In an instant, Jennie withdrew her hand from mine and ran into the room and over to Peg's bed at full speed. "How did you know it was me, Mommy?"

"I could hear little feet coming down the hall," Peg answered, wrapping her arms around Jennie's torso, "and I knew they belonged to you."

Peg was sitting up in bed in one of her own nightgowns. She still wore her makeup from earlier in the day, but her mascara was badly smudged, probably from crying, and her hair was in disarray. She looked tired, but she was calm. For some reason, she had been assigned a private room, so the three of us were alone.

Peg and I said nothing about my meeting with Dr. Goldstein, and I didn't bring up my conversation with Dave. Instead Jennie and Peg talked as only a three-year-old and her mommy can, with Jennie rambling on about this and that as Peg hung onto every word.

The minutes passed, and too soon it was time for us to go. It was almost nine, way past Jennie's bedtime, and I still had to go back to the house and pack an overnight bag before taking her over to my parents' house for the night.

"Hon, we should go," I said.

"I know. I know," Peg replied, nodding rapidly to emphasize that she understood.

"I don't want to go home, Mommy," Jennie piped in. "I want to stay here with you."

"I know, honey," Peg said, holding her close with one hand and stroking her head with the other, "but it's past your bedtime, and I think Daddy should take you home now."

"But I'm not tired, Mommy," came the automatic response as Jennie pulled away from Peg and looked squarely at her.

"I know, honey, but Mommy is, and I think Daddy is too."

Jennie looked at Peg as if she were ready to cry. "Will you come home tomorrow, Mommy?"

"I don't think so. But soon, I promise."

"You promise?"

"Yes, I promise."

"I miss you, Mommy."

"I miss you too, sweetheart," Peg replied, starting to lose her composure.

She gave Jennie a kiss on her forehead, then on the top of her head and then gave her a long, silent hug. As if on cue, I picked Jennie up off the bed and put her back on the floor next to me.

I had no idea what thoughts were going through Peg's mind at that moment as she felt her little girl slide out of her arms. She must have been in agony, terror-stricken, but she gave no indication of any of that. She just bit her lower lip, quickly wiped away a tear and tried to smile, first at Jennie, then at me.

I bent down to kiss her good night. "I'll call you in the morning," I said as I straightened up.

I took Jennie's hand, and we started to leave.

"Good night, Mommy," Jennie called out when we reached the door.

"Good night, sweetheart."

"I love you, Peg," I said as I always did just before we turned out the light and went to sleep.

"I love you too," Peg answered quietly from her bed, her hand up to her mouth, her fingers pinching her lips.

A second later and we were in the hall, Jennie's hand again in mine, on our way back to the elevator. And as we walked down the hall hand in hand, I listened to the slap, slap, slap of Jennie's sandals, and I wondered if Peg were listening too.

Nineteen

I stayed with the children at my parents' house that Wednesday night and decided not to go into the office the next morning. Instead, I called Peg shortly after breakfast and told her of my conversation the night before with Dave about Dr. Werner.

"So," I said in conclusion, "Dave's going to call me here as soon as he gets in touch with Dr. Werner, and we need to be ready with a decision. Assuming Dr. Werner's willing to treat you, that is. So... what do you want me to say to Dave when he calls?"

"I don't know," Peg replied after several seconds of thought.

"Well, we have to make a decision, hon, one way or the other."

"I know. I just don't know what the right thing to do is." She paused. "What do you think about Dr. Goldstein?"

"He seems competent, and he's certainly confident, but he's young. Hell, Peg, he's younger than I am, which makes me wonder how much experience he's got."

"I know," Peg agreed. "I've been thinking the same thing. And what about the hospital? Huntington Hospital, I mean?"

"Well, it's probably a good enough hospital for normal stuff, Peg, but I don't think what you've got is normal stuff. So I'm not sure Huntington Hospital is up to the task of taking care of you."

Peg said nothing in response, so after a second or two, I continued. "On the other hand, if you transfer into Manhattan for treatment, it's going to be a whole lot more difficult for people to visit you. You won't see people as often as you would if you were here in Huntington. Especially Jennie and John. But the question is, what's more important? Visitors, or the quality of care you get?"

"So you think I should go into New York and let Dr. Werner treat me if I have the chance?"

"I didn't say that. Anyway, it's more important what you think."

"I don't know what to think," she said softly. "I don't want to be a million miles away from everyone and not be able to have people visit me, especially the kids. But at the same time, I want to beat this thing, and I'm not sure Dr. Goldstein and Huntington Hospital are going to give me my best chance. But maybe I'm wrong. Maybe he's the best there is, and maybe a small hospital like Huntington will give me the kind of care a big city hospital can't. I don't know. I just don't."

We were both silent for a moment before Peg continued.

"I think what I'd really like is for you to make the decision. Can you do that for me?"

"If that's what you want, yes. That's not like you, though."

"I know, but I'd like to leave it up to you," she repeated. "I know you'll do what's right."

"Then that's what we'll do," I replied. "I'll let you know what's happening as soon as I hear from Dave. Okay?"

"Okay," Peg replied, barely audibly.

"I'll do my best, Peg."

"I know you will. You always do."

Twenty

Dave called at ten-forty. "Hi. How are you?" he said, beginning the conversation as he always did in his crisp military way.

"I'm all right. You?"

"I'm good."

"Did you get to Dr. Werner?" I asked.

"Sure did. Got to him just before he started his morning rounds."

"Did he remember you?"

"Yeah, he did," Dave replied, a touch of pride evident in his voice.

"So how'd it go?"

"Pretty good, I think, but I'll let you be the judge. We had a good conversation. And a long one. I told him all about you and Peg, how I came to know you. Told him about the family. You know, about Jennie and John. Stuff like that. I told him about Peg getting sick and about your concerns with Dr. Goldstein and Huntington Hospital. Basically tried to appeal to any compassion he might have for someone in trouble. Anyway, it worked, I guess, because even though he's not accepting any new patients right now, he's going to take on Peg.

"He asked me to let him know this morning if Peg wants to transfer to New York Hospital," Dave continued. "If she does, he'll arrange for her to be admitted tomorrow morning. He said you should arrange for an ambulance to bring her into the city, and you should plan to arrive at the hospital around ten-thirty. That way, he'll have time to examine Peg and still have all afternoon to run the necessary tests before they start her chemotherapy. Which, by the way, he'll probably start on Monday morning, if he agrees with Dr. Goldstein's diagnosis."

Dave paused. "So now, good buddy, the ball's in your court. If you want Dr. Werner to treat Peg, just say the word. He's there for you."

Dave waited for an answer, offering nothing more. He knew he shouldn't; he knew he couldn't.

And I knew a decision had to be made, and it had to be made now. But the enormity of that decision was terrifying. Peg had literally entrusted her life to me. She had put her life in my hands to do with it as I thought best.

"Okay," I suddenly heard myself saying. "Decision's made. We'll get Peg out of Huntington and into New York Hospital tomorrow morning. Call Dr. Werner and tell him he's got a new patient."

"Will do," Dave answered. "And for what it's worth... I think you're doing the right thing."

"I hope so, Dave. Because God help me if I'm not."

Twenty-one

I didn't see Peg until seven forty-five that evening, even though I had intended to visit her after lunch. I had called her room around one o'clock to tell her I was on my way, but there was no answer. I tried every twenty minutes or so from that point on, but each time, no answer. When I finally reached her at five twenty-five, after what must have been fifteen calls, she explained that she had been out of the room all day being subjected, it seemed, to every test known to modern man. Given the hour, I told her I'd see her as soon as I had grabbed a bite to eat.

When I arrived at her room that evening, she was in bed, propped up on two pillows that rested against the headboard, with a magazine in her lap and her eyes closed. She wore another one of her own nightgowns, a pale blue silky thing with thin shoulder straps. The left strap was off her shoulder and hung down against the outside of her upper arm. Where the strap should have been was a large bandage held in place with broad strips of adhesive tape. A clear plastic fitting, similar to the type used on intravenous lines, but much larger, protruded from its center. She looked so much paler and more tired than the night before, it was hard to believe barely twenty-four hours had passed. Her hair looked unkempt, she wore no makeup, and for the first time, she looked truly sick.

She opened her eyes as soon as she heard my footsteps at the door and greeted me with a tired smile. I pulled the room's single armchair over to the side of her bed, and she began to tell me about her day; a day that had included numerous blood tests, a spinal tap, the taking of a bone

71

marrow sample from her hip, urine samples, X-rays, electrocardiograms, more blood tests and still more blood tests. She put her hand to her shoulder and said Dr. Goldstein had installed the central line around two-thirty that afternoon in preparation for her chemotherapy scheduled to begin Saturday morning. She asked about the kids and how they were doing, but seemed to be somewhat more at ease with the idea of being apart from them.

"Did you hear from Dave?" she asked, suddenly changing topics.

"I did. He called me this morning."

"And…?"

She listened quietly as I told her about my conversation with him and didn't interrupt until I got to the part where Dave told me Dr. Werner had agreed to accept her as a patient.

"What did you say?" she asked, breaking in sharply.

I looked at her for several seconds before answering and then, watching her face for her reaction to what I was about to say, answered her question. "I told him to tell Dr. Werner he's got a new patient. And that we'd meet him, Dr. Werner that is, at New York Hospital tomorrow morning. At ten-thirty."

Peg made no comment. She just sat perfectly still, looking into my eyes as intently as I was looking into hers, waiting for me to continue.

"I've arranged for an ambulance to be here tomorrow morning at eight-thirty. To take you into the city. I'll go in with you."

Still no response, and still no indication from her face or her eyes as to what she was thinking. No grimace indicating disappointment. No smile indicating agreement. Nothing.

"You okay with this?" I asked, anxious for some kind of feedback.

Peg looked hard at me but remained silent.

"You told me to make the decision," I pressed, "and I did. Now, are you okay with it? Because if you're not, we'll change it."

I waited a second or two and asked my question again.

"So are you okay with it or not?"

Peg finally answered, but too late to give me the comfort level I had been looking for.

"Yes," she said slowly. "Yes, I'm okay with it. If you think it's the right thing to do."

She put her hand up to the bandage on her shoulder again. "I just can't help wishing we hadn't already started with Dr. Goldstein."

"Should I tell Dr. Werner we've changed our minds?" I asked.

I knew that wasn't what she was saying, but I desperately needed some kind of assurance that I had done the right thing.

"No. No," she replied emphatically. "The decision's been made, and I'm sure it's the right one. I just wish we had been able to make it last night. Then I wouldn't have had to go through all these tests today, which now I'll probably have to go through again with this new doctor. That's what bothering me. That and I've spent all day getting used to Dr. Goldstein being my doctor. And now he's not."

She paused and seemed to reflect on what she had just said. "But I can't have everything, can I?" she said, looking over at me with tears welling up in her eyes.

I looked down at my hands and realized I was sitting on the edge of the armchair, hunched over tensely, hands clasped between my knees.

"No, we can't have everything," I answered quietly. "If we could, we wouldn't be here, would we?"

We both sat in silence for several minutes, me on the edge of the chair, Peg in her bed, wondering how we had come to be in this place, for this reason, so quickly.

I was the first to speak. "I should call Dr. Goldstein and tell him what we've decided."

Peg nodded.

I took his card out of my wallet, walked over to the telephone on the far side of the bed and dialed his office number.

"Dr. Goldstein's office," a woman's voice announced after the fourth ring.

"Yes. My name is John Herbert. I'm the husband of Peggy Herbert, Margaret Herbert, who's a patient of Dr. Goldstein."

"Yes, sir. I'm afraid Dr. Goldstein is not in the office right now. This is his answering service. May I take a message for him, or is this is an emergency?"

"No, it's not an emergency, but I do need to talk to him tonight. Could I ask you to contact him and ask him to call me either here at Huntington Hospital in my wife's room, Room 512, or at my parents' home any time after, say, nine-thirty?"

"Yes, sir. I can do that. May I have that other number, please?"

"Of course. 516-922-6889."

"Very good, sir. You should be hearing from the doctor shortly."

"Thank you. Good night."

"Good night, sir."

I put the receiver back in its cradle and looked at my watch. It was eight-fifteen. I walked back around the foot of the bed to the armchair and had just sat down when Peg's phone began to ring. I leaped up, quickly walked back around the bed to the nightstand and picked up the receiver.

"Hello?"

"Mr. Herbert?"

"Yes, this is Mr. Herbert. Dr. Goldstein?"

"Yes. I'm returning your call. Is everything all right with Mrs. Herbert?"

"Everything's fine, doctor. Thank you for getting back to me so quickly."

I waited a moment before continuing, and as I did I saw that Peg was watching me. "Dr. Goldstein, I… apologize in advance for what I'm about to say, but my wife and I have… decided she should transfer to New York Hospital to be under the care of another physician there. We … we think we'll feel more comfortable having her treated in the city… in a larger hospital… by someone with a little more experience. So I've arranged for my wife to be transported by ambulance tomorrow morning to Manhattan—the ambulance arrives here at eight-thirty—and I'd really appreciate your arranging for her discharge before then."

I paused again.

"I'm sorry to have to tell you this after you've already begun treating Peg, but hopefully you understand."

He waited until I had finished talking and then gave a sigh that was audible over the phone. "Well, Mr. Herbert, the decision is yours and your wife's to make. But I must say I think both of you are making a very serious mistake. Huntington Hospital can give your wife the kind of personal one-on-one care she requires better than a large city hospital can— precisely because it is a small community hospital. As for the need for a physician with more experience… my credentials are exemplary, as any number of physicians in this community can confirm. But you've obviously made up your mind, so we should leave it at that."

I heard him sigh again. "Mrs. Herbert's discharge papers will be ready for you by the time you're ready to leave tomorrow morning. I wish you both the best of luck. Good night."

I was about to wish him a good night as well when I realized he had already hung up.

Twenty-two

We arrived at New York Hospital at ten minutes after ten on Friday morning, August 1st. The ambulance entrance was on the north side of the building and was accessed from Second Avenue by means of a cobblestone-paved alley between the hospital and the adjoining building. The alley was only wide enough to permit the passage of one ambulance at a time and opened into a small courtyard, also paved in cobblestone, large enough to accommodate three, perhaps four ambulances. Both the alley and the courtyard were shrouded in deep shadow by the building walls that surrounded them, even though the day was bright and sunny.

The hospital was a twenty-nine-story, stone block and brick edifice, probably dating back to the turn of the century. It covered more than two-thirds of a city block and could only be described as huge. Frighteningly huge.

Peg and I and the attendant waited in the ambulance while our driver went inside to log in Peg's arrival and transfer her to New York Hospital. After five or six minutes, he reappeared with a hospital orderly pushing a wheelchair, walked to the rear of the ambulance and opened the rear doors.

"Mr. Herbert, I've got Mrs. Herbert checked in for the moment," the driver announced as he and the orderly started to roll Peg's gurney out of the ambulance, "but Admissions would like you to see them as soon as you can. Okay?"

"Sure," I replied. "If I can find Admissions. This place is huge. Where is it?"

"First floor lobby, sir," answered the hospital orderly.

"Thanks. I'll go there after we get my wife to her room. I assume that's okay?"

"Yes sir, you can do that," the orderly replied crisply.

He turned to our driver as soon as Peg's gurney was out of the ambulance and onto the cobblestones. "Does the lady need a gurney, or is the wheelchair all right?"

"The wheelchair will be fine," the driver answered. "We brought her down to the ambulance this morning in a chair. That's okay, isn't it, Mrs. Herbert?"

"That's fine," Peg said, speaking for the first time since we had turned into the cobblestone alley. "I don't really even need the wheelchair."

"Oh yes you do, ma'am," the orderly quickly said with a laugh. "Hospital rules say you've got to be in a chair or on a gurney."

While the orderly was helping Peg slide off the ambulance gurney and into the chair, the attendant got out of the ambulance and walked back to me with Peg's overnight bag in one hand and a large, thick manila envelope in the other. "Mr. Herbert," she said, "don't forget your wife's suitcase and her hospital paperwork. I'm pretty sure the attending physician here is going to want to see Mrs. Herbert's test results and all."

"Thank you for remembering," I said with relief. "I forgot all about them."

"Well, you've got a lot on your mind today," she replied over her shoulder as she climbed back up into the ambulance.

"Got that right," the hospital orderly agreed. "We all set now?"

"We're set if you are," I answered, trying not to let my growing anxiety show.

He deftly turned the wheelchair around in spite of the rough cobblestones and began to wheel Peg inside. I quickly extended my hand to the driver, thanked him for his help and caught up with Peg and the orderly.

We passed along one side of the emergency room, thankfully empty at this hour of the morning, and reached a bank of elevators. The orderly wheeled Peg into one, held the door open for me and two other people, punched the third and fourth floor for them at their request, and then punched nine for us.

"Floors seven through nine are for cancer patients," he volunteered when the second of the two people who had gotten on with us left the elevator. "Floor seven is the pediatric cancer ward; floors eight and nine are for the adults. Mrs. Herbert will be on nine."

A cancer ward, I thought. *How in God's name did we wind up here? In a cancer ward!*

I reached out and touched Peg's shoulder. In an instant her hand came up to mine, and she lightly squeezed my fingers. Somehow I knew she was wondering the same thing.

The elevator doors slid open, and the orderly signaled me to step out first. I did as he asked and found myself at the end of a long corridor with dark brown linoleum floor tiles, beige concrete walls and a high, vaulted concrete ceiling that had once been white. Ornate dark bronze lighting fixtures, each supporting five large milky-white glass globes, hung from the center of the ceiling every sixty or seventy feet.

God, this place is old, I thought, looking down the length of the corridor. *Look at the ceiling height. Don't see that anymore. And the walls must be a foot thick. Built like a fortress. But God, it's old.*

I waited until the orderly had wheeled Peg out of the elevator and then followed him a couple hundred feet down to a nurse's station. He brought the wheelchair to a stop, walked over to one of the nurses and said something to her. She looked at Peg and me while he was speaking and then at a clipboard on her desk. Apparently finding what she was looking for, she pushed back her chair and came out to greet us.

"Good morning, Mrs. Herbert," she said warmly, extending her hand first to Peg and then to me. "And good morning to you, Mr. Herbert. My name is Janet Reinart. I'm the head day nurse. We've been expecting you, Mrs. Herbert, and your room is all ready for you.

"This way, Jerry," she said to the orderly over her shoulder, and she started to walk down the corridor back towards the elevators. Then she stopped and pushed open a heavy oak door on the right side of the hall.

"Here we are," she announced cheerfully. She stepped aside to allow the orderly to wheel Peg into the room. I followed the orderly, and Janet followed me.

While Janet and the orderly helped Peg into bed, I looked around at what was to be Peg's new home for as long as it took for her to get well. The room was on the east side of the building and, thanks to three over-sized double-hung windows, offered a wonderful view of the East River and of Queens and Brooklyn beyond. The bed was placed against the south wall, and a large corkboard hung on the north wall at the foot of the bed. The ceiling was at least twelve feet high, and a lighting fixture with a single glass globe hung from its center. Off-white walls, ceiling, and vinyl floor tiles made the room bright but stark.

"I'll bring in some pictures of the kids tomorrow," I said after the nurse and the orderly had left the room and as I was taking Peg's things out of her overnight bag. "This place needs a little decorating, a little softening, don't you think?"

"I'm hoping I'm not going to be here long enough for that to matter," Peg said, her voice suddenly quivering.

"I'm sorry," I said, seeing the terror-stricken look on her face and realizing how she had taken my comment. "I didn't mean to imply that. I just meant..."

"I know. I know," Peg replied, waving my words away as she reached for a tissue. "I'm just scared to death that I'll never get out of this room alive, John."

"You're going to get well in this room, sweetheart," I assured her. "Not die in it. And you're going to walk out that door, healthy again, and come home to Jennie and John and me. Believe me."

I wrapped my arms around her, and she buried her face in my chest and began to cry.

"I don't want to die," Peg whimpered into my shirt. "I just don't want to die."

Twenty-three

He came in without knocking and was halfway across the room before Peg or I realized he was there.

"Mrs. Herbert," he announced, "I'm Dr. Werner, Chief of Blood Oncology here at New York Hospital."

Before Peg could respond, he turned to me and gave me a quick nod, acknowledging that he was introducing himself to me as well. "Mr. Herbert."

We each muttered a quiet hello, almost simultaneously, and waited for him to continue. But instead of saying anything more, he opened the manila envelope containing the record of Peg's stay at Huntington Hospital and stood next to her bed for several minutes, silently reviewing its contents.

He was a wiry man, medium height, about five-eight, probably forty-five or fifty years old, and his hair was salt and pepper. He came across as an intense man, and from the way he skimmed through Peg's file, I could tell that he was a man in a hurry. He didn't smile, and he made no attempt at warmth. When he was finished, he slid the folder back into the envelope and threw the envelope down onto the bed in what I took to be a disdainful gesture.

"So," he began, "welcome to New York Hospital. I trust your trip in this morning was uneventful?"

"It was fine, thank you," Peg replied uneasily.

"Good. Well, I see Dr. Goldstein ordered the standard range of tests. Unfortunately, we're going to have to do most of them again so I can be absolutely certain we're working with accurate information. I'll try to avoid taking another bone marrow sample, because I know that's a very uncomfortable procedure. But whether that's possible will depend on the quality of Huntington Hospital's slides. If they're not as good as we need, then we'll have to take another sample."

He stopped talking for a second and looked at the bandage on Peg's shoulder. "Sometime this afternoon I'll remove that central line. I don't know what Dr. Goldstein had in mind when he installed it, but there's no need for one as far as I'm concerned."

He looked at his watch. "It's ten-forty now. We probably won't be able to start any procedures until after lunch, but I'll write up the orders now, and that should let us get started early this afternoon. If Dr. Goldstein's diagnosis is correct, the treatment regimen, as I presume you know, will be a form of chemotherapy, which we should be able to start sometime tomorrow. Questions?"

Somehow the tone of his voice made it clear we shouldn't have any and that he wouldn't be thrilled about answering them if we did. But suddenly, his behavior changed completely, almost as if controlled by a switch, and he let a small smile creep across his face as he looked down at Peg.

"You must be very scared, Mrs. Herbert," he said softly, "but I want you to know that you're in one of the finest hospitals in this country staffed by some of the finest physicians in this country, and we're going to do everything humanly possible to make certain you walk out of here a healthy lady. You just remember that, okay?"

"I will," Peg murmured.

"Good. I'll see you this afternoon then."

He patted her shoulder, and I found myself wondering which Dr. Werner was the real Dr. Werner. He picked up Peg's envelope from the foot of the bed, turned around abruptly and walked towards the door.

"Have a good day, Mr. Herbert," he added as an obvious afterthought, and he closed the door behind him.

Neither Peg nor I said anything for a moment or two. We just stared at the door, half expecting him to come back and continue what had been an all-too-brief introduction.

"Well," I finally said when it was obvious we were alone, "Mr. Personality he's not, is he?"

"No, he isn't," Peg answered with a faint smile. "But then again, that's not why we're here, is it? For jokes, I have you."

I gave a little chuckle. "Yeah, for jokes you have me. Seriously though," I said, looking over my shoulder at the closed door, "are you okay with him?"

"First of all," Peg replied, "what choice do we have now? We can't go back to Huntington Hospital, can we? So we're committed to New York Hospital and to Dr. Werner. And yes, I'm okay with him if he can make it possible for me to come home to you and my children. If he can do that, he could be Attila the Hun for all I care."

I looked at Peg for several seconds, wondering what to say. And as I did, I realized her eyes were telling me everything she was feeling at that moment—sadness, fear, resignation. But perhaps most importantly, resolve. The look in her eyes told me she was getting ready to fight. As far as she was concerned, Dr. Werner's brief visit had been akin to a referee's instructions before a bout. And for her, the bell for round one was going to ring sometime early that afternoon.

Twenty-four

It is said that one can get used to anything. There was a time when I would have taken exception to that maxim, but Peg's ordeal at New York Hospital proved the adage to be true as we quickly settled into a routine that, if not comfortable, was at least workable.

My first step was to move into one of my parents' guest rooms so I could spend at least a few minutes each day with Jennie and John. I stopped all overnight business travel and started leaving work every afternoon at three so I could be at the hospital by four-thirty. I stayed with Peg every night until seven-thirty and then drove back to Long Island. Occasionally I arrived home in time to see Jennie before she went to bed, but I saw John only in the mornings at breakfast.

My mother always had a hot dinner ready for me no matter what time I came home, and she and my father would sit with me while I ate and gave them the latest report on Peg's condition. After I had eaten, the three of us would watch the ten o'clock news on Channel 5 and go to bed. Every day the routine was the same.

The shortened work day took a toll immediately, so I brought my office paperwork with me when I visited Peg. This worked rather well for the first few days and enabled me to keep up with most of my work. But by Thursday, August 7th, as the chemotherapy progressed, I found myself spending more time tending to Peg than to the paperwork. On Tuesday, August 12th, I opened the first of two briefcases only after she had fallen asleep and shortly before I left for home. And on Wednesday,

August 13th, I realized I was kidding myself. When I left for the hospital at three o'clock that afternoon, I left my desk piled high with unseen reports, unanswered memos and unread mail. The briefcases stayed in my office closet.

The chemotherapy was brutal. Day after day the IV tube dripped poison into Peg's body; poison intended to kill her cancerous bone marrow—hopefully at a faster rate than the poison was killing her. It penetrated every cell in her body and killed not only cancer cells, but also good, healthy cells, including white blood cells, the cells that defend us from attacks by bacteria, mold spores, fungus spores and all sorts of other invaders. With fewer and fewer white cells in her blood to ward off these attacks, Peg became increasingly vulnerable to the infectious agents that surround each of us every day.

As a result, Peg developed fungal infections, which in less than two hours progressed from a single black spot on her tongue or roof of her mouth to a growth large enough to cause her difficulty speaking or swallowing. She developed bacterial urinary tract infections so painful she was barely able to urinate without crying out in pain, and vaginal fungal infections—each in turn or simultaneously appearing as if from nowhere and rapidly blossoming into full-scale attacks.

The bacterial infections brought fevers. In less than thirty minutes, Peg's temperature would soar from normal to over one hundred two and a half as the bacterial attack of the moment progressed, unchallenged by defending white blood cells. As soon as her temperature began to rise, an antibiotic drip was added to the chemo drip. Sometimes the antibiotics worked rapidly, and within twenty or thirty minutes Peg's temperature would start to drop. Sometimes the antibiotics worked more slowly, and the fever would persist for several hours. And sometimes they didn't seem to work at all—capable of holding the offending bacteria at bay but incapable of overcoming them—and the fever would remain, unabated.

Whenever this happened, if the attending physician decided the fever couldn't be allowed to remain at its current level any longer, Peg was placed on a chill blanket, a contraption that matched the barbarity of chemotherapy, but mechanically rather than chemically. The chill blanket was basically a rubber pad interlaced with tubing through which water ran, refrigerated by a stand-alone chilling unit brought into the patient's room. The patient was placed on this ice cold rubber pad, usually naked, in the hope that mechanical refrigeration would accomplish what antibiotics could not—reduction of the fever.

The good news was that it worked. The bad news, judging from Peg's convulsive shivering and the look of outright agony on her face, was that it was a brutally painful treatment for a patient already weakened by sickness and burning with fever.

Thankfully, I only saw Peg on the chill blanket once—although she was placed on it several times—and I could do little to ease her suffering that afternoon other than rub her hands and feet to stimulate circulation and take her mind off the pain of the cold.

But the nausea was the worst. The chemicals that dripped into her arm stimulated the portion of her brain responsible for nausea and vomiting, and as long as the chemotherapy continued, so did the nausea and the vomiting—long after her stomach was empty.

For the most part I could do little to help Peg win her battle. The doctors, the nurses and the drugs were her allies, while I was relegated to being an observer. But the nausea let me be a part of the effort, although a small one. Each afternoon, sometimes for hours on end, Peg would retch again and again into the white enamel pan that I held under her chin. When she thought she might not throw up for a few minutes, I emptied and washed the pan in her bathroom sink and then returned to my post as the retching started again.

At one point Peg stopped eating, her logic being that if she had nothing in her stomach, she would have nothing to throw up. Human physiology, however, is not so easily thwarted. She continued to retch convulsively, dry heaves the nurses called them, and quickly realized having something to bring up was better than the alternative. She decided to resume eating. But deciding to eat was easier than finding the will to eat. So I assumed the roles of cheerleader and coach when dinner came, coaxing her, convincing her she had to eat to stay strong; and she had to stay strong to get through the chemotherapy.

And so it went. When she wasn't throwing up or racked with fever or convulsively shivering from having been on the chill blanket, she was lying in bed either asleep or trying to sleep, summoning up enough energy to fight for another day.

The days passed, and Peg's chemotherapy continued. The "bad cells" continued to die. Unfortunately, but unavoidably, so did the "good cells."

Twenty-five

Even though I visited Peg every day, I didn't see Dr. Werner as frequently as I had hoped. It always seemed that he had either just seen her moments before I arrived or stopped in moments after I left. So each day, within minutes of my arrival, I asked Peg for a recap of whatever he had said and tried to track her progress on the basis of her reports.

But a few times luck was on my side, and Dr. Werner was either with Peg when I arrived or came in to see her during my visit. Each time this happened, I took the opportunity to ask him how she was doing, what we could expect over the coming days, and what her long-term prognosis was. And each time his report was short and devoid of any of the details that give one a true sense of how things really are. As a result, he generally failed to give me a clear picture of where we were. But still, my sense each time was that Peg was fighting a good fight and had more than a reasonable chance of winning it.

Our exchange on Tuesday, August 12th, was typical.

"So how's our patient doing, doctor?" I asked.

He had just finished taking Peg's blood pressure and was now reviewing her chart on the clipboard that hung at the foot of her bed. "She's doing well," he replied without looking up.

"How well is well?"

"As well as can be expected."

"Meaning?"

He hung the clipboard back on the hook at the foot of the bed, slowly, deliberately, and looked at me as if he were trying to decide if I were challenging what he understood to be his absolute authority within the hospital. "Meaning her white cell count is coming down as it should. She's tolerating the chemo as well as can be expected. And her fevers are no worse than expected."

His tone was flat; his delivery robotic. I knew it was intentional, and I knew it was meant to convey some sort of message to me, but I pressed on.

"This is good?"

"Yes. She's progressing according to plan."

"Anything we need to be concerned about over the next few days?"

"Nothing other than what we've been concerned about all along. And that's infection and Peggy's reaction to the chemotherapy. Those are our two main concerns."

"Any idea yet as to when she'll be able to come home?"

"No."

"Are we winning?"

"Winning?"

"Are we winning the fight? Against her leukemia?"

"We're not losing."

"So we're winning."

Dr. Werner sighed loudly, making it clear he was trying to be patient with me.

"Mr. Herbert, a lot can happen between now and the day Peggy goes home. So I'm happy just to be able to say we're not losing. I'll see you tomorrow morning, Peggy. Good night, Mr. Herbert."

He turned and left the room. The question and answer period was over, and I had been suitably chastised.

Twenty-six

Peg slept through many of my visits—sometimes because of medication, and sometimes because sleep had been impossible earlier in the day because of nausea or a fever.

Some nights, however, she was able to stay awake, at least for a little while. But even on these nights I did most of the talking, because she didn't have the energy to do much more than ask simple questions. So Peg would ask her three- or four- or five-word questions, and I would try to tell her through my answers what was happening in the world she had left behind.

"How are my babies?"

"They're okay. They miss you terribly, of course. Especially Jennie. But they're doing fine. Mom doesn't go into the office anymore, so she's home with the kids all day. And Dad leaves the office for home around the time I leave to come here. To give her a little help. Jennie's in the pool every day, learning how to swim, and Dad bought John little arm floats that you blow up and attach to each arm. So now even he's in the water, happy as a pig in mud. But most important, they're having fun, and they're okay. The folks are taking great care of them. That's one thing you don't have to worry about."

"Does Jennie ask about me?"

"Every night when I come home and every morning before I leave for work. 'When is Mommy coming home?' 'Is Mommy feeling better, Daddy?' 'If she's feeling better, why isn't she coming home?' 'Will you bring Mommy home with you tonight?' 'Won't Mommy be surprised to see how I swim?' 'Does Mommy miss me, Daddy?' 'Tell Mommy I miss her.' 'I love Mommy a whole lot. Do you love Mommy a whole lot too, Daddy?' Does that answer your question? Yeah, Jennie asks about you. All the time."

"Is she frightened?"

"Most of the time, no. But sometimes… yeah, I think she gets scared. Like last night. Mom was putting her to bed just as I came home from here, and Dad told me the two of them were just about to say prayers. So I go down the hall to the kids' room and there's John in his crib, fast asleep, and there's Mom and Jen on their knees next to Jennie's bed saying the Our Father. And when they're finished, Jennie says 'And God, please bless Mommy, and please let her come home.' And when I heard that… I started to come apart at the seams. So Jennie sees me standing at the door, wiping my eyes and blowing my nose, realizes I'm crying, and the next thing I know she's crying and asking Mom why I'm crying. Guess daddies aren't supposed to cry, huh? Anyway, I don't think she's frightened unless I give her reason to be. So I've really got to work on that."

"And how's my little guy?"

"Probably five pounds heavier than when you last saw him. No, not really, but seriously, he's great. He's happy. He smiles all the time, and when he's not smiling, he's giggling. And Mom is loving him to death. Frankly, I think he's doing better than the rest of us combined."

"Can I see them?"

"Who? The kids?"

"Who else?"

"I've asked, sweetheart, but children under twelve aren't allowed on the adult cancer floors. Not even to visit parents. I called one of the administrators yesterday to see if there was any way they could make an exception for us. But she said if they make an exception for us, they'll have to do the same for anyone else who asks, and they can't do that. So for now, I'm afraid we're stuck. But I brought some pictures Mom took of the kids in the pool. I'll show them to you later. Okay?"

"Did you water my roses?"

"No, I didn't. I'm sorry, but I haven't been to the house since Saturday, and then only for a few minutes to pick up some clothes. But I'll call Dave tonight and ask him if maybe he can set up the sprinkler over the weekend."

"How is Dave? And Beth?"

"They're good. Dave said they're going to try to come in next Saturday to see you, but that'll depend on how Beth's feeling. She's due in a couple of weeks, so Dave's a little uncomfortable about making the trip into the city with her. But they're going to try."

"How's your father?"

"Not good, hon. He's taking all of this really hard. Harder than I ever would have thought. He just can't believe his 'sweet patooty' is sick. So no, he's not doing too well."

"How about your mother?"

"Well, you know Mom. She's tough. And she keeps her thoughts pretty much to herself, so it's hard to tell how she's doing. But she's determined to make life as good as she can for the kids while you're here. Sometimes I think she's afraid you're going to grade her or something when you get home. But really, I think she's all right. The kids keep her mind off you, and that's a good thing, I guess."

"How's work?"

"Well, it's a little crazy. I'm obviously not putting in the hours that I should be, so I'm behind on just about everything. But people understand. They really do. I've told a lot of our customers what's happening, and after they wish us luck, they tell me to take care of you and not worry about them. And they mean it. Kind of nice. And everyone at the company obviously knows what's going on, and they're all doing whatever they can to be of help. So work's okay."

"And how are you?"

"Me?"

"Yes, you."

"I miss you... so much. You have no idea how much I miss you. In the morning. In the evening. In the middle of the night. And when I think of you and all you're going through… it tears me apart, Peg. I… to be honest… I try not to think about you during the day, because it hurts too much when I do. And then I can't work. Can't focus. Can't function. And I keep asking myself why. Why has this happened? And I keep coming up empty. But I'm getting through it. God knows, if you can get through your end, I can get through mine. But I do miss you, and I love you. More now than ever before."

But one night, Wednesday, August 13th, Peg was wide awake, alert, almost vivacious. Our conversation that night was anything but one-sided and focused on a time before Dr. Werner and New York Hospital and chemotherapy and cancer. Instead, our conversation centered on memories—good memories—memories that we shared and which had come to define us.

"Do you remember the first time we made love?" I asked that night. Peg smiled.

"When was it? March? April?" I asked.

"April," Peg answered without any need for reflection. "The first Sunday in April, to be exact. Sunday afternoon. Anne Baker and Jane Goldberg had gone somewhere for the weekend, and Sarah and Jerry had gone out to the Island. And we had the apartment to ourselves."

"I guess you do remember."

Again Peg smiled. "Do you remember what happened afterwards?" she asked. "Do you remember what we did?"

"I sure do. We got dressed, and we went for a walk. West up 67th Street to Madison Avenue and then north up Madison. I don't remember how far. But I do remember that I was flying. I mean I felt great. And more in love than I ever thought possible. And I remember that as we walked along, we wondered if we looked any different to the other people on the street. We wondered if they could tell what had happened just by looking at us." I shook my head in amazement at the clarity of the memory and looked over at Peg.

"And I remember," she added softly, "that at one point during that afternoon, you were so deliriously happy you threatened to stand in the middle of the sidewalk and shout the news to everyone around us." She paused for a second and looked over at me, her eyes sparkling like they used to. "I'm kind of glad you didn't do that," she said with a little giggle.

And before we knew it, we were laughing. At each other and at the silly things people in love do.

When the laughter subsided, we both fell silent and looked out the window, watching the shadows of the buildings on the east side of Manhattan slowly stretch across the East River as the sun moved lower in the western sky.

"Do you remember Dr. Amann?" I asked, turning away from the window to face Peg again. "Dr. Richard Amann?"

"I remember," she replied. "The male fertility specialist."

"He's the one."

Peg rolled her eyes. "I also remember his waiting room," she said, "and how tiny it was. And how embarrassing it was for you to be sitting there, holding your semen sample in a test tube, with all those other people who were just as embarrassed as you because they were there for the same reason. And I remember all those letters and baby pictures from patients who had babies after seeing him, all over the walls of the waiting room and on both sides of the hall leading down to his office. Yes, I remember Dr. Amann."

"Do you remember what he said after he examined the sample we brought in?" I asked. "After he had spent probably ten minutes telling us all about sperm counts and maturation stages and motility levels? When I asked him if I was sterile?"

Peg shook her head no.

"He said, and I quote, 'Well, let's put it this way. In the eyes of the law, no, you're not sterile. But, practically speaking, if you ever spent an evening in the back seat of a car and worried about it the next morning, you didn't have to.' "

Again we laughed. Not just at the recollection of Dr. Amann's words, but also at the thought of where we had been, faced with the possibility of never being able to have children, and where we had ended up, with not one but two beautiful, healthy children.

"Do you remember the sign outside that church on the way back to our car after we saw Dr. Amann?"

"I do," Peg replied thoughtfully. "I've thought of what that sign said many times in other situations. 'God's delays are not necessarily God's denials.' Right?"

"That's right. And that was true, wasn't it? A little surgical help from Dr. Amann… what was it called? A varicocoelectomy? Yeah, that was it. And here we are, five years later, with Jennie and John."

Peg gave a tired little chuckle. "I remember when it looked like we'd never have any children even after Dr. Amann," she said quietly. "After your operation. Months and months after when I still wasn't pregnant. I remember us deciding that if we weren't going to have children, we could still have fun. So we booked our trip to France on the *QE 2*."

She looked over at me with a sad smile. "God, that was a great trip. Remember? A week on board ship and then two weeks in France. One week in Normandy and the Loire valley and the second week in Paris. I remember we couldn't afford the trip, but we figured we'd have the rest of our lives to pay for it. Then we came home; and three, four months later, I'm pregnant with Jennie."

"Four months later," I said. "We came home from France near the end of July, and you went to the doctor the Wednesday afternoon before Thanksgiving. I remember that because they said you wouldn't have the test results until Friday since the next day was Thanksgiving. And I was pissed. I wanted to know so badly."

"That's right," Peg agreed. "I'd forgotten about that. You really were pissed."

We looked at each other for a moment in silence, each of us again wondering how we had come to be here.

"Maybe we should take another trip to France on the *QE 2* when you get out of here," I suggested, happy to have come up with a way to push aside the gloom that had started to build—the gloom that always seemed to hover over us these days, right at the edge of our every thought, day after day, ready to wash over us at any moment for any reason. "Would you like that?" I asked.

Peg looked at me for a long time before answering. It seemed as if she were trying to read my thoughts, trying to judge if I were serious or simply pretending to be optimistic for her sake.

Apparently unable to decide, she sighed deeply, looked down at her hands and then over at me. "Maybe," she finally replied. "We'll see. We'll see."

I waited for her to add something, but instead she seemed to lose interest in what we had been saying, and she turned to look out the window again, deep in thought. I watched her, wondering where she was at that moment and what she was thinking, knowing that the forces of gloom were winning.

When she spoke again after several minutes of silence, she spoke without looking at me, still staring out the window, as if I weren't even there. "I wonder if I'll ever see my babies again," she said matter-of-factly, without emotion.

"Peg! Come on!" I shouted.

She turned away from the window to look at me.

"What a terrible thing to say! Why would you ever say something like that? Look at how far you've come. If you've made it this far, chances are good you'll make it all the way. It's just a matter of time, Peg. We just have to be patient. Have to give Dr. Werner and his people time to turn this thing around. That's all."

She nodded quickly, as if she were trying to shake off the thoughts that had led her to ask the question in the first place. Then she began to smooth the sheets nervously with both hands, and her eyes filled with tears. "I know. I know you're right. I just have to be patient. I keep telling myself that. I really do. Hour after hour. Day after day. It's just that I miss them so much, John. You have no idea what it's like to lay here and know my babies are out there with someone else. Not me. And to wonder if the last time I'll ever see John was in our kitchen the afternoon I went to Huntington Hospital. Or if the last time I'll ever see Jennie was when you brought her up to see me that night. You can't imagine what that's like, John. No one can."

She reached for a tissue from the box on her night table, wiped her eyes and blew her nose. "You know," she continued, "I keep thinking about what a wonderful life I've had—we've had."

"Have," I interrupted. "Not 'had.' 'Had' makes it sound like it's over, and it isn't."

Peg ignored me and kept talking. "And then I find myself wondering if maybe that's the problem. That maybe our life was just too damn good. Maybe we're paying now for having had such a great life."

"What are you talking about, sweetheart? You're being silly."

"I'm not being silly, and I'll tell you why. You've heard the expressions. 'There's no such thing as a free lunch.' 'Pay me now, or pay me later.' 'Into every life some rain must fall.' You've heard them. You know the sayings as well as I do. And maybe there's some truth to them. If there weren't, why did people create them in the first place? Adages reflect people's beliefs, John, and those beliefs, I have to think, are based on experience. And if that's true, then why did we expect to be so lucky in life when other people aren't? When so many other people have such difficult lives with so much pain? What makes us different from them? Why are we so surprised this has happened to us? What made us think we'd get through this life without having to pay some dues?"

She stopped talking and stared at me, demanding an answer with her eyes. I sat there speechless, not knowing what to say, because, in a way, everything she had said made sense.

"I never thought of what's happened in those terms," I stammered finally. "I've never thought of life in those terms either. I guess the truth is... I just thought... we were lucky. Never gave it much more thought than that."

"Well, guess what, sweetheart," Peg said sleepily, suddenly out of energy. "We've just run out of luck. It's time to pay some dues."

I started to protest, started to say something encouraging, but realized I was too late. She was already fast asleep.

Twenty-seven

Friday, August 15th, was the two-week anniversary of Peg's arrival at New York Hospital. I left the office that afternoon at five after three and arrived at the hospital at twenty after four. As I walked down the corridor from the elevators towards Peg's room, I saw that her door was closed, usually a sign that someone was with her. I knocked lightly on the door before opening it, hoping Peg's visitor was Dr. Werner and not one of the nurses. I hadn't seen him since Tuesday, and I was anxious to get a first-hand report from him before the weekend.

I peeked in around the door; sure enough, there he was, sitting on the edge of Peg's bed, one leg crossed over the other, arms folded across his chest, looking more relaxed and more approachable than he had at any of our prior meetings. To my surprise, he smiled when he saw me and waved me in with his hand. "Your timing is perfect," he exclaimed.

I walked over to Peg's bed and bent down to give her a kiss. "Why's that?" I asked, taking off my suit jacket and hanging it on one of the hooks next to the bathroom door.

"Well, I was just about to tell your wife the results of the tests we did on the bone marrow sample we took this morning."

"I didn't realize you were scheduled for a bone marrow test today," I said, turning to Peg.

"Me neither."

"Well, anyway," Dr. Werner continued, "we took a bone marrow sample this morning to determine the extent to which you're responding to the chemotherapy. We obviously expected to see some improvement, but quite frankly, I didn't expect the kind of results we got."

"Is this going to be good news or bad news?" I interrupted in spite of myself.

"Good news," Dr. Werner responded with a self-satisfied smile. "Very good news."

He paused for a second, looking first at Peg, then at me, then back at Peg. "In short, on the basis of the bone marrow sample we took this morning, I am pleased to report that you, Mrs. Herbert, are in complete remission."

"Remission?" Peg repeated.

"What does that mean?" I asked. "Does it mean what I think it means?"

"It means we saw no cancer cells in your bone marrow sample. None whatsoever. In other words, the chemotherapy you've been receiving for the last thirteen days has successfully destroyed all of the cancerous tissue in your body, so your bone marrow sample showed no clinically detectable signs of leukemia. You're cancer-free."

"Oh my God," Peg whispered, hugging herself with one arm and pressing her other hand, balled up into a fist, against her mouth.

"Holy shit!" I exclaimed, stunned at this totally unexpected news.

"Oh my God, my God," Peg whispered again as she started to cry.

"Does this mean she's cured?" I asked, trying to control the elation that threatened to overwhelm me.

"In the clinical sense, yes, she's cured," Dr. Werner answered.

"But how is that possible?" I asked, still unable to believe what I was hearing. "I mean, she's only been here for two weeks."

"You'll recall that the type of leukemia Peggy has, I should say had, was an extremely aggressive form. The bad news with this type of leukemia is that, left untreated, it can overwhelm the body very quickly, resulting in death of the patient. The good news is it's very susceptible to aggressive chemotherapy if the therapy is started early enough in the disease cycle. We were lucky in that we were able to start treating Peggy's leukemia early enough to get a jump on it, with the result that as of this afternoon, she's cancer-free."

"Unbelievable!" I exclaimed. "Absolutely unbelievable!"

"Now a couple of words of caution are in order here," Dr. Werner continued, addressing Peg. "The good news, as I said, is that all of the cancerous cells in your body are dead. The bad news is all of the tissue in your body that normally produces white blood cells is also dead. Which means that until this tissue has a chance to regenerate itself, you have no white cells available to fight an infection."

"And what does that mean?" I asked.

"It means that it's more important now than ever before to keep Peggy free from infection—long enough to give her body a chance to regenerate the white blood cells she needs to fight infection on her own. Infection's been a risk ever since she started the chemo, but less of a risk than it is now, because although her immune system was impaired, it was still existent and functioning. Now it's not. So for the next several weeks, we have to do whatever we can to prevent her from being exposed to infectious agents. That means I'm going to ask you to limit visits to immediate family members only—and then only if they are completely healthy. In other words, if they even have so much as a head cold, I do not want them in this room. Understood?"

"Understood," I replied.

"I'll advise the floor staff of Peggy's status and will request that everyone who comes in contact with her over the next few weeks—doctors, nurses, aides, everyone—be gowned, masked and gloved to minimize the chances of someone transmitting something to her. So don't be alarmed if you see someone in here wrapped up from head to toe. And that will include all guests too," he added, looking at me. "Even you."

"Okay. But what happens if Peg does get an infection?" I asked, afraid to hear the answer but knowing I had to ask the question.

"Well, first of all, the likelihood is very good she will get an infection of some sort. It can't be helped. We're surrounded by infectious agents every day of our lives. What we're going to do, though, is monitor her very, very carefully throughout each day. That way we'll note the first sign of an infection, which will probably be a fever, early in its cycle, and we'll be able to respond immediately with the appropriate antibiotics before it gets out of control.

"One more thing," Dr. Werner said with an audible sigh, looking at each of us to make certain we were listening. "And please, neither of you should quote me on this. We're notoriously short-handed on weekends. Especially on summer weekends. And as I just said, I want Peggy monitored day and night. So I strongly suggest that we arrange for a private nurse to be here around the clock from this afternoon, say from six or six-thirty, until six o'clock Monday morning. And we should do this every weekend from now until Peggy's out of danger. Is that okay with the two of you? It's not going to be cheap, but I think it's something you have to do."

"If you think that's what we should do, that's good enough for me," I replied without hesitation.

"Good. I'll take care of that on my way out. They'll bill you directly, Mr. Herbert. I'll give them your home address. So," Dr. Werner concluded, slapping both hands on his thighs, "we're not out of the woods yet, but we've come a long, long way, and today's news couldn't be any better."

He turned to face me. "To use your words, Mr. Herbert, we're winning. Definitely winning. Not just 'not losing,' but winning."

"Thank you, doctor," I mumbled, still trying to absorb the last two minutes of conversation. "Thank you. Thank you for the news, and thank you for everything you've done. You have no idea how grateful I am. No idea whatsoever."

"Well, hold the thanks until we put Peggy in a car on her way home. But needless to say, this is the kind of news I love to give."

He turned back to Peg. "You probably won't get a lot of sleep for the next few weeks, because the nurses will be examining you and taking your temperature every two hours, twenty-four hours a day. But that's a small price to pay, isn't it?"

"It certainly is," Peg said, tears again running down her cheeks.

Dr. Werner stood up, patted Peg lightly on the cheek and extended his hand to me. "I'll leave the two of you alone now," he said as we shook hands. "I imagine you have a few things to talk about."

He was halfway to the door when he stopped and turned around. "I knew I forgot something. I'll be off this weekend, so Dr. Porter will be covering for me. Just so you know."

"Okay. Have a good weekend, doctor. And again, thank you."

He gave us a quick wave, turned back towards the door and was gone.

For several seconds, neither Peg nor I spoke. We just stayed where we were, her propped up in her bed, me standing a few feet away, both of us immobile, both of us too stunned to know what to say or do next. We stayed like that for fifteen or twenty seconds, until Peg lifted up her arms and reached out to me. In an instant, I was standing next to her bed, bending down to her, feeling her arms wrap around my shoulders, burying my face into her neck, now wet with tears as she sobbed uncontrollably. By the time we finished our hug, we were both crying and laughing at the same time.

"Do you realize what happened a few minutes ago?" I asked. "Do you realize what Dr. Werner told us?"

"I do. I do," Peg said between sniffles and giggles. "I do."

"You're coming home, Peg. To me. To Jennie. To John."

"I'm going to see my children again. I'm going to be their mommy again. Oh God, John. I can't believe it. I just can't believe it."

"Well, you better believe it, because it's true."

Peg nodded, blew her nose a few times, wiped her eyes and then laid her head back on her pillow.

"You know what's funny? The things I've missed most and want to do most when I get home are the simplest, silliest things you can imagine. I want to bury my face in Jennie's hair and smell it. I want to pick up John and feel his warm little body. I want to sleep in our bed. I want to take a hot shower whenever I want to. I want to listen to Jennie's non-stop nonsensical chatter. I want to feed John and watch him swallow his food and watch him smile as he tastes it. I want to unfold little shirts and little pants and little dresses and little sweaters and dress my kids. I want to tuck my children into bed. I want to hear Jennie say her prayers."

She stopped to blow her nose again. "I want to see my roses. I want to see the sky and the sun. I want to smell fresh air and feel the breeze on my face."

She looked up at me. "I want to come home. And I want to live."

Peg and I had what could only be described as a victory celebration that night. We both knew she wasn't out of trouble yet, but we also both knew she had cleared the toughest hurdle. For the first time in two weeks we talked about how life would be when she came home. She even brought up the trip to France on the *QE 2* and told me she'd love to go again someday.

It was an evening focused on the future instead of on the moment or the past. It was as good an evening as one can have in a cancer ward.

Twenty-eight

On Saturday morning, August 16th, Peg developed a fever.

Although expected, the fever was nevertheless frightening, because it meant she had already contracted an infection, even though twenty-four hours had not yet passed since Dr. Werner had declared her in remission. She was given massive doses of antibiotics intravenously throughout the morning and into the early afternoon, but her fever continued to rise. As a result, around two o'clock, she was once again placed on a chill blanket.

By the time my parents and I arrived shortly after five, Peg's temperature was almost back to normal, and she had been taken off the chill blanket. But she was a wreck. She was soaked with perspiration, she was shivering uncontrollably even though she had been off the chill blanket for over an hour, and she was exhausted from the fever and the antibiotics. So the visit was short and nothing like the night before. But the good news was that Peg had won another round.

As we prepared to leave, I remembered I had wanted to tell Peg that Dave had called.

"When did he call?" she asked with obvious effort.

"This morning. Just before lunch."

"How is he?"

I gave a half chuckle, half snort. "He's good. So is Beth. And he asked me to give you a hug for the two of them."

"What else did he say?"

"What do you mean 'what else'?"

"You laughed when I asked you how he was," she answered, eyes half closed.

"You don't miss a trick, do you?"

"Mmm-mmm," Peg whispered.

"He wanted to know if I'd like to go sailing on our boat."

Peg looked at me, her eyes now fully open, questioning, confused.

"What he wanted to know was," I continued, "would I like to go sailing tomorrow with Beth and him? He thought maybe I could use a few hours of relaxation and thought some time on *Windsong* might do the trick."

"What'd you say?"

"I told him no."

"Why?"

"Because if I went out on the boat, I wouldn't be able to visit you tomorrow."

Peg smiled. Weakly, but she smiled. "You should go," she said softly, eyes again half closed. "He's right. It would be good for you." She took several shallow breaths before continuing. "And given the way I feel right now, I probably won't be very good company tomorrow anyway. Seriously. Go. I don't mind."

"I'm not going to do that. Especially not after what you've gone through today."

"You really should. You can't do anything for me, and I could use the rest."

"You can't rest while I'm here?"

"Of course I can," Peg replied with a heavy sigh. "But I try not to. I try to stay awake when you're here. So I can see you. But tomorrow I should sleep. Go. I mean it. Call Dave when you get home, and say yes."

I smiled but shook my head. "I can't do that."

"Yes you can. Enjoy the day for both of us, and tell me all about it on Monday." She reached out for my hand and squeezed it. "Go. It's okay."

She closed her eyes, and a moment later she was asleep.

We stayed in Peg's room for over half an hour—my mother in the one chair, my father and I leaning against the windowsill—watching her sleep, not talking for fear of waking her. And when we were finally certain she was asleep and resting comfortably, we tiptoed out of the room, retrieved our car and began another trip home to Long Island.

Twenty-nine

The telephone rang at ten minutes after seven on Sunday, August 17th, as I was about to leave my parents' house to meet Beth and Dave at the yacht club.

"Who in hell could be calling at this hour on a Sunday morning?" I asked out loud as I ran to the desk next to the refrigerator, trying to answer the phone before either my folks or the kids woke up.

"Jesus, maybe it's about Peg."

I picked up the receiver on the third ring, suddenly afraid to put it to my ear. The voice at the other end asked for Mr. Herbert.

"Which one?" I replied automatically, knowing with a sinking feeling that I recognized the voice.

"Mr. John Herbert," the caller answered.

"Is this Dr. Werner?"

"Yes, it is," the caller replied.

"You've got me, Dr. Werner. John Herbert. Is something wrong? Has something happened?"

"Mr. Herbert, I'm afraid Peggy's taken a turn for the worse. I think you should come to the hospital right away."

My throat tightened. My heart began to race. My pulse pounded in my ears. And in the space of a second or two, question after question rose up in my mind, demanding answers.

What's he mean by 'a turn for the worse'? How bad a turn for the worse? What's 'right away' mean? How much time have I got to get into the city? Is Peg dying?

But I asked no questions, and Dr. Werner offered nothing more. "I'm on my way," I heard myself saying instead.

"Good," Dr. Werner replied. "I'm leaving for the hospital now and should be there in about thirty minutes. I'll see you there."

He hung up. I stood next to the desk for ten, maybe fifteen seconds, staring at the phone, trying to collect my thoughts. The house was totally quiet except for the hum of the refrigerator next to me. Then, aware that seconds were passing, I turned and ran across the kitchen, through the family room and down the hall to my parents' bedroom. I knocked hard on the door and after the third knock heard a sleepy response from my father.

"Yes?"

"That was Dr. Werner on the phone, Pop. He says Peg's taken a turn for the worse, and he wants me to come to the hospital right away. I'm leaving now, so can you call Dave and Beth and let them know? Tell them I won't be sailing with them this morning?"

There was silence for a moment, then the rustling of sheets and the sound of slippered footsteps walking across the floor. "Mom will do that," he answered from the other side of the door. "I'll go with you."

"What's the matter, Bill?" I heard her ask before I could reply.

"Dr. Werner just called John and asked him to come to the hospital right away."

"Pop," I called through the closed door, "I appreciate the offer, but I'm dressed and ready to go now. I don't want to waste time waiting for you. All right?"

"I'll only be a minute," he replied. "Just give me a minute."

"A minute, Pop," I agreed reluctantly.

He was true to his word. In just about a minute, he opened the bedroom door—gray stubble on his cheeks and chin, his hair barely combed, but dressed—and came out into the hall, followed by my mother. He gave her a kiss, looked at me with sleepy eyes, and without a word to either of us, began walking down the hall.

"Drive carefully," my mother said as she reached up to give me a kiss. "I'll be praying for you."

I gave her a hug and hurried to follow my father. I caught up with him in the kitchen, and we went into the garage. He hit the door opener, and we stood side by side watching the garage door roll up. We stepped out into a picture perfect August morning—cloudless blue sky, light breeze gently ruffling the leaves overhead, surprisingly cool—a day that would have been a great day for sailing or anything else.

"Want me to drive?" my father asked when we reached my car.

"No. This is going to be a fast trip, and I'll feel more comfortable behind the wheel than next to it."

He looked at me over the roof of the car and shrugged. "I won't press it, but take it easy, will you?"

I nodded, unlocked the doors and slid behind the wheel.

At seven-twenty we turned onto an empty Oyster Bay Road, the first of several winding, tree-lined two-lane roads that we would be taking and which were typical of Long Island's North Shore. Within seconds I was approaching sixty miles per hour, as fast as I dared given the curves and far in excess of the posted thirty-mile-per-hour speed limit.

Oyster Bay Road to Chicken Valley Road. Chicken Valley Road to Wolver Hollow Road. Wolver Hollow Road to Route 25A. Four and a half miles in just under six minutes.

We turned right onto Route 25A—straight, four lanes wide, almost empty—heading west towards New York City. I increased our speed to seventy-five, easing up only when we approached intersections, and even then only to fifty-five or sixty. If the traffic lights were red, I drove through them as fast as cross traffic allowed. Dr. Werner's "right away" kept sounding in my head.

A left on Roslyn Road towards I-495, the Long Island Expressway, also known as the LIE to hundreds of thousands of weekday commuters. I was down to fifty now, and traffic was starting to build. We had been on the road twelve minutes.

A right off Roslyn Road onto the service road for the Expressway, then up the access ramp and onto the LIE, again heading west into New York. I left the acceleration lane at over sixty, moved into the inside lane, the center lane, then the outside lane and was quickly up to seventy-five, then eighty, then a little faster. My father looked over at me as we inched past eighty.

I turned my headlights on and started switching my high beams on and off as we overtook other cars in the outside lane. Most people sensed something was wrong in the car that had suddenly appeared behind them from out of nowhere; they seemed to know its speed had a purpose. A flash of our high beams and these drivers quickly moved over to the center lane. But if a driver didn't move over immediately, I passed on the inside, refusing to be delayed. Outside lane to center lane to outside lane to center lane and back again. At times there was almost a rhythm to it.

As we got closer to the city, the traffic continued to build, and in spite of my best efforts our speed began to drop, not down to the speed limit, but slower nevertheless. At one point I found myself half hoping a patrol car would see us so he could run interference for us if the traffic got too bad. But then I realized if a patrol car saw us, he'd pull us over; and we'd have to explain our speed, perhaps successfully, perhaps not, and we had no time for that. I stopped hoping for a patrol car.

From the Long Island Expressway to the Grand Central Parkway to the Triborough Bridge to the toll plaza at the city end of the bridge. Incredibly, it was only five minutes to eight as we paid our toll and drove down the curved exit ramp to the southbound lanes of the FDR Drive. Three minutes later, we got off at the 96th Street exit, headed west on 96th to Second Avenue, and then left on Second and south to New York Hospital.

And then we were there. Our first left off Second Avenue brought us onto the hospital's main drive. Our second left, halfway down the drive and past a permit-only staff parking area, brought us into the deep shadows of the cobblestone courtyard in front of the hospital's main entrance. In a few hours this courtyard would be packed with cars, clogged with visitors coming and going. But right now at six minutes after eight on Sunday morning, the courtyard was empty. No cars. No people.

I stopped in front of the hospital lobby's revolving glass doors, and we got out of the car. In sharp contrast to the conditions out on Long Island, the air in the courtyard was hot and heavy and still. High above us and all around us, a thousand air conditioners in a thousand windows roared, keeping the heat and the humidity at bay.

As we got out of the car, a parking attendant came out of his booth at the end of the courtyard and walked towards us. "Visiting hours don't start 'til one o'clock," he declared aggressively when he was still several feet away.

"I'm afraid this is an emergency," I replied. "My wife's doctor called and told me to come to the hospital right away."

The attendant looked at me for a long moment. "Well, you gotta have a claim ticket if you're gonna leave your car. Wait here."

He turned, walked back to his booth and a few seconds later was back, claim ticket in hand. He tore off my part of the ticket and handed it to me, this time without eye contact. "How long you gonna be?" he asked.

A simple question, but that morning a hard one to answer.

"I'm not sure," I answered. "I guess we could be a while."

He seemed to soften, to understand, and wrote something on his half of the ticket. "Well, whenever you're ready, I'm here. At least 'til four, and then I'll let the night man know."

Before I could thank him, he got into my car and drove out of the courtyard, leaving my father and me standing there, separated by what had been the width of the car.

My father looked at me. "You okay?" he asked.

"Yeah, I guess. How about you? You ready?"

"As ready as I'll ever be, son. You lead. I'll follow."

Thirty

We walked across the lobby to a bank of elevators along the opposite wall, our footsteps reverberating on the granite floor. The lobby was cool and quiet and devoid of any sign of life except for a yellow plastic "Danger. Slippery When Wet" sign in the middle of the room. No one at the information desk. No one on either side of the counter in the coffee shop. No one sitting on any of the sofas. The lobby was empty. At this level, the hospital was still asleep.

Two of the eight elevators stood with their doors open. We entered the closest one, punched the button for the ninth floor, and the doors closed silently. The time was ten minutes after eight.

A moment later my father and I stepped out onto Peg's floor. We had walked only a short distance down the hall when a nurse, hearing our footsteps, peered around the corner of the nurses' station to see who the intruders were. When she saw my father and me, she immediately came toward us and intercepted us before we reached Peg's room. From where we stood, I could see that Peg's door was closed.

"Mr. Herbert?" she asked.

"Yes."

"I'm glad you're here. Dr. Werner is expecting you. He's with your wife now, but he should be able to see you shortly."

"May I go in?" I asked as I looked down the hall towards Peg's room, trying to keep my voice from trembling.

"I think it'd be better if you waited here," she replied. "Can I get either of you something to drink? Coffee? Juice?"

I ignored her offer. "I'd really like to see my wife. I'll behave. I promise."

"I don't think that would be a good idea, Mr. Herbert," she said.

She looked at my father to give him the opportunity to agree with her, but he didn't respond, and his expression gave no indication of what he was thinking.

"Please," I repeated, surprised that I was almost whispering. "I won't get in the way, and I won't make a scene. I promise. I just want to see my wife."

She sighed, started to say no again, and then seemed to think better of it. Several seconds passed. Finally she gave me a tight smile and a barely perceptible nod and reluctantly turned towards Peg's room, indicating that I should follow her.

"I'll be with you in a few minutes, Pop," I said, turning away from the nurse. "Okay? There's a bench down by the nurses' station," I continued. "Why don't you sit there until I come out?"

"Yeah, I'll do that," he agreed. But he didn't move. Instead, he remained where he was, looking at me.

"I'll be all right," I told him. "Really. You just wait for me on the bench."

Reassured, he reached out, softly patted my arm and started to walk down the corridor. I turned back to the nurse, let her know I was ready, and fell into step behind her as we walked to Peg's room.

The nurse opened Peg's door without knocking, and one of the people inside looked up and started to say something. She put a finger to her lips, signaling silence, shook her head dismissively, and entered the room. I followed her and stepped into chaos.

Peg was lying on her back, no pillow under her head, naked, her legs apart. Her arms were at her sides, palms up. An intravenous line ran into each arm and a third ran into the right side of the base of her neck. Her shoulders and chest were smeared with blood, and she had numerous large purple bruises on her arms, legs and stomach. A catheter tube ran from between her legs to a urine bag that hung off the base of the bed at her feet. She was staring blankly at a spot on the ceiling, blinking only occasionally and then slowly, almost patiently, as if she were no longer involved in what was going on around her.

Eight people were in the room, not including Peg or me or the nurse who had met us, all of them clad in white. Dr. Werner was on the far side of the bed, preparing to inject something into the intravenous line in Peg's neck. He was standing just behind a man on the telephone giving someone numbers describing levels of potassium, calcium, oxygen, carbon dioxide and the like. An orderly was trying to lean past Dr. Werner to draw blood from Peg's arm, while a nurse standing on my side of the bed was taking Peg's blood pressure and calling out the results to everyone in the room. A nurse at the foot of the bed was in the process of hanging another IV bag onto a second stand at the bed's corner post. In the far left corner of the room, one technician was adjusting knobs and pushing buttons on a large instrument on a cart, while a second technician uncoiled its wires and cables. Still another nurse was adjusting Peg's oxygen.

Litter was everywhere—rubber gloves, bandage wrappers, bloody gauze pads, pieces of adhesive tape, paper towels, needle covers, IV packaging, a broken syringe, cotton swabs—all over the floor, the night table, even the windowsill.

I stood just inside the door, taking it all in, trying not to panic.

This is unbelievable, I thought as I surveyed the room and the people. *All these people. All this equipment. What the hell's going on?*

Several seconds passed, and then came understanding.

We're in trouble. She's dying.

Dr. Werner looked up and saw me. "Mr. Herbert, you shouldn't be here," he said with obvious annoyance. "Please wait outside."

I shook my head no.

"Mr. Herbert, please. There's nothing you can do here except get in someone's way."

The tone of his voice broke through my shock. "I won't get in the way," I said as convincingly as I could. "I'll stay out of the way. Really."

He started to respond, but before he could, Peg stopped staring at the ceiling and turned her head towards me. "Hi, hon," she said softly.

For an instant, all activity in the room stopped.

"Well, well," Dr. Werner exclaimed. "Good to have you back."

"Hi, sweetheart," I replied, looking from her to Dr. Werner, then back to her. "How're you doing?"

"I'm okay," she whispered, "but my feet are cold."

"Want me to rub them for you?" I asked.

"Mmmmm, yes," Peg answered groggily.

Dr. Werner looked like he was about to say something to me, but instead, he turned away and directed his attention again to the IV line in Peg's neck.

The decision had been made. By Peg, not him. I was allowed to stay.

I took the chair that had been pushed into the corner of the room, positioned myself at the base of Peg's bed where she could see me, and began to rub her feet. I tried to ignore the catheter tube running past her instep and focused on rubbing first one foot, then the other, blocking out everything else happening in the room around us.

Almost immediately, Peg went back to staring at her spot on the ceiling while the doctors and nurses and technicians continued to work on her. I didn't talk to her because I was concerned that I would interfere with communications between the rest of the people in the room, so rubbing her feet was my only way of letting her know I was still there. I didn't look at her face because her stare was frightening, and I was un-nerved by the blood on her shoulders and chest, her nakedness in front of all these strangers, and by all the paraphernalia to which she was now connected. Instead I kept my eyes down; and when I needed to change focus from her feet to something else, I looked at the clock on the wall and watched the second hand glide silently around its face.

The minutes passed, and gradually the level of activity declined as Peg's condition stabilized. The man on the telephone hung up and started to fill out a form on his clipboard. The two technicians in the far corner of the room turned off the instrument on the cart, re-coiled the wires and cables, and wheeled the cart past me and out of the room. The orderly said something to Dr. Werner, and then he left too, followed by two of the three nurses. Only the nurse who had been taking Peg's blood pressure remained. She walked over to the far side of the bed where Dr. Werner and the man who had been on the telephone were still standing and adjusted one of the IVs hanging from a pole attached to the headboard. She wiped off most of the blood on Peg's shoulders and chest and then pulled a sheet over her. While she was lifting up the side rails of the bed, Dr. Werner came over to where I was sitting and indicated with a nod of his head that he wanted to see me outside of Peg's hearing.

I stood up and followed him out of the room and across the hall, closing the door behind me. As I waited for him to speak, he massaged his temples with his eyes closed. "Peggy went into toxic shock sometime early this morning," he began finally. His voice was low, and he sounded exhausted.

"Why?" I asked. "She seemed okay last night after her fever broke."

"Well, she was," he explained. "And she wasn't. As I've told you, we've destroyed Peggy's cancerous bone marrow, but we've also destroyed her white blood cells and therefore her ability to fight infection. When her temperature started to climb yesterday morning, that meant some sort of infection was setting in. Some sort of infection she couldn't fight. Dr. Porter ordered intravenous antibiotics, and by early last night, according to her chart, her temperature had returned to almost normal. Unfortunately, whatever bacteria started the fever stayed in her system after being killed by the antibiotics. Now, normally Peggy's white blood cells would have destroyed these dead bacteria. Would have rendered them harmless and gotten them out of her system. But Peggy doesn't have any white blood cells. So the dead bacteria stayed in her body and then broke down, releasing their toxins into her blood.

"As a result, sometime early this morning, she went into what we call toxic shock. Her blood pressure plummeted, and she began to hemorrhage subcutaneously. Under the skin. That's the reason for the bruises all over her body. At six forty-five this morning, one of the nurses went into her room to take her blood pressure, could barely get a pulse, saw that she was bleeding subcutaneously and assumed, rightly so, that she was in severe shock. She called the duty nurse, the duty nurse called me, and I called you."

Dr. Werner ended his dissertation like he always did, in a way that signaled he had, in his opinion, addressed all issues and answered all questions and that there was nothing left to be said.

"When did Peg start to go into shock?" I asked.

"As I said, one of the nurses went into her room at six forty-five and found her in shock."

"Great," I said, suddenly impatient with his attitude and feeling anger rise. "That's when one of the nurses found Peg in shock. That doesn't tell me when she went into shock. That's what I'm asking. When did she go into shock? At six forty-five this morning?" I started to wave my arms in exasperation. "Or at ten-thirty last night? In other words, how many times during the night did someone check on Peg? Or was the six forty-five visit the first time anyone went into her room all night? That's what I'm asking, doctor."

More questions flooded into my mind as I tried to catch my breath. "And what about the private nurse we arranged for? The one who's supposed to make up for the lack of staff over the weekend? What about her? Where was she? Why didn't she realize Peg was going into shock?"

"I don't know," Dr. Werner responded quietly.

"Don't know what, doctor? When Peg went into shock, or whether anyone checked on her until this morning?" I could feel tears welling up.

"Mr. Herbert," Dr. Werner replied with a sigh, "I understand that you're upset and that you have questions you'd like answers to. I understand that. But right now the most important thing is Peggy and keeping her stabilized. So you're going to have to excuse me. We're getting ready to move her down to the intensive care unit on the fifth floor, and I want to be with her while we do that."

"One more question. Is she going to be all right? Will she live?"

"I think she'll be fine," Dr. Werner answered. "She gave us a bit of a scare, but I think she'll be fine." He patted my arm reassuringly. "We'll talk more later. As soon as we get Peggy settled in the ICU. Okay?"

Before I could answer, the door to Peg's room opened, and the foot of her bed appeared. Dr. Werner turned away from me and walked across the corridor to help the nurse negotiate the bed through the door. Our conference was over.

As Peg's bed came into view, I could see that it had been freshly made. The top sheet, crisp and wrinkle-free, was stretched taut over her body, leaving only her head and bare shoulders visible. Her hair was still flat and wet with perspiration, but her head now rested on a clean white pillow. The IV bottles swung from side to side over her head, the result of the turn into the corridor.

Dr. Werner moved to the head of the bed, put a hand on Peg's arm and looked down at her. Her eyes were closed. "We're moving you to another part of the hospital, Peggy," he said quietly, gently, "where we can keep a closer eye on you for the next few days." He waited for a moment. "Your husband's right here. Once we've got you settled, I'll bring him in to see you. Would you like that?"

Peg opened her eyes at these last words and turned her head first to the right and then, seeing only the nurse and Dr. Werner, to the left, where I was standing at the side of the bed.

"Hi," she whispered.

"Hi again, sweetheart. I'll see you in a little while. Okay?"

"I'll be waiting for you," she answered tiredly, closing her eyes again as she spoke.

"You should be able to see her in about thirty minutes," said Dr. Werner after a quick glance at his watch. "Come down, and wait for me in the waiting room. The ICU's on the fifth floor. Just follow the signs when you get out of the elevator."

"I'll see you there," I replied.

The nurse began to push the bed down the hall, and I fell into step next to Peg, my hand on her shoulder.

"I love you," I said softly.

"I love you too," Peg whispered, her eyes still closed.

I walked next to her for another seven or eight steps, and then I stopped and watched her bed move down the hallway towards the eleva-

117

tors. I watched Dr. Werner punch the elevator call button, and I watched him and the nurse stand there in silence, their faces raised as they tracked the progress of the illuminated floor lights over each set of elevator doors. I heard the ding signaling an elevator's arrival, and I watched them maneuver Peg's bed in the direction of the opening doors. And then the doors closed, and they were gone.

I felt a hand on my shoulder. Startled, I turned around and found myself facing my father.

"Where have you been?" I asked, surprised at his sudden appearance.

"Down the hall," he said, looking over his shoulder in the direction from which he had come. "On the bench, where you told me to wait."

"Right. I knew that. They're moving Peg down to the fifth floor. To the intensive care unit."

"I know," he replied. "I overheard one of the nurses who came out of her room. So now what?"

"Dr. Werner said we should go down to the ICU and wait for him there. He said I'd be able to see Peg in about thirty minutes. So I guess we find the ICU, and then I guess we just wait."

"I've got a better idea," my father said as we started to walk towards the elevators. "Neither of us has had anything to eat yet this morning. Why don't you go down to the intensive care unit and wait for Dr. Werner while I try to scrounge up breakfast for us, and I'll meet you there?"

"You'll be able to find the intensive care unit?" I asked.

He seemed amused at my concern. "Don't worry," he assured me. "I'll find it, and I'll find you."

I pressed the down button, and the two of us stood staring at the bank of closed elevator doors in front of us, listening to the sounds coming from the elevator shafts behind them, the sounds of hissing cables and clunking doors opening and closing above and below us. It was five minutes after ten.

Thirty-one

I got off the elevator at the fifth floor and followed the signs directing me towards the intensive care unit. The waiting room was surprisingly small, but comfortably furnished with a large maroon leather sofa, two deep-cushioned matching leather armchairs, and gray tweed wall-to-wall carpeting. A wooden parson's table covered with magazines stood against the wall at one end of the room, a small desk at the other end. A door next to the desk, presumably leading to the intensive care unit itself, was marked "Positively No Admittance" and "Authorized Personnel Only." Windows high above the sofa filled the room with natural light, but were too high to permit a visitor to look out.

The waiting room was empty. I stood in the middle of the room for several seconds, trying to decide what to do, then went over to the table and picked up a magazine. But realizing I couldn't possibly focus on reading, I threw the magazine back onto the table, walked over to the sofa, and sat down to wait. I listened for sounds coming from behind the door to the ICU, but all I could hear was the sound of rushing air from the ventilation system.

Five minutes passed, then ten, then fifteen.

Suddenly the door opened, and a man who appeared to be a physician entered the room. "Mr. Herbert?" he asked.

"That's me."

He was a young man in his late twenties. He was dressed in blue jeans and a blue-and-white checkered shirt, over which he wore the regu-

119

lation mid-thigh white lab coat. His stethoscope was draped around his neck and hung down on either side of his chest. His black hair was rumpled, and he needed a shave. As he came through the door his expression was one of fatigue; but when he saw me get up from the sofa, his expression changed to one of discomfort, perhaps even one of pain.

I walked across the room to meet him, searching his face for some inkling of what he was about to tell me. But as I got closer to him, I saw that he was searching my face, and I wondered why. We met more or less in the middle of the room, and I extended my hand.

"Mr. Herbert, I'm Dr. Porter, one of the resident physicians assigned to your wife's care."

He let go of my hand, jammed his hands into his pockets, lowered his head and stared at the floor between us. When he finally raised his head and allowed his eyes to meet mine, I could see he was a very uncomfortable young man. He hesitated, visibly, before continuing.

"Mr. Herbert, I'm sorry to have to tell you this, but… Mrs. Herbert has passed away. She died about twenty minutes ago."

Book
Two

Thirty-two

The wind has picked up considerably since I first got here, and I pull the collar of my overcoat up and across my face in an attempt to protect my cheeks from the bitter cold. The predicted snow has arrived, and the first tiny flakes ride the wind down to the frozen ground.

I stare at the bronze plaque in front of my feet. "Margaret Ellen Herbert," the inscription reads. "June 1, 1946 ~ August 17, 1980," and below that, "I love you ~ forever."

I look up and look around me to confirm that I'm still alone. I am.

"I have so much to tell you, Peg," I say out loud, directing my eyes once again to the grave marker in front of me. "A lot happened after you died that you don't know about, and there's so much you should know. So many things I've wanted to talk to you about for so long. Where to start?"

I wait a moment to collect my thoughts, to let my mind go back to that terrible morning on the 17th of August, 1980. I remember that I felt as if I had been kicked in the stomach, my knees threatening to buckle under the weight of Dr. Porter's words.

I struggled to breathe. I squeezed the sides of my forehead with one hand, hard, as if I could purge my brain of what I had just heard if only I could squeeze hard enough. And then the tears started.

"I knew it," I said when I was able to speak. "I knew it. I just knew it. I knew this was going to happen the minute I walked into her room this morning. I knew they were playing catch-up ball up there. And I knew they were too late. I knew it, and they knew it, and now my wife is dead."

Dr. Porter continued. "She'd only been in the ICU a few minutes, and we had just finished moving her to one of the ICU beds when she stopped breathing. She didn't give us any warning. She just stopped breathing. We did everything we could, Mr. Herbert, but she didn't respond at all. Not at all. She was just too weak, I guess, and didn't have any strength left after what she went through last night. Anyway, her heart stopped, and she died."

He paused for a second. "Mr. Herbert, I don't know what else to say other than I'm sorry. Sorrier than you can ever imagine. She was doing so well. I really thought she was going to make it."

Again he paused, this time for several seconds, and he shook his head slowly. "They tell us never to get involved with our patients, and most of the time we don't. But every once in a while someone special comes along, and whether you want to or not, you find yourself pulling for him or her. You find yourself getting involved. And Mrs. Herbert—Peggy—was one of those people. A really special lady." His voice trailed off. "Again, Mr. Herbert, I'm very sorry."

He seemed to be searching for something else to say, something that would fill the deafening silence in the room. "Oh, I almost forgot. Dr. Werner asked me to apologize to you for his not being here, but he's got another emergency on the eighth floor. He got the page just a few minutes ago and had to race up there. He wanted to tell you about Mrs. Herbert himself, but he couldn't, and he hopes you understand."

I stood in front of him, my eyes closed. Crying. Unable to move. Unable to speak. Unable to think. I tried to swallow, but I couldn't. I kept trying to take a full breath, but I couldn't.

"Are you okay, Mr. Herbert?" Dr. Porter asked. "Can I get you something?"

I tried to answer him, to tell him I needed nothing. Nothing he could give me, anyway. But I couldn't.

"Mr. Herbert?" he called out, his voice louder now.

I opened my eyes and looked at the young Dr. Porter and tried to clear my throat so I could speak.

"What do I do now?" I asked.

"We'll keep Mrs. Herbert here until you've made the necessary funeral arrangements," Dr. Porter responded, thinking he knew what my question meant. "Once you've made those arrangements, someone from the funeral home will contact us, and they'll take care of everything. You won't have to worry about anything." He continued to look at me, oblivious to the irony of what he had said.

Nothing to worry about? I thought as I stood there. *Nothing for me to worry about? My God! I can't begin to comprehend all I have to worry about. A nine-month-old son. A three-year-old daughter. Two families about to be shattered. Life without the best friend I ever had. No, nothing to worry about. Nothing at all!* I thought bitterly, still staring at the young Dr. Porter.

His voice broke into my thoughts. "Mr. Herbert, I need to get back into the ICU. I have another patient there I should be attending to. Are you sure you're okay? Because if you're not, I can get someone to stay with you for a while."

"No, I'm fine. Really. I just need a few minutes to pull myself together."

I took several deep breaths and felt myself starting to regain my composure. "There is one thing you can do for me," I said. "I'd like to see my wife before I leave. Say good-bye. If that's possible. Can you do that for me?"

He hesitated before answering. "I can do that," he replied after a few seconds of thought. "If you think you're up to it."

"I'm up to it," I assured him.

"Just give me a few minutes to make sure everything's in order back there, and then I'll come back and bring you in to see her. All right?"

I nodded.

"Just wait right here," he repeated nervously as he turned to go back into the ICU. "I'll be right back."

I stood in the middle of the room, still unable to move. My mind was now strangely blank. I wasn't thinking about anything, I realized. I was focused only on waiting for Dr. Porter to return and on seeing Peg. Nothing more. The news of Peg's death had overwhelmed the circuitry of my brain, making it impossible for me to handle anything at that moment other than the most immediate tasks. So I just stood in the middle of the waiting room, right where Dr. Porter had left me, staring at the door to the ICU, waiting for him to return to take me to Peg.

In less than five minutes, the door to the ICU opened, and Dr. Porter once again stood in front of me. He seemed stronger now, more in control, more professional. "Ready?" he asked. "We're all set if you are."

"I'm ready," I answered, surprised at the weakness of my voice. "I only need a minute. Just enough time to see her and to say good-bye."

"Take all the time you need," said Dr. Porter, holding the door to the ICU open for me. "We understand. Believe me, we do."

We walked down a short hallway past a nurse's station and towards sliding glass doors that opened automatically as we approached. When we were inside the ICU, Dr. Porter guided me to a nearby bed almost completely surrounded by curtains. I walked up to it and stopped. I was vaguely aware of fifteen to twenty other beds in the dimly lit unit, most of them occupied and all without the encircling curtains. The large room was silent except for the periodic hiss of respirators and the asynchronous beeps of heart monitors.

Dr. Porter reached past me and pulled back the curtain just enough to let me stand next to the bed. Peg was lying on her back, covered by a sheet drawn up to her neck, her arms at her sides outside the sheet. Her hair, which had been flat with perspiration when she left the ninth floor, was now dry and frizzy. Her lips were tightly compressed, unnaturally so, and a thin line of blood was visible between them. Dried caked blood lay in the recesses of her left ear. Her skin was much paler than it had been earlier in the morning, and the bruises on her arms from the subcutaneous bleeding were now a dark purple.

I stood next to her bed, not moving, not feeling, not believing.

I felt Dr. Porter's hand on my arm and wondered if he were trying to comfort me or signal me that it was time to go. I ignored him and stared at Peg. His hand stayed on my arm, the grip a little tighter than it had been a few seconds ago, but I continued to stare at Peg's face, trying to burn her image onto my brain so I would never, ever forget what she looked like. I didn't want to remember her like this, but I knew the next time I would see her she would look even less like my Peg than she did at this moment.

I gently but purposefully disengaged my arm from Dr. Porter's grasp and took a step forward. Dr. Porter watched me warily, not knowing what I was about to do and not knowing how to respond. Slowly I bent down and kissed her. Really just a brush of my lips on hers, but enough of a kiss to tell me her lips were no longer soft and warm, but were already cool and hard. Confirmation, as if I needed it, that she was dead.

I looked at her one more time and whispered my good-bye, wishing with all my might that I was alone and that Dr. Porter wasn't standing behind me.

"I'll always love you, Peg. And I'll always remember you. I promise. Good-bye, sweetheart."

I turned away from the bed and stepped outside the curtain. Without a word, Dr. Porter pulled the curtain closed and led me through the sliding glass doors, down the hallway and back into the waiting room.

"Are you all right, Mr. Herbert?" he asked as he pulled the door to the ICU closed behind him. "Do you need anything?" Again his hand was on my arm.

"No. I'm all right," I answered. "I just need some time to let all this sink in. I feel like I'm having a nightmare, and I'm going to wake up any minute now."

"I understand," Dr. Porter replied.

"Can I wait here for my father?" I asked, suddenly remembering he was still somewhere in the hospital. "He's getting breakfast for us, and this is where we said we'd meet."

"Sure. Stay as long as you need to."

A moment of silence.

"Mr. Herbert... I have to go. Again, I'm sorry. My thoughts will be with you and your family."

We shook hands awkwardly, and he went back into the ICU.

127

My family, I thought. *What's left of it, he should've said.*

I stared at the closed door and wondered whether Peg was still inside or if they had already taken her to wherever they take the dead. I pushed the thought out of my mind and walked back to the sofa to wait for my father.

It was now five minutes to eleven. I had left the ninth floor at five minutes after ten. In less than fifty minutes, the world I knew had ceased to exist.

Thirty-three

I saw the paper bag first. A large brown paper bag with a grease stain in one corner. And when I raised my head, I saw my father, standing just inside the doorway to the ICU waiting room, holding the paper bag in one hand and closing the door behind him with the other. He took a few steps across the room before he saw my face. When he did, he stopped and looked at me, his expression one huge question.

I looked up at him, not knowing where to start or how to say what had to be said. Then, after what must have seemed like an eternity to him, I answered his unasked question.

"I don't think we'll be needing breakfast, Pop," I began, my voice breaking as I tried to form the words I needed to say. "Peggy's dead."

He looked at me incredulously, unable to comprehend what I was telling him.

"She died about half an hour ago. Heart failure, they think. The doctor said there was nothing they could do. She was just too weak. From the chemo. From the infection. From last night. Whatever. I don't know. Anyway, it's over."

His face crumbled first, then his body, as he grasped what I was saying. He opened his mouth to speak, but no words came. His lower lip started to tremble, and his eyes filled. He put out a hand and guided himself into one of the armchairs, still holding the paper bag that contained our breakfast. Then he leaned forward, his elbows on his thighs, bowed his head and began to sob.

We sat in the waiting room for almost ten minutes, me crying on the sofa, my father crying in the chair. Each of us struggling with our own pain, neither of us able to comfort the other. Both of us alone even though we were together. Both of us grappling with terrible thoughts, struggling to come to grips with a new reality.

"We should call Mom," I said finally, "and Peg's mom, and tell them what's happened. And then we should go home. There's nothing else we can do here."

He nodded in agreement, wiped his eyes with his handkerchief and blew his nose.

"Will you call Mom? I don't think I can handle that right now."

Again he nodded.

I tried desperately to focus, to think organized thoughts. "I'll call Peg's mom first. Then you call Mom. And while you're doing that, I'll go back upstairs to Peg's room and pick up her stuff. Then we can meet downstairs in the lobby. All right?"

He stood up and looked at the crumpled handkerchief in his hand, but he didn't answer me.

"You okay, Pop?" I asked.

We were both standing now, about eight feet apart. He raised his head, and his eyes answered my question. He was in no physical danger. I could see that. But his eyes showed me an almost unbearable pain, and they reminded me that his Peggy was gone too, not just mine. His eyes told me his heart was broken.

He looked so sad, so alone, suddenly so old, I instinctively raised my arms and held them out to him. We each took a step forward, wrapped our arms around each other and held each other as tightly as we could.

He pulled away then, and when he did, he looked at me and spoke for the first time since he had come into the waiting room. "We'll get through this, son," he said. "Just like we've gotten through everything else that's come our way. Your mother and I are always here for you. No matter what. You know that. And as long as we all have each other, we'll be okay."

"I know we will, Pop," I said for his sake, knowing it wasn't true. "I know we will."

He smiled at me, and I did my best to smile back.

"Right now, though," I added, "I better call Peg's mom before I lose my nerve."

I walked over to the phone on the desk, read the dialing instruction card and picked up the receiver. I dialed nine to get an outside line, entered my credit card number, the area code and the first three digits of Maureen Reilly's number, and immediately put the phone down.

"My God, Pop. What the hell am I going to say to her?" I asked, my hand still on the receiver.

"You're going to tell her what's happened."

"Just like that?"

"Just like that, son. There's no other way."

"Jesus," I muttered, and I started to dial again.

The telephone on the other end of the line rang once, twice, three times. "Maybe they're at church," I said out loud, half hoping no one would answer.

A voice cut the fifth ring in half. "Hello?"

"Maureen? This is John."

"What's the matter? Is Peggy all right?"

"No, she isn't."

"Oh my God... my God... my God..."

The voice trailed off, and I heard the sound of the receiver hitting wood.

Another voice came on the line. "John, this is Erin. What's happened?"

"Peggy's dead, Erin."

"Oh, no, no, no."

I heard her repeat my words in answer to a question from someone else in the room. "When did this happen?" she asked when she came back on the line.

"A little while ago."

"Why? What happened?"

"They think she died of heart failure. Erin," I continued before she could ask any more questions, "I'm sorry, but I've got to get off. I just can't do this now. I'll call you as soon as my father and I get back to Long Island. Is that all right?"

"Where are you now?" she asked, not answering my question.

"I'm at the hospital. In the intensive care unit. I'll call you later. All right?"

"Yeah. Sure. Oh, God..."

The line went dead. I wiped my eyes and tried to blow my nose, but I couldn't. Too much crying.

"I'm going upstairs, Pop. You better call Mom. I'll see you in the lobby in a few minutes."

I started to walk towards the door, and as I passed him, he gave me a couple of soft pats on the back. "I'm with you, son," I heard him say just before I pulled the door closed behind me.

Thirty-four

The elevator doors opened, and I stepped out onto the ninth floor for the second time that morning. The corridor was now bustling with activity as nurses walked in and out of patients' rooms with medication trays, and aides went from room to room changing bed linens, emptying wastebaskets and retrieving the last of the breakfast trays. At the far end a janitor was mopping the floor. It was eleven-twenty.

As I started to walk to Peg's room, the nurse who had met us earlier that morning came out of the room next to hers. When she saw me, she stopped and waited for me to reach her. "Mr. Herbert, I'm so sorry," she said with genuine feeling when I was still a step or two away. "Dr. Porter called a few minutes ago and told us what happened. We were wondering if we'd see you before you left the hospital."

"I just came back to pick up my wife's personal things, pictures of the kids, get-well cards, stuff like that. Is everything still there? Can I go in the room?"

"Yes, of course. No one's been assigned to the room yet, and we held off the cleaning staff until we knew whether you were coming back. Do you need any help?"

"No, that's all right. I can do it alone. Should only take me a few minutes. Really not that much to collect."

"Well, let me know if you need anything. And again, I'm sorry." She smiled hesitantly and turned to a medication cart next to the wall. She checked the list on her clipboard, picked up a tray for a patient across the hall, and left me standing next to the door to Peg's room.

I pushed the door open and started to walk in, but I stopped almost immediately. Because of its eastern exposure, the room was bathed in bright sunlight, as it had been on the day we'd first arrived, but it now looked like a war zone. All of the litter—the rubber gloves, the bandage wrappers, the bloody gauze pads, the pieces of rolled-up adhesive tape, the crumpled paper towels, the needle covers, the IV packaging, the broken syringe, the cotton swabs—was still on the floor, the night table, the windowsill. The only part of the room that was litter-free was the floor where Peg's bed had been.

With the bed out of the room, I could now see a pool of dried blood on the floor between where the bed had been and the window. Bloody footprints traced the path of someone who had stepped in the blood and then walked to the foot of the bed.

I stood frozen, looking at what had been Peg's home for the last two and a half weeks. I shuddered, and trying to ignore the fear that was enveloping me, went over to the night table, opened the bottom drawer and took out a plastic laundry bag. I went first to the closet and took the three nightgowns hanging in it off their hangers and put them in the laundry bag. I went into the bathroom and took Peg's makeup bag, toothbrush, toothpaste, hairbrush and shampoo from the shelf and put them in the laundry bag.

I took her magazines, two books and her address book from the top drawer of the night table and put them into the laundry bag. I went to the bulletin board and took down the scores of get-well cards and letters, promising myself I would read each one when I had more time. I took down the pictures of the kids my folks had taken for Peg. Jennie in the pool. John in the pool. John asleep in his high chair at the kitchen table. Jennie asleep in the guest room bed. Jennie hugging Jackson, my parents' golden retriever. John sitting in the corner of his crib, head back as he drained the last drop of milk from his bottle. Each one a small slice of everyday life, preserved on Polaroid film. Each one a small window into young lives outside the walls of the hospital.

I put everything into the plastic laundry bag except for the brightly colored thumbtacks in the bulletin board. I decided to leave them for the next person. I picked up the framed pictures of Jennie and John last— the ones that had been sitting on the windowsill next to Peg's bed, right where she could see them—and tucked them under my arm. Then I was done. Everything that had belonged to Peg was now either in the laundry bag or under my arm.

I looked around once more to make certain I hadn't missed anything. My eyes were drawn again to the pool of blood on the floor and the bloody footprints, and I wondered why the blood was there and what had happened.

I looked out the window and saw a tug slowly pushing a barge up the East River. On the far side of the river, I saw that traffic was moving on the Triborough Bridge. Slowly, but moving. I saw blue sky without a cloud in sight and realized that outside Peg's window Sunday morning was beautiful.

I looked around the room one last time and shook my head sadly, and then I turned and left.

Thirty-five

The elevator came to a soft stop, and the doors slid silently open. I stepped out and was momentarily taken aback at how the lobby had changed since my father and I had arrived just a few hours earlier.

Even though it was only eleven-forty and visiting hours did not officially start until one o'clock, every available seat was taken. Those not fortunate enough to sit stood either alone or in groups. A line of people had formed in front of the two guards who now sat behind the information desk, and the coffee shop was full. The noise produced by a multitude of different conversations, some far louder than they needed to be, was considerable and reverberated off the granite floor and stone walls. But in spite of the confusion, I spotted my father standing next to the revolving glass doors that opened into the courtyard where we had left the car.

"Got everything?" he asked as I walked up to him.

"Yeah, I've got everything," I said without realizing the irony of my response. I held up the bulging laundry bag. "It's all in here. Did you get to Mom?"

My father nodded slowly.

"How did she take the news?" I asked.

"Surprisingly well. But... I think she kind of expected something like this after Dr. Werner's call." He paused. "She's very concerned about you, though."

I searched unsuccessfully for a suitable response.

"Want me to drive?" he asked.

"No," I replied flatly.

He shrugged, and with nothing left to say, we went into the court-yard. As we stepped outside, we hit a wall of heat and humidity made worse by exhaust fumes hanging in the motionless air. August in Manhattan. We stood next to the doors for a minute or two before one of the parking attendants came to take my claim ticket. Five minutes later he parked the car on the far side of several cars that were discharging passengers. He held the door open for me, accepted a dollar tip with a quiet "thank you," and wished us a nice day. I waited until my father buckled his seat belt, and then I drove out of the shadows and confusion of the cobblestone courtyard. Down the hospital's drive, past the staff parking area, and away from New York Hospital. Forever.

We turned left onto Second Avenue heading downtown and left again on the first eastbound cross street to York Avenue. A left on York heading uptown to 96th Street, a right on 96th to the northbound FDR Drive, and a left lane exit to the Triborough Bridge toll plaza. We paid our toll and began to drive across the bridge to Long Island and home. The time was exactly noon.

The bridge was eight lanes wide—four lanes in each direction—and as we settled into the flow of the traffic, I looked at the people in the cars to the right and left of us and in the cars that we passed and that passed us. And as I looked at the people, I felt a combination of anger and envy. Anger because they were doing whatever they were doing without even a second's thought for Peg or me or our family or what lay ahead for us. And envy because they could. I looked through the windshield and the side windows at all the activity around us, and I realized nothing had changed for anyone else. The world was exactly the same at twelve noon as it had been at eight o'clock this morning. No changes. No big deal. The world was unaffected by Peg's death. It didn't know, and it didn't care. Somehow that didn't seem right. But that was how it was. Like it or not, Peg was dead, and even though my world, my kids' world, my parents' world, would never be the same, the rest of the world would keep on going. Same as always. It didn't know. And it didn't care.

Thirty-six

I turned into my parents' driveway at twenty after one Sunday afternoon—exhausted and terrified. Exhausted from the incredible tension of the past six hours, and terrified of what was to become of my children and me.

I pulled up to the garage, turned off the ignition, and sat motionless behind the steering wheel, trying to summon the courage to face my mother and Jennie. My father must have shared the feeling because he, too, sat perfectly still, staring straight ahead through the windshield.

We sat like that for perhaps half a minute before Father Bob, the priest from my church, came around the corner of the house from the pool deck and headed towards my side of the car. Seeing him, I opened the door and slowly started to get out.

"Hello, Father," I said, concentrating on greeting him instead of on the terrifying thoughts that had been torturing me for the last two and a half hours.

"John, I am so sorry."

"Thank you, Father. I didn't expect to see you here so soon. How did you find out?"

"Your mom called the church office, and one of the ladies called me."

"Well, I'm sure glad you're here," I admitted, and I started to cry.

I closed the car door behind me, and he put his arm around my neck, steering me towards the pool deck. As he did, he pulled my head down so my ear was close to his mouth. "John," he whispered, "I know at this moment it's hard to accept, but sometimes God takes the most beautiful flowers for his own garden."

I recoiled. I knew he meant well, but his words brought me anything but comfort, the thought that Peg had been chosen to leave us just as painful as thinking her death had simply been a random event, devoid of meaning or purpose.

Fortunately, I had little time to reflect on what he had said, because as we rounded the corner of the house, I saw my mother just a few steps ahead of us, sitting with Jennie on one of the lounge chairs. When she saw us, she patted Jennie's head and got up. She met me halfway across the pool deck and gave me a long, tight hug. No hysterics. No tears. Just a long, tight hug.

When she finally released me from her embrace, she held me at arm's length and looked at me intently. "I'm so sorry, son," she said, shaking her head as if she were still trying to believe the news.

She looked over her shoulder at Jennie, who was still sitting on the lounge chair, very much aware something was terribly wrong. "I haven't said anything to Jennie," she said quietly, "but she knows something has happened. Anyway, I thought you might want to be the one who tells her. Or I can if you want me to."

"No," I said more emphatically than I'd intended. "I have to tell her. Not you." I took a deep breath, trying to stay calm. "Where's John?"

"He's inside taking a nap. He was in the pool all morning, and he's tuckered out."

I looked over at Jennie. "Hi, sweetheart," I called out as normally as possible. "Just sit there for another minute, and then I'll come over to talk to you. Okay?"

Jennie nodded, almost imperceptibly.

Father Bob put a hand on my shoulder. "John," he said, "why don't I take your mom and dad inside and talk to them while you talk to Jennie?"

Before I could respond, he turned to my father. "Bill, come inside with Dorothy and me for a few minutes."

My father, looking like a beaten man with his hands in his pockets, head down, shoulders hunched forward, didn't answer. He just put out a hand for my mother to take, then turned around and walked towards the back door. Father Bob gave my arm a few reassuring rubs and followed my parents inside the house.

I was now alone, standing on the pool deck in the brilliant sunlight, with Jennie staring at me, eyes wide with apprehension. I walked over to her and sat down. I tried to smile, but I couldn't. She looked steadily at me, but knowing I couldn't look at her without breaking down, I turned away and stared at the shimmering pale blue water in the pool. But she was not to be put off any longer.

"Daddy," she said in a very small voice, "is Mommy going to be all right?"

Oh God, I thought, watching the ripples the breeze made on the water's surface, *how do I say this to my little girl?*

"Is she, Daddy?"

I turned back to her and somehow found the strength to look directly at her, right into her eyes. "Yes, sweetheart," I answered. "Mommy's going to be all right now, because Mommy went to heaven this morning to be with God. And now that she's in heaven, she's not sick anymore. And she's not in pain anymore. Now she's one of God's angels."

I started to cry. I didn't want to. I wanted to be strong for Jennie, but I couldn't be. I couldn't look at her and tell her this and be strong all at the same time. So I took her hands in mine, looked into her eyes and cried.

But Jennie didn't cry. She just sat on the lounge chair watching me. "Does this mean we'll never see Mommy again?" she asked.

I freed one of my hands from hers and wiped my eyes with the back of it. "I'm afraid so, sweetheart. But we'll always remember Mommy. I'll make sure of that. We'll have our pictures of her. We'll have our memories of her. And she'll always be with us, inside our hearts, forever."

"But she promised…" Jennie reminded me, her voice filled with confusion and pain. "She said she'd come home soon."

God help me, please, I prayed silently to myself as I looked at her little hand entwined in mine. *Help me say the right thing.*

"And Mommy told you the truth when she said that," I began carefully, ever so carefully. "She thought she'd be coming home to us. Really soon. But she didn't know how sick she was."

We sat looking at each other, Jennie without questions, me without answers.

"I miss Mommy," she said finally.

"Me too, sweetheart. Me too."

The seconds continued to pass, and as they did, I realized there was nothing else to say. I had told Jennie her mother was dead. What more could I say? At least for now. There would, of course, be questions—hundreds, maybe thousands over the coming days, months, years—but for now there was nothing else to say.

I got up slowly. "Why don't we go inside and give Grandma and Grandpa a big hug? I bet they could really use one. What do you think?"

Jennie climbed off the chair without a word. Like her grandmother, no tears, no hysterics, just a terribly heavy sadness radiating from inside her little body. I put out my hand for her to take and felt her cool little hand slide into mine as my fingers wrapped around it protectively.

"We'll be okay, sweetheart," I said as the two of us walked across the pool deck. "You and me and John. We'll be okay. I promise."

Thirty-seven

Father Bob left the house a little after two. He gave Jennie a big hug and a kiss and told her to listen to Grandma and Grandpa. He told my father to be strong for the rest of us, and he told my mother how lucky Jennie and John and I were to have her on our side. Then he put his arm around my shoulders and looked first at me and then at my parents.

"I'm going to ask John to walk me to my car," he said. "He'll be back in a minute. John," he continued, "come with me. I want to talk to you before I go."

I followed him out of the kitchen onto the pool deck and around the back corner of the house to the driveway. I thanked him again for coming and for all his support. He didn't respond, but when we reached his car, he turned around and looked deeply into my eyes, first one, then the other, before he spoke.

"Remember, John," he said, "God is with you. Always. Wherever you go. Whatever you do. There will be times when you'll feel you're alone, but you're not. He's always there. Watching you. Guiding you. Protecting you. Don't ever forget that."

I nodded and tried to give the impression that I agreed with him, that I knew he was speaking the truth. But I said nothing. I knew if I did, my words would fail me; and he would know that I knew God had turned his back on me and my children. So I just looked at him and nodded, hoping my eyes were not the window to my soul.

We stood next to his car for several seconds, and from his expression I suspected Father Bob was wondering if he'd succeeded in getting his departing message across to me. And that made me wonder how he could expect me to believe God had any interest whatsoever in protecting me or my family after what He had allowed to happen this morning.

Finally, Father Bob patted the back of my head and opened his car door. "Take care of yourself and the children, John," he said as he got in. "And call me if there's anything I can do."

"I will, Father. And thank you again."

I watched his black sedan go down the driveway until it reached the street, and then he was gone.

As I came back into the kitchen, I heard my mother telling my father they should try to rest for a few hours. "I'm tired, Bill," she said as she wiped the dinette table. "I'm tired, and I'm drained. I don't know what's ahead of us tonight, and tomorrow's going to be tough. So I think we should use this afternoon to get our strength up if we can."

"You're probably right," my father agreed quietly. "How about you, son?" he asked, looking past my mother at me. "You look like you could use a few hours of rest."

"No, not now, Pop. I'm tired, but I can't sleep. You and Mom go ahead. Maybe I'll sit outside for a while with the kids."

"I think you could use some time alone," my mother countered. "John's still asleep, and maybe Jennie would like to take a nap for a while with Grandma and Grandpa."

"Can I sleep next to you, Grandma?" Jennie asked, obviously taken with the idea.

"As long as you lay still so Grandma can rest."

"I can lay still, Grandma," Jennie assured her.

So before I knew it, my parents and Jennie were heading across the family room, leaving me in the kitchen, grateful for the quiet but immediately uncomfortable with the prospect of being alone. I watched them walk down the hall, and then I went out onto the pool deck. I stood in the sun, feeling its warmth on my face and on the top of my head, and decided to move one of the lounge chairs out of the shade. After dragging a chair over to where I'd been standing, I sat down, took off my sneakers and put my head back. I closed my eyes, sighed deeply and tried to focus on all that had happened in the last few hours and on what I needed to do now.

The silence around me was broken only by the occasional chirp of a bird or the rattle of a locust or the swish of the breeze in the pines around me. And the silence was frightening, because it underscored my solitude, my aloneness. I opened my eyes, hoping to see something that would lessen my fear, but the expanse of cloudless blue sky only made me feel smaller and more insignificant and more isolated.

I lay on the lounge chair for the better part of an hour, thinking one minute about the kids, trying to figure out how I was going to take care of them, and the next minute about myself, trying to figure out how I was going to live without Peg. I tried desperately to gain control of my racing thoughts and rising panic—to think logically, to make plans—but after a while I realized my efforts were doomed to failure. I sat up and swung a leg over each side of the chair.

"I should start calling people," I said out loud. "That's what I should be doing. No one knows Peg has died. None of our friends. None of the people at the bank. Somebody has to tell them, and I guess that somebody's me."

I considered the enormity of the task before me and thought about how each call would affect someone—some just a little bit, some a lot, some probably more than I could ever imagine. But I knew the calls had to be made, so with what seemed like the weight of the world on my shoulders, I put on my sneakers and went into the house.

I decided to use the phone in the library rather than the one in the kitchen because the library had a door I could close for privacy. I walked through the family room and down the back hall and past the guest room, where the kids were staying. I peeked in; John was flat on his back in his crib, still fast asleep. Across the hall my parents' bedroom door was ajar; judging from the silence, they and Jennie were asleep too. Other than the muted whine of the air conditioning unit outside, the house was silent. Again the silence and loneliness pressed in on me.

I went into the guest bedroom where I was staying, retrieved both my address book and Peg's, and crossed the hall to the library. Carefully shutting the door behind me, I sat down at the desk, opened my address book first, and started to make my calls.

Oddly, most of the calls were the same, which made them easier to make after the first few, their sameness acting as a kind of anesthetic, numbing the pain of having to deliver this kind of news.

"Dave?" "Mike?" "Bob?" "Frank?" "Hi. It's John Herbert."

Always a question as to how I was doing.

"Well, I'm not doing too well, really, which is why I'm calling."

A deep breath every time for strength and composure.

"Peg died this morning, and I knew you'd want to know."

Another question, always the same. Different words sometimes, but always the same question.

"We don't know what happened. She seemed to be doing pretty well last night when I saw her; but she had a high fever all day, and they think that caught up with her some time Saturday night or early Sunday morning." Another deep breath. "Anyway, I wanted you to know. We don't know anything about funeral arrangements yet, but as soon as we do, someone will give you a call."

Always an expression of sympathy, sometimes barely understandable through the sobbing.

"I know. I know. I'm going to miss her too. More than anyone can imagine. Look, I've got to go. I've got a million calls to make, and I'm going to come apart if I stay on here any longer."

Then a good-bye, the receiver placed back in its cradle, a finger finding the next name and the next number; and I started all over again. And again. And again.

Thirty-eight

We had dinner Sunday night at the kitchen table at seven-fifteen—my parents, Jennie, John and I. Neither my parents nor I felt like eating, but my mother was a great believer in the palliative effect of food, so dinner was served at the usual time regardless of the events of the day.

Dinner was eerily different from any we had ever shared before—not just because Peg wasn't at the table with us, but because of the almost total absence of conversation. I think neither of my parents knew what to say, either about Peg's death or about the days ahead, and chose to remain silent rather than say the wrong thing. I said nothing because I knew anything I said would reflect the fear and confusion that filled my mind, and I didn't want to add to the pain and suffering around me. And I think Jennie said little because she was taking her cue from the adults. Even John was lured into being uncharacteristically quiet by the absence of anyone else's voice and by the hypnotic clink and scrape of utensils against plates.

We finished eating about seven forty-five and were about to start clearing the dishes when my mother got up from the table and went over to where Jennie was sitting. Without a word, she lifted Jennie out of her booster seat and onto the floor, took her hand and started to lead her down the hall in the direction of the back door.

"Where are you going, Mom?" I asked.

"Outside," she replied. "I want to show Jennie something."

"It's gonna be dark in a few minutes," I pointed out. "Can't it wait until morning?"

"No, it can't," she replied matter-of-factly.

Curious as to what was going on, I left my father sitting at the table drinking the last of his coffee and followed the two of them. I came outside just in time to see my mother kneel down beside Jennie.

"Look up at the sky, sweetheart," I heard her say. "Do you see that star there, just over the trees? The really bright one?"

"Uh-huh," Jennie replied quietly, looking first at the star, then at her grandmother, then back at the star.

"Well," my mother continued, "now that Mommy's in heaven, that star is Mommy's star. And do you know what that means?"

Jennie shook her head somberly, still looking up at the star.

"It means that whenever you want to talk to her, all you have to do is find that star, and she'll be right there listening to you. Any time you want."

Jennie turned away from the star and looked intently at my mother. "Will she be able to talk to me?"

"No, sweetheart. She won't be able to talk to you. But she will be able to hear everything you say to her."

Jennie turned back to the star and stared at it thoughtfully for several moments. "I love you, Mommy," she said softly.

Oh, Jesus, I thought. *I can't handle this. Not tonight. I just can't.*

But before I could go back inside, Jennie turned away from the star towards me, and in spite of the fading light, saw my face and realized I was about to cry.

"What's the matter, Daddy? Don't you want to talk to Mommy?"

A deep breath and another silent prayer for strength. "Nothing's the matter, sweetheart. I just got a little sad when I saw Mommy's star."

A second of silence as I wondered what to say next. "Why don't you talk to Mommy with Grandma for a few minutes, and then I'll see you inside when you're done?"

Jennie nodded and looked again at the star just over the tops of the trees. And for the next four or five minutes she and my mother had a

147

conversation with Peg while I stood just inside the back door, trying to pull myself together and wondering what the two of them were saying.

At first I marveled at my mother's ability to listen to her granddaughter talk to a tiny point of light in the early evening sky. Then I found myself wondering if maybe Peg could hear the two of them. And then I wondered if maybe I were losing my mind.

Thirty-nine

I got out of bed early Monday morning, August 18th, knowing I had a lot to do and worried about not having enough time. For starters, I had to complete the last of my telephone calls to friends and co-workers. I had stopped making calls shortly before dinner Sunday night and hadn't been able to summon the strength to continue making them after dinner. I estimated I had at least twenty-five calls still remaining. I could have asked someone else to make them—several people had volunteered the day before on hearing the news—but I felt this was something I had to do, something that couldn't be delegated to someone else.

I also had to call the funeral home to make certain the hospital had released Peg's body. If not, I had to find out why and deal with the problem. I had to go home and pick out a dress and some jewelry for Peg to wear at the wake, and I had to bring everything to the funeral home and then select a casket. I had to ask a few people to let everyone know the first viewing was tonight and provide information regarding time, location, directions and so forth. And last, I needed to call the florist and then Father Bob about the funeral service to be held at Saint John's Episcopal Church in Huntington on Wednesday.

At five after seven I found the next name in Peg's address book. I picked up the receiver and started to dial. The Monday morning calls were different from the Sunday afternoon calls. Sunday afternoon, I had the distinct impression again and again that my call had shattered an otherwise peaceful and relaxing summer weekend. People had answered their telephones expecting the call to be simply another little event on their path to Sunday dinner, bed and the beginning of a new work week. But the people who answered their telephones on Monday morning shortly after seven o'clock—some obviously awakened by my call, some awake but not yet functioning, others moments away from leaving the house for work—answered warily, seemingly already prepared for bad news.

Throughout the morning my folks took turns watching the kids and calling their friends whenever the line was free. The emotional strain on the two of them was evident in the way they looked, moved and talked. Neither of them had slept well, and dark circles under their tear-reddened eyes dominated their faces. My mother still managed to move around the house with purpose, albeit a little more slowly than usual, but my father seemed to find the task of moving himself from point A to point B almost more than he could handle.

By shortly after one o'clock everything was done, and my folks and I and the children sat down for lunch. Conversation between my parents and me was sporadic at best and centered on the details of the day—what we had each done during the morning and what we predicted lay ahead that night—rather than on the larger issues facing us, which was definitely fortunate and perhaps intentional.

"What are you going to do this afternoon?" my mother asked as she started to clear the dishes from the table.

"Believe it or not, I was thinking I might lie down for a while," I replied, swallowing the last bite of my tuna sandwich. "This morning really took a toll on me, I guess."

"I know it's taken a toll on me," she answered. "And on your father," she added while she watched him slowly sip his coffee. "A few hours of rest would probably do us all good."

Ten minutes later, the lunch dishes stacked in the sink, John in his crib, Jennie with my folks, I stretched out on the guest room bed. I lay on my back, hands clasped on my chest, eyes closed, for fifteen minutes before accepting the fact I couldn't will myself to sleep. With a sigh, I rolled over onto my side, wondering what I should do. *I should sleep*, I thought. *Or maybe I should call the funeral home and make sure everything's okay.*

Another moment of consideration and the decision was made. I rolled off the bed, put on my sneakers and went into the library. I quickly scanned a yellow pad still on the desk and found the number for the Tarasan-Virag Funeral Home and the name of the director I had met earlier that morning. I dialed the number.

"Good afternoon," a woman answered quietly. "Tarasan-Virag Funeral Home."

"Good afternoon. My name is John Herbert. I'm calling for Paul Virag."

"Oh, I'm sorry, but Mr. Virag isn't here at the moment. Could someone else help you perhaps?"

"I don't know. I'm calling about my wife, Peggy Herbert. I dropped off her things this morning. Is there someone I can talk to about her?"

"Yes, of course, Mr. Herbert. Just one minute."

In seconds, a man's voice came on the line. "Mr. Herbert? This is Jerry Crandall. How can I help you?"

"Well… I was calling to see if you had finished getting my wife ready for tonight."

"We're just about finished, Mr. Herbert. With the dress and the jewelry you dropped off this morning, I think your wife is going to look lovely."

"That's good to hear. I appreciate your efforts."

"Please. That's what we're here for."

I hesitated, not knowing how to broach the next topic, and Crandall assumed the call was over.

"Mr. Herbert, if there's anything else we can do for you tonight during the viewing, please let me know. I'll be on duty when you arrive."

"Well, as a matter of fact, there is one more thing I'd like to ask of you."

"Of course, Mr. Herbert. What is it?"

"I'd… like to come over now… or whenever you're finished getting my wife ready… to look at her. To make certain she looks the way she should. The way she did. If you know what I mean."

I could feel Crandall pulling away from me before he said a word. "Really, Mr. Herbert, that isn't necessary. We do this all the time. I'm quite certain you'll be very pleased with the result."

"I'm sure I will be," I replied, "but I'd still like to see my wife before tonight to make certain she looks like the woman everybody knew. That's not a problem, is it?"

"No, of course not, Mr. Herbert. It's just that this usually isn't done, and as I said, it's not necessary. Really it isn't."

"I understand that, Mr. Crandall. But it's very important to me. The lady your people are working on is my wife."

I imagined him rolling his eyes and looking up at the ceiling. "Well, if you think you're going to want to change anything, you'll have to get here before the makeup artist and hairdresser leave. I can't ask them to make a second trip."

"I can be to you in twenty-five minutes," I said. "Is that soon enough?"

"That'll be fine, Mr. Herbert," Crandall replied with obvious reluctance. "Come to the front door and ring the bell. I'll be waiting for you."

Before I could thank him, he hung up.

A minute later, after leaving a quickly written note to my folks on the kitchen table, I slipped out the back door and drove to the funeral home to inspect the remains of my wife.

Forty

Twenty-seven minutes later I turned into the empty parking lot of the Tarasan-Virag Funeral Home and pulled into a slot to the right of a columned portico over the front entrance. Crandall must have been watching the lot, because he opened one of the double doors for me before I was halfway up the front steps.

"Mr. Herbert?"

"That's right."

"Jerry Crandall."

We shook hands just inside the door, and I could tell he was trying to judge my state of mind before he let me come too far into the building.

"I really appreciate this," I said, hoping I sounded calm and reassuring.

He closed the door behind me without answering and turned the deadbolt. He then gave the door a single pull to make certain it was locked, looked at me once more and started to walk down a hall to the right of where we were standing. "Come this way, please. We just finished preparing Mrs. Herbert, but both the makeup artist and the hairdresser are still here if there's anything that's not to your liking."

We walked side by side, our footsteps silenced by the deep pile carpet. Midway down the hall we turned to the left through a set of open double doors and went down two steps into an enormous chapel. At first I thought the room had a low ceiling, but I quickly realized the ceiling was at least ten feet high and only appeared low because of the size of the room. At least one hundred fifty padded folding chairs were arranged in perfectly straight row after perfectly straight row across the expanse of carpet. Around the perimeter of the room were a couple dozen high-backed upholstered armchairs as well as several large sofas. Only a few of the room's many wall sconces were lit, but the light was more than enough to illuminate the multiple shades of gold, bronze and cream in the room's carpet and wallpaper.

Peg's casket, its lacquered mahogany reflecting the light from the wall sconces, was centered against the wall opposite the double doors. A middle-aged, overweight woman and a slim man at least ten years her junior stood perfectly still at the head of the casket, waiting for the next few minutes to unfold.

Crandall and I walked down the side of the room towards the casket, Crandall nervously looking first at me, then at the man and woman, then back at me. When we got to within about five feet of the casket, he stopped and nervously indicated I should continue forward alone.

I took two steps and stopped. I intentionally avoided looking at Peg's face. Instead, I looked first at the casket and took in the beauty of the wood and ran my hand over the flawless finish. Then I looked at Peg's carefully folded hands. I noticed her left hand was on top so that her wedding band was clearly visible, and I nodded approvingly. I looked at her dress, her favorite blue dress, and tried to distinguish between the curves in the material that belonged to the dress and those that belonged to Peg. And then, I looked at her face.

And as I did, I realized that the last two images I would have of her and which I would remember forever were as inaccurate as they could possibly be. In one, only a day old, her face was ashen, her mouth and ears were ringed with blood, and her once thick, lustrous hair was tangled and frizzy. In the other, the one before me now, she looked like a glamorous stranger, a stranger with too much eye shadow and too much mascara, a shade of lipstick too bold and with hair teased and sprayed, something Peg had never done. Neither image was the Peg I had known. And yet, although both were totally false, both were completely real.

I looked at Peg for several moments before finding the will to speak. When I did, I spoke to the man and woman still standing at the head of the casket. "I'd like you to take off some of the eye shadow, if you don't mind. As I told Mr. Virag, she always wore it, but because her eyes were so blue, she didn't need very much. And I'd like you to take off most of the mascara too. Again, she didn't use much. And... I'm sorry, but the hair isn't her either. It's... too fancy. Too glitzy. She never teased her hair, and she never used hair spray. Her hair was so thick, she didn't need to. It should just... kind of hang, in waves, gentle waves, if you know what I mean."

Neither the man nor the woman responded. They didn't nod in agreement or even signify they understood what I was saying. Nor did they shake their heads in protest or give any sign that they were angry or insulted. They just looked at Crandall in awkward silence and waited for him to respond. Finally Crandall took a deep breath and, without seeming to exhale, addressed each of my comments.

"Mr. Herbert, we can certainly remove some of the eye shadow if you'd like, and we can remove most of the mascara if that's what you want. But the hair is a problem. I don't know how to say this delicately, but... we lost a great deal of your wife's hair while we were shampooing it, and the only way we could correct for that was to tease her hair the way you see it and then use hair spray to keep what hair was left in place. I'm afraid if we do anything more with your wife's hair now, we might wind up with a much worse problem." He let this sink in and then continued. "I do hope you understand that we've done our best."

"I understand," I replied, hearing my voice crack. "I do. You can't erase the fact she's gone through hell. I should have realized that. I just wasn't thinking. I'm sure you've done all you can." I extended my hand. "Again, thank you for letting me come here today. I truly appreciate it."

I looked once more at the stranger in the casket who was once my wife, shuddered in disbelief, and left the chapel without another word.

Forty-one

One of the many telephone calls I made on Monday was to Don Brady, a college buddy since my freshman year who now lived outside of Chicago. As soon as Don heard the news, he told me he'd come to New York for Peg's funeral, but added that his wife, Lynne, wouldn't be able to join him because she'd just given birth to their first child, a boy. I had known Lynne was due sometime in August, but I hadn't given her pregnancy a thought since Peg went into the hospital. Anyway, I told Don I understood and thanked him profusely for being willing to make the trip.

He flew into LaGuardia Airport late Monday night, picked up a rental car and checked into a bed and breakfast in Cold Spring Harbor, a small village just west of Huntington. Shortly before eleven the next morning, the back doorbell rang, and there was Don. He talked with my parents and me for a while and then suggested the two of us grab lunch somewhere.

"I don't know if I'm up to that, Don," I replied dismissively. "I had a terrible night's sleep last night, my nerves are shot and I feel like hell warmed over. Maybe some other time?"

"I think you could use a break now," Don pressed. "Come on. A change of scenery for a few hours. A little fresh air. It'll be good for you. Isn't there some place you'd like go?"

"Well, we could go to the yacht club, I suppose. It's a weekday, so it won't be crowded, and we could eat outside. Not the worst idea, I guess, but... I don't know, Don. Doesn't seem right somehow."

"Come on," Don urged. "We'll be gone an hour or two at most. Trust me. You'll feel better if you go."

"What do you think, Mom?" I asked, hoping she'd been listening to Don's entreaties.

"I think it's a good idea. You should go."

"You'll be okay with the kids?"

"I'll be fine. Go."

"Guess that settles it," I said, turning back to Don. "But I still think I'm going to be lousy company."

"You're not going out to lunch to entertain me," Don said with a smile as he got up from the kitchen table. "I'm supposed to entertain you."

We arrived at the club around twelve-fifteen and entered the club-house from the side entrance. Ellen Walsh, the wife of the club's general manager and the hostess for lunch that day, was standing on the far side of the dining room talking to one of the waitresses. When she saw me, her eyes opened wide in surprise and then filled with tears as she rushed over to me, arms outstretched. She hugged me for several seconds before pushing herself away to speak.

"I just heard about Mrs. Herbert not even half an hour ago," Ellen exclaimed, wiping away her tears. "I couldn't believe it. I said to the woman who told me that she must have made a mistake, but she said no, it was true. Oh, Mr. Herbert, I am so, so sorry."

"Thank you, Ellen," I replied, not knowing what else to say.

The three of us stood awkwardly in the corner of the dining room, Ellen trying to regain her composure, me trying not to lose mine, and Don wondering what was going to happen next.

Ellen wiped her eyes once more and shook her head. "I'm sorry," she said. "You don't need people carrying on like this, I'm sure."

"Don't worry about it," I assured her. "There've been a lot of tears the last two days, and I'm sure there'll be a lot more before this is all over."

She nodded but appeared to be regretting her show of emotion. "Will you be having lunch today, Mr. Herbert?" she asked, her normal businesslike demeanor returning. I said yes, and she led us to a table on the outside patio.

"And can I get you something to drink, Mr. Herbert?" she asked as she handed us our menus.

"I'll have a Myers dark rum and orange juice, please," I answered, instantly feeling guilty. Guilty for ordering a drink I enjoyed, and guilty for even being here in this beautiful spot on this beautiful day.

"And you, sir?"

"I'll have a Budweiser, please," Don answered, true to form.

We sat and waited for our drinks, looking out at Northport Harbor. The yacht club was positioned halfway up a hill overlooking the harbor, so from our vantage point on the patio, we could see hundreds of boats below us on their moorings. The water was a brilliant blue, reflecting the sky above, and looked alive as the breeze ruffled its surface. Little puffs of white cloud skittered across the blue sky as the boats swung on their mooring lines, almost in perfect unison—first in one direction, then in another, always trying to head into the wind, always one step behind. The club's flags waved crisply while halyards on dozens of boats slapped in the breeze against aluminum masts. The scene before us was so beautiful and peaceful—so different from the chaos and white noise I felt inside.

Our drinks arrived, and I lifted my glass and tilted it in Don's direction. "To health," I toasted. "Nothing else matters."

"Got that right," Don agreed, tapping the mouth of his bottle against the side of my glass.

"So tell me about your son. You and Lynne must be excited."

Don looked at me for a second and then looked out at the harbor. "We are," he answered softly.

"What's his name?"

"Donnie," Don replied, turning to face me again. "Donald Brady III, to be exact. After my dad and me."

"That's great. I'm happy for you. Happy for you both."

"Thanks. Unfortunately, though, not everything turned out like we had hoped." He looked out at the harbor again before continuing. "Donnie has Down's syndrome. Which, needless to say, came as a bit of a shock to us. We never expected to have a baby with a problem like that. Never gave the possibility a thought. And yet here we are, parents of a Down's syndrome child."

"Holy shit, Don."

"Yeah, my reaction exactly. When the obstetrician came out of the delivery room and told me about Donnie, I knew he'd made a mistake. Or was talking to the wrong father. And then I realized there wasn't any mistake, and he was talking to the right father."

"Jesus, Don, I'm sorry. I don't know what to say. Except I'm sorry."

"There is nothing to say," Don answered matter-of-factly. "That's the way it is. Period."

"Simple as that?" I asked. " 'That's the way it is'?"

"Hey, it's bad news," Don replied. "Real bad news. There's no other way to describe what's happened. But the world hasn't come to an end. And worse things could have happened." Don paused, looking for the right words. "I think... Fate deals most people a bad hand sooner or later," he continued. "The hand Fate's dealt to Lynne and me with Donnie may not be the hand we wanted, but that's the hand we got and the one we're going to live with for the rest of our lives, whether we want to or not. The important thing is how we deal with that hand. We can either believe our situation is as bad as it could possibly be, and wallow in that thought, or we can be thankful our situation isn't any worse."

We both looked out at the harbor, each of us deep in thought.

"You know what I'm thinking?" I asked, breaking a silence that had lasted several minutes.

Don looked at me from across the table, eyebrows raised, questioning.

"I'm thinking what you said applies to me, too."

"Applies to everyone, my friend. No exceptions."

Don picked at the label on his empty beer bottle while I stared at what was left of my drink.

And then we both started to cry.

Forty-two

Peg was buried on Wednesday, August 20th. Paul Virag, the funeral director, told me Tuesday night that if I wanted to have a few minutes alone with Peg before they closed her casket, I needed to be at the funeral home by nine Wednesday morning. He made a point of saying I couldn't stay long. We had to be at St. John's at nine forty-five, he explained, and his people needed time to remove all the flowers from the chapel, seal Peg's casket, load it into the hearse and travel the mile and a half to the church in summer morning traffic.

So at nine sharp, I pulled into the Tarasan-Virag parking lot with my father and mother, the children at home in the care of one of my cousins. Peg's mother had become extremely upset during the wake the night before, and Peg's sisters decided it would be best if they all went directly to the church rather than to the funeral home first. I hadn't asked anyone else to join me, so the three of us were the only people there. As we reached the top of the steps, Paul opened one of the doors. He reminded us of our limited time and shepherded us down the hall to our chapel.

Except for Paul and one gray-haired man standing in the corner, his hands clasped behind his back, we were alone in the huge room. Somehow understanding the order in which something like this should be done, my mother and father approached the casket first, hand in hand. They stood in front of it for perhaps a minute, heads bowed, shoulders bent under the weight of their sadness. My mother sighed several times and shook her head. My father stood rigidly, tears running down his cheeks. They then each laid a hand on the casket and slowly walked to the far side of the room.

As they moved away, I walked up to the casket with leaden feet, each step an effort as I struggled to believe this was all really happening. When I reached the casket, I stood motionless—not praying, not thinking, just staring at Peg's face and form, trying desperately to insure I would never forget what she looked like, even in death. I'd had difficulty remembering the sound of her voice that morning, and I was terrified to think the memory trace of her was already fading. I couldn't let that happen. So I stood, and I stared.

Fingers lightly touched my elbow. "Mr. Herbert?"

I turned and saw Paul Virag standing behind me. "Mr. Herbert, we need to get ready."

"I know. I know. Just give me one more minute."

Paul nodded understandingly and stepped back.

I turned again to Peg and looked down at her face for the last time. My eyes filled, and my vision blurred as I admitted to myself that our time together in this life was over.

"I love you, Peg," I whispered, laying my hand on top of hers. "Forever."

I wiped my eyes and turned away.

"Why don't you all have a seat in the lobby for a few minutes while we get Mrs. Herbert ready for the trip to St. John's?" Paul said as he ushered us to the rear of the chapel. "Mr. Herbert," he added, facing me, "we're going to load as many of the floral arrangements as we can, but we won't be able to take them all. There are too many. So we'll take the largest and nicest ones with us to the cemetery, and the rest we'll deliver to nursing homes in the area. Will that be all right?"

I said yes, but I wasn't listening to him. I was looking at Peg's casket, and I was thinking that in a few seconds, someone would lower the lid, plunging her into eternal darkness. Then someone would crank the bolts that drew the lid down tight, so tight that neither air nor water would enter for—what had Paul said? One hundred years? And I was thinking once that happened, the beautiful Irish girl with the thick black shining hair and the brilliant blue eyes would be sealed away forever.

Forty-three

We arrived at St. John's at nine forty-three, my parents and I in the rear seat of a Tarasan-Virag limousine, Paul Virag in the front seat with the driver. When we were within a hundred feet or so of St. John's, Paul got out of the car, walked up ahead of us and moved the yellow "No Parking" cones onto the sidewalk so our driver could park directly in front of the church. As soon as the car came to a stop, he opened the rear passenger door and helped each of us out of the car. The hearse pulled in front of our limousine while Paul was helping us disembark, and the driver of our car, along with three other men, all in the requisite black suits, slid Peg's casket out of the hearse and onto a rolling gurney.

While the three of us stood on the sidewalk in front of the church watching Paul give the four men last-minute instructions, passing cars slowed and their occupants stared at us, probably thankful, unconsciously, that we were standing there and not them.

A rivulet of sweat ran down the small of my back, and I shivered. I wondered if I needed to use the bathroom, but I couldn't make up my mind.

Somewhere a police siren sounded, and it startled me because until that moment I hadn't been aware of any sounds. Not from the traffic passing by, not from birds in the trees around us, not Paul Virag's voice. Nothing. Until that moment, I realized, I'd been standing on the sidewalk shrouded in total silence.

Numb, I thought. *That's how I feel. Numb. But more than that. I feel like I'm not really here. Like I'm watching all this from somewhere else. Like I'm not even a part of it.*

Don't I wish.

I wonder if the kids are all right? I asked myself. *I wonder if I should've brought Jennie? No,* I decided a second later. *I did the right thing leaving her home. This is no place for her. No place for me either,* I thought cynically.

But before I could take that thought any further, Paul left the four men and walked down the sidewalk towards us. "Mr. Herbert," he said to me when he was still a few feet away, "the pallbearers will bring the casket in first. They'll walk slowly down the center aisle of the church, two men on each side, and they'll position the casket at the base of the steps in front of the choir stalls. You'll follow the pallbearers up to the front of the church, and you'll take the first pew on the right along with your parents, your mother-in-law and your wife's sisters. I'll bring your parents in now, and then I'll come back for you." He turned to my mom and dad. "Mr. Herbert? Mrs. Herbert? May I ask you to join me now?"

My father reached for my mother's hand, but as he did, she extended her hand to me instead. She gave my hand a tight squeeze and looked at me for a long time before kissing me on the cheek. "I love you, honey," she said simply, and then she took my father's hand and followed Paul up the steps into the church.

A minute later Paul was again at the bottom of the church steps. "Are you ready, Mr. Herbert?" he asked.

"I'm ready," I answered, dreading what was to come next.

He turned to the pallbearers and gave them a quick nod, their signal to carry the casket and the gurney up to the top of the steps. When they had done so, he guided me up the steps behind them. He gave another quick nod, and the two men in front opened the double doors to the church and put down the doorstops. They carefully lifted the front wheels of the gurney over the doorsill and rolled it about ten feet into the back of the church, just behind the last row of pews.

I stepped into the relative darkness and the cool interior of St. John's and saw hundreds of heads turned towards the back of the church. I stared in amazement as I looked from one side of the church to the other; not a seat was to be found. The church was filled to capacity, and dozens of people stood in the back and halfway up the right-hand aisle.

The pallbearers started to walk up the center aisle. I fell in step behind them. *This is like a wedding procession,* I mused, *but without the music and without the bride. Well, the bride is here,* I thought bitterly the next second. *It's just that she's dead.*

We walked up the center of the church towards the choir stalls and the altar, and I tried to ignore the sounds of people crying, whispering, blowing their noses. I tried instead to concentrate on the creaks the old wood floor made under our feet and on a tiny squeak coming from one of the wheels of the gurney. I looked straight ahead, focusing on the foot of Peg's casket, knowing if I made eye contact with the people who pressed in on either side of the aisle, I would lose what little control I still had. But in spite of my best efforts, the sounds of mourning filled my ears, and I couldn't avoid seeing the contorted faces, the unchecked tears and the shaking heads.

No, I thought, halfway down the aisle, wiping away tears, *this is no wedding procession.*

Forty-four

Two and a half hours later, after Peg's funeral service at St. John's and her burial at Pinelawn Memorial Park, I sat in the limousine with my mother, my father, Peg's mother and her three sisters on the way back to Beth and Dave's house for lunch. We sat in silence, watching first countryside, then strip malls and then suburban neighborhoods slip past our blackened windows.

As I looked out the window, I became conscious of the wedding band on my finger and slowly began to turn it against my pinkie with my thumb. I looked down at it and remembered how excited I'd been when Peg had first slipped it on my finger. I remembered how I had looked down at my hand hundreds of times for weeks after we were first married, marveling at how it looked and staring at it in wonderment. I thought about how it had never been off my finger in the nine years Peg and I had been married. And then I began to wonder if it still belonged on my finger, because I had just buried everything it had ever symbolized.

What do I do with you? I thought as I stared at the gold band. *If I take you off, what does that look like? Makes it look like I couldn't wait to get you off, that's what. You know that's not true, and I know that's not true, but no one else does. But why on earth should I wear you? Because if I take you off now—not even half an hour after I've buried Peg—people won't understand. That's why. But if not now, when? And why then and not now? Nothing's going to be any different next week or next month or next year, except maybe next week or next month or next year, people will understand and won't get upset. But that's not enough of a reason for me. Sorry, but it isn't. I hope you understand, Peg.*

I looked at Peg's mother; she was still staring out the opposite window. Then I carefully pulled the ring off my finger and slid it into my jacket pocket.

Book
Three

Forty-five

The day after Peg's funeral I went back to work. Not because I was ready to, but because I had to. I knew if I stayed home, my thoughts would automatically spiral inward and downward, until the pain of losing her would become unbearable.

I dismissed the idea of moving back to our house in Huntington. I worked for a living, and my children needed someone to take care of them. They needed a mother. So they got mine. And that meant I had to live with my parents if I wanted to be with my children.

The following Tuesday, August 26th, after the kids were in bed, I decided to go through the paperwork that had accumulated since Peg had gone into the hospital and which I had been throwing into the top drawer of the guest room dresser. The drawer was filled with hospital bills, insurance statements, lab reports, receipts for everything under the sun, the normal mail from home, the cards I'd removed from the bulletin board in Peg's room, and scores of unopened condolence cards and letters.

I didn't have the energy to pore over the hospital paperwork or the mail from home, so instead I pulled together the unopened cards and letters, sat down on the edge of the bed and started to read. Most were typical sympathy cards with typical personal messages—"We were so saddened to learn" or "Our thoughts and prayers are with you"—touching and nice to receive, but... typical.

However, a few really stood out. A neighbor from across the street wrote that she had not only prayed for the repose of Peg's soul, but had also asked Peg to remember us here on earth. She said she believed that those we love continue to have powerful influence on our lives after they die, and she was certain Peg would help me in death just as she had helped everyone in life by being a wonderful wife, mother, friend and neighbor.

Another neighbor who had recently come to the States from England wrote that Peg was the prettiest, funniest, most life-enhancing person she had met since moving to America. She said she was always amazed at Peg's immaculate house and her beautiful needlepoints and wondered how she managed to do everything so perfectly and still be a loving and caring mother. She felt blessed to have known Peg and was certain that life on Dewey Street was going to be much duller without her. She closed by assuring me that, hard though it may be to understand now, God has his reasons. He must, she said, or else the world is a very cruel place indeed.

An assistant vice president at Chemical Bank where Peg had worked wrote that Peg was not just respected by her colleagues for her intelligence and candor. More importantly, he said, she was loved for her humanity and her warmth. He knew Peg would be sorely missed by her Chemical family, but he could not imagine the magnitude of her loss to me, my children and my family.

One of Peg's closest friends said the letter I was reading was the last of several she had written to me since Peg's death. The others she had discarded because they were too laden with sorrow and pain. She said she had never told Peg how much she meant to her or the extent to which Peg had influenced her life, but she wanted me to know. She said she would always remember Peg for her sense of perspective, especially in times of crisis, her sense of humor, her good judgment, her ability to separate reality from image and the important from the unimportant, and her constant availability to her friends.

A friend of one of Peg's sisters whose husband had died two years earlier warned that the coming weeks and months would be terrible for me and others who loved Peg. But she had some advice to offer—advice based on what she had learned after her husband's death and which had more than once pulled her out of depression and self-pity. She said that although my children and I must not allow ourselves to live by guessing at what Peg would want us to do, we should remember that Peg would never want to watch us suffer or be unhappy. Instead she would want us to celebrate her life and her spirit by immersing ourselves in life and all it had to offer as soon as we possibly could.

One of Peg's sisters wrote that she had always marveled at Peg's consistency in that the dreams Peg expressed while playing childhood games and in teenage fantasies were the same ones she worked towards and attained as an adult. She credited me with enabling Peg to become the person she always wanted to be and said that I had helped her in ways no one else could have. She ended her letter saying that if we could measure quality in life, we would find that Peg had experienced a lifetime's worth in the short time she had. I should have no regrets, therefore, she said, and I should at least take comfort in that.

But the most memorable letter of all was from a man who used to be the sales manager for one of our largest customers and who had lost his wife to cancer several years before. His letter was dated August 19, 1980. Cal said that although he never had the pleasure of knowing Peg, he knew me, and he knew of my respect and love for her, so he knew she must have been a very special person. He wished that he could give me a simple formula for peace of mind or tell me that my adjustment would be easy, but he knew this simply was not possible. But life does go on, he assured me, and he was certain I would find each passing day to be a little more bearable.

He then told me of an elderly friend of his mother's who, having outlived two husbands, gave him some advice when his wife died that he treasured to this day. She told him he had just finished a good book and he should close it and put it on the shelf. Then he should open a new book and begin reading from it as soon as possible. He would always re-member passages from the old book, she said, but they would become dimmer as he became absorbed in the new book. He admitted that his mother's friend's advice was easier said than done, but he had found it invaluable nevertheless and hoped it would be of value to me.

I sat on the edge of the bed holding Cal's letter in my hand, staring at his words, wondering what he was trying to tell me. Was he telling me to find someone to take Peg's place as soon as possible? No, that couldn't be. Cal would never think like that. But then, what *was* he saying? I read the words again. "You have just finished reading a good book." That had to be a reference to his just deceased wife and, indirectly, a reference to Peg. And if it was, what else could "open a new book and begin reading from it as soon as possible" mean?

I shook my head in confusion and frustration. *Well, the letter's beautiful and worth saving,* I thought, *even if I don't know what it means.*

I got up off the bed and collected what I'd read. Ever the one for order, I stacked the cards so all the spines were to the left, smaller ones on top, larger ones on the bottom, and jogged them into a neat stack. I stacked the letters in size order too and threw away all of the envelopes. All except Cal's. I read his letter one more time and then carefully slid it back into its envelope and placed it on top of the letter pile. I opened the dresser drawer and pushed the rest of the paperwork aside to clear a space for what I'd read, cards in one pile, letters in another. At least now, I reasoned, I had a clear line of demarcation between read and unread.

But as I was about to close the drawer, I saw two groups of yellow lined pad paper protruding from under a hospital bill in the unread pile. One group consisted of several pages held together by a paper clip, while the other was considerably thicker, legal-sized and stapled. I pulled the smaller one out first and saw that the handwriting was Peg's. In the left-hand margin she had written days of the week beginning with Wednesday, and next to each day she had written a paragraph. I realized I was looking at a diary of sorts, a day-by-day accounting of her stay in the hospital, beginning with the Wednesday she had checked into Huntington Hospital. I went back to the bed, sat down and started to read.

Wednesday—To Dr. Goldstein for exam and consultation. So young. Only thirty-three! Took a blood sample. Low count on white, red and platelets. He tells me I have leukemia. He wants me in the hospital. Amy Bennett took me back to the Emergency Room. Impossible to describe my feelings as they ran from hysteria to confusion to disbelief. How can I be so sick? He says my chances are good.

John brought Jen up. Wonderful therapy. John looked like he was going to break into tears any minute, but I didn't cry at all. Just enjoyed the chatter. Her million questions. Her hurried hugs to tell me that she's frightened too. The little guy couldn't come. Too late for him. What if tonight in kitchen with Linda was last time I'll ever see him? Can't think like that. Mustn't!

Dave and Beth and the folks know, and they're all trying to keep things normal with the children. Folks took kids home with them.

I can't sleep. I just cry and cry. Seems like no one wants to answer my call button. Two transfusions of blood.

Thursday—I wake up crying. I feel so alone. I question and keep thinking how I've always felt so damned blessed. Everything. School, marriage, my beautiful babies that weren't possible. Sooner or later I knew I'd pick a wild card.

Father Bob came in to see me. He was consoling and promised many prayers. I asked him to pray for Mom because I know her faith will be so shaken again.

Dr. Goldstein came to talk to me. He outlined everything I have. AML...acute myelogenous leukemia. I have an excellent shot because of my age and physical condition. The therapy... DAT... is straightforward. Kill all the bad cells and at the same time, all the good cells and come back from there. The complications and infections could kill me. In the meantime, lots to look forward to—nausea, vomiting, mouth sores, no hair, fever, etc. One day at a time.

The day is a torture of tests. Blood, a tube into my vena cava, spinal tap, X-rays, EKG, more blood tests. Finally I can lie flat on my back for two hours.

People are mobilizing all over. Dave put John in touch with a Dr. Werner at New York Hospital. People calling with other recommendations. Blood drives at Chemical and in the neighborhood. Beth and Dave organizing all sorts of things. I keep breaking down but got good reports on my behavior during all the tests. I'm pretty cried out today so I guess they thought I was being brave.

So many thoughts. Should I write letters to my babies in case I die? Should I hurry up and finish the family albums? Morbid, but I can't help it.

Tomorrow I'm moving to New York Hospital. I'm scared, but I think it's right.

Friday—Left Huntington Hospital at eight-thirty. New York Hospital is very intimidating at first, but I have a pretty good room. River view. I guess that will be important later when I'm here for a long time. The bone marrow slides from Huntington Hospital were not good enough, so everything was done again. That was horrible, but what a team! Dr. Werner (old before his time, very serious, very thorough), Dr. Levy (very compassionate, also seems good, a woman and I think I'll appreciate that), Dr. Porter, Dr. Burton, Dr. Graff. All went over me with a fine-toothed comb. More X-rays. Another EKG.

Dr. Porter came back later in afternoon and took out neck IV. Back in right arm.

Phone ringing off hook. Erin here for a long time. John here at seven to talk to Dr. Werner. Dr. Werner's not in agreement with Huntington Hospital's diagnosis. All results aren't in. Can't start treatment until Monday.

Saturday—Slept well. No pills. Ring of interns around me this morning. Dr. Werner in to see me. Kind of gruff but nice. I should anticipate fever over weekend. He's surprised I don't feel sick. (Good sign?)

John called early. I talked to Jen. "When you come home next week, I can splash you." She's getting a lot of swimming done. Erin and Mom here for a couple of hours. They're calm now too. Beth and Dave sent "Anatomy of an Illness," and I caught the author on TV. I'll be getting fruits and vegetables from home. Mike called. Very understanding having been in this position one month ago. Only low moment was after they started transfusion at four. Slight fever. Dizzy trying to eat dinner. Reality of it creeping back. Seeing John, I burst into tears. He and folks brought goodies... pictures of kids (John Jr. with a beer can), fruit, etc. I'm really getting settled in. Thank God for my own room. Two pints of red blood today.

Monday—Fever last night. They started antibiotics. Sweated most of the night. This morning I had my first shower. Wonderful! Broke down talking to Jennie. "Mommy, maybe tomorrow Daddy and me could pick you up, and you could come home and make my lunch..."

That was the last entry.

I sat on the bed as I had with Cal's letter and stared at her words, at her precise yet flowing script, and wondered why she had stopped making entries. Was the pain or the nausea or the fever simply too much by Tuesday?

I shook my head in sadness and bewilderment.

It was time for bed.

Forty-six

I learned quickly that keeping busy was the key to sanity, and that keeping busy was most important during those two or three hours after dinner and before bed. So Wednesday night, August 27th, after putting Jennie and John to bed, I decided to go through more of the paperwork in the top dresser drawer. I again ignored the hospital-related material and instead pulled out the stack of legal-size paper I had passed over the night before. The yellow sheets were numbered, page one to nineteen, and entitled "Blood Donors." With no recollection of ever having seen these sheets before, I decided to scan the names before throwing the list away.

As I leafed through the pages, I was stunned to see the number of people who had been contacted by Peg's friends and co-workers, and who had agreed to donate blood or plasma on her behalf. Hundreds upon hundreds of names appeared on the yellow pages, most of them unknown to me. All of the entries were handwritten. Some looked like they had been entered by the person listed, but most of the names, judging by the similarity of the handwriting, had been entered by only four or five people. I shook my head in amazement at the realization that all these people had agreed to help Peg and in sadness that they never got the chance.

On the fourth page I noticed a name I recognized—Nancy Charlton, the daughter of Shirley and Donald Charlton, our next-door neighbors. But the address wasn't Shirley and Don's; the address was in Roslyn, a town fifteen miles to the west of Huntington. I wondered if maybe this was another Nancy Charlton, but decided that would be too much of a coincidence. I was surprised my eye had caught Nancy's name out of the hundreds of names listed, because although Peg and I knew who she was, neither of us had ever spoken to her. She was for all intents and purposes a stranger.

And yet perhaps I shouldn't have been surprised that her name stood out, because in one sense Nancy Charlton was anything but a stranger. To the contrary, she was a joke Peg and I had shared many times. A nice joke, but a joke nevertheless.

For reasons I could never explain to myself or to Peg, I was intrigued by Nancy Charlton from the moment I first saw her washing her car in her parents' driveway. Peg said the wet shirt had caught my eye, but there was something else. I could never figure out what that something else was, but Peg knew I thought Nancy was special in some unspecified way.

Peg also knew I watched Nancy turn out of her driveway almost every morning on her way to work. I didn't know why, but something made me go to the window as soon as I heard Nancy's tires crunch on the driveway gravel. And something made me watch her stop at the end of the driveway, carefully look both ways up and down the street, then turn left and drive slowly past our house on the way to the railroad station, peering intently over the hood of her ancient gold Chevy Impala sedan.

And Peg knew how angry I had gotten one Saturday night when a date pulled up in front of Nancy's house, sat in his car and beeped his horn for her. I stopped getting dressed, went to the side window of our bedroom and waited for Nancy to come out of her house while this clown leaned on his horn. Even though I had never said a word to Nancy Charlton, I was annoyed that this guy sat in his car expecting her to respond to his horn instead of treating her like a lady and getting out and ringing her doorbell. I watched Nancy walk down her front walk and get into the guy's car, and then I turned away from the window and made some comment to Peg about the situation. I remember her asking why I cared, and I remember I had no answer for her. I just knew I did.

Anyway, here she was again. Her name, her address, her daytime phone number, her evening phone number. I looked at her line on the page and felt almost like a voyeur, privy to information not really mine to know. But I continued to stare at the listing and wondered who had called her and when and what she had said when she was called and why she had agreed to help. And then I decided I would call her at work the next morning. To thank her for agreeing to donate blood to Peg. That would be a nice thing to do, I thought.

Whoa, John, a voice said, somewhat harshly, from somewhere in my head. *Tell me again why you're going to call this woman.*

"To thank her," I said to the voice.

Great, it replied. *And what about the other four or five hundred people on the list? You gonna call all of them too?*

"No, I couldn't possibly do that."

Yeah, I know that. I also know there's no goddamn reason on earth why you should call this young lady. Bad idea, my friend. Bad idea.

"Why is it such a bad idea?" I asked the voice. "All I'm going to do is call this Nancy Charlton and thank her for being willing to donate blood to Peg. That's all. Where's the harm in that?"

No harm in that at all, the voice agreed, *if that's the reason you're calling her. But I think there's more to it, which means this is a call you shouldn't be making. Like I said, it's a bad idea, my friend. A bad idea.*

"Maybe," I thought to myself, "but I'm still going to call her."

I shook my head to end the conversation, put aside the sheet with Nancy's name and address and telephone numbers, and continued to go through the paperwork in the dresser drawer.

Forty-seven

On Thursday, August 28th, the single sheet of yellow legal paper remained on the left side of my desk all morning. I looked at the sheet countless times and picked it up several times, but each time I picked it up, I put it down almost immediately, deciding that the time wasn't yet right for me to make my call.

The sheet of paper was still on the left side of my desk when I got back from lunch. I picked up the sheet again and was about to put it down again when I heard the voice from somewhere deep inside.

What the hell is going on here?

"What do you mean, 'what the hell is going on here'?" I asked. "I'm just trying to decide if now is a good time to make my call."

Why are you waiting for a "good time" to call? the voice shot back. *I thought all you were going to do was thank the young lady for agreeing to donate blood. Or am I missing something here?*

"You're not missing anything."

So again I ask why you have to wait for a "good time"?

"I don't know," I replied, suddenly feeling foolish.

I stared at the yellow paper in my hand, at Nancy Charlton's name and business number, and wondered if she were there now.

"Probably," I said to myself, still staring at the sheet of paper.

My intercom buzzed. I ignored it.

This is absolutely ridiculous, chided the voice. *You know you shouldn't make this call. That's why you're stalling. Admit it, for Christ's sake, and forget about calling Nancy Charlton.*

A moment of mental silence.

So are you going to stop the bullshit and get on with your work? the voice asked.

I rubbed my lower lip for several seconds as I deliberated.

"I'm going to call her right now," I said to the voice finally. "There's no reason to be nervous, and there's no reason to put off my call. I'm just being stupid."

Before I could change my mind, I quickly picked up the receiver and dialed Nancy Charlton's number.

One ring, two rings, three rings, then a woman's voice. "Good afternoon, Nancy Charlton's office."

"Uh, good afternoon. My name is John Herbert. I'm calling for Nancy Charlton. Is she available?"

"I'm sorry, but Miss Charlton isn't back from lunch yet. May I take a message?"

A split second of hesitation. *Should I leave a message,* I wondered, *or should I just forget the whole thing?*

Decision made. "Uh, yes. Please. If you would. Would you let her know I called, and ask her to give me a call back when she gets a minute?"

"Of course. May I have your number, Mr. Herbert?"

"Sure. 516-334-6500."

"Fine. I'll see that she gets your message. Thank you for calling."

"Thank you. Have a good day."

I placed the receiver back in its cradle, put my hands behind my head and leaned back in my chair. I had made the call. I looked at my watch. It was one thirty-five.

I wondered when Nancy would return my call. Then I wondered if she would return my call. Then I decided to stop wondering anything and got to work.

Forty-eight

Thirteen, fourteen, fifteen, sixteen, finally seventeen. The elevator doors slid open, and Nancy Charlton stepped out of the elevator onto the deep piled carpet of the seventeenth floor of the Exxon building and the New York sales offices of *National Geographic* magazine. She looked at her watch as she started to walk to her office. "Five minutes of two," she said to herself. "I could've sat in the sun another couple of minutes."

A left at the end of the elevator lobby towards the east side of the building, and then a right down the hall, past her boss's office and the salesmen's offices on the left and the secretarial cubicles on the right.

She walked into her office and was halfway to her desk when the secretary who had covered for her during her lunch hour bolted out of her cubicle waving a pink "While You Were Out" telephone message slip.

"Nancy, wait. You had a telephone call while you were out to lunch!" she exclaimed excitedly.

Nancy stopped, turned around and took the message slip from the secretary's extended hand. "Thanks, Judy," she said, dropping the slip on her desk without reading it.

Nancy walked behind her desk and tossed a paper bag containing an empty yogurt container and an empty soda can into her wastebasket. She bent down, opened the bottom right hand drawer of her desk and took out her pocketbook. When she straightened up, she saw the secretary still standing in the doorway.

"It didn't sound like a business call," the secretary volunteered. "It sounded more like a personal call."

"Really?" Nancy asked disinterestedly as she looked into her compact mirror, pursed her lips and put on fresh lipstick.

"He sounded very mature."

"He?" Nancy asked. She closed the lipstick tube and began to apply makeup to her cheeks and nose.

"A John Herbert. Do you know a John Herbert?"

By now, a second secretary had joined the first, and the two of them stood half in, half out of Nancy's office.

Nancy stopped applying her makeup, snapped the compact case closed and picked up the message slip with her free hand. The message was simple.

Mr. / Ms.—John Herbert

From—Judy

Phone No.—516 334 6500

The "Please Call" box was checked, and the Message portion read "personal (?)."

Nancy swallowed hard. *My God*, she thought. *Why is he calling me? Shit!*

The two secretaries remained where they were, watching her face intently, trying to read her every expression. "Do you know him?" the second secretary asked.

"I know of a John Herbert," Nancy replied. "He's my parents' neighbor. Lives next door to them. Anyway, thanks for taking the call."

The answer didn't satisfy either of the two women, but they realized Nancy Charlton was not going to reveal anything more. Reluctantly, they withdrew from the doorway and returned to their cubicles.

Nancy sat down at her desk, put her lipstick and compact case back in her pocketbook, and closed the open desk drawer. Then she picked up the pink message slip again and stared at the name, carefully printed in block letters.

"John Herbert," she said aloud to herself. "Why are you calling me? And what can I possibly say to you?"

She swung her chair around and stared out the window at the office building opposite hers across the Avenue of the Americas.

Maybe I shouldn't return the call, she thought. *Maybe I should just pretend I didn't get the message. That would certainly be the easiest thing to do. I mean, after all, what am I supposed to say to a guy who's just lost his wife?*

She turned away from the window and noticed for the first time seven other pink telephone message slips spread across her desk. A little smirk crept across her face as she scanned them. *Funny no one hand delivered these to me,* she thought.

She sighed and picked up the John Herbert message again. "I can't not call you," she said, staring at the name. "I just can't do that."

She picked up the receiver and started to dial.

Forty-nine

At five minutes after two my intercom buzzed. I picked up the receiver and heard my secretary announce that Nancy Charlton was on line 3 returning my call. I thought I detected a question somewhere in her delivery, but I ignored it and punched 3.

"Hello?"

"Hi. This is Nancy Charlton. I'm returning John Herbert's call."

"Hi, Nancy. This is John Herbert. Thanks for getting back to me so quickly."

She didn't reply, so I plunged ahead. "I... uh... called earlier just to thank you for agreeing to be a blood donor for Peg. That was very... kind of you, and I... I wanted you to know I appreciated it."

"Well... that was the very least I could do," Nancy replied. She paused, then continued. "I just wish I had had the chance to actually be a donor."

Another pause, but longer this time. "I'm sorry about Peggy. My mother told me she was sick, and then last week she told me what happened. I really am sorry."

I could tell from the tone of her voice she was being sincere, and I wondered what I should say in response that I hadn't already said a hundred times. I wanted to say something meaningful—something I hadn't already said, something that would let her know I appreciated her sincerity—but I realized almost immediately I wasn't going to come up with anything earth-shattering at that precise moment.

186

So I simply said, "Thank you." And then, "I appreciate your saying that."

Several seconds passed before Nancy spoke again. "How are your children doing? I know your little boy's too young to know what's happened, but what about your daughter? Is she okay?"

I hesitated before answering, because I didn't know for sure how Jen was doing. But I couldn't say that. "Jennie's okay as far as I can tell. My mom and dad are taking care of her and my son, and I think that's making things better than they might be otherwise."

"Still, this must be very hard for her. I mean, she's only...what—two, three?"

"Three. Just turned three on August third."

"So she's old enough to know what's happened."

"I'm afraid so," I agreed. "Uh... I hope you won't misinterpret what I'm about to say," I continued, suddenly reaching a decision I didn't even know I was considering and ignoring all the rules of propriety, "but ... I was wondering if by any chance you might like to join me for dinner Saturday night. I realize it's probably a crazy idea, but... I could really use someone to talk to."

Nancy took a deep breath before she answered. "I'm... I'm sorry, but I'm busy Saturday night."

"Ahh. Okay. Not a problem. I understand."

What the hell did you think she would say? the voice in my head yelled. *You've just lost your wife, for Christ's sake. You're a widower! With two little kids!*

"But I'm free Sunday night if that works," Nancy added.

What did she say? the voice in my head cried out.

"Yeah. That'll work," I answered, allowing a grin to creep across my face. "Absolutely, that'll work. Great. What time is good for you?"

"I don't know. Whatever's good for you."

"How about seven?"

"Seven's fine."

"Seven it is then. And where will I pick you up? At your parents' house?"

"No. You can pick me up at my apartment. In Roslyn."

"Okay. Fine. How do I get there?"

"Do you know where Roslyn Road is?"

"Sure do."

"Well, my apartment's on Elm Street, which is off Roslyn Road, three blocks north of the Expressway. I'm the third house on the left. Number 66."

"Got it."

"Oh, one more thing," Nancy continued. "Don't go up to the front door of the house. That's my landlord's door. There's a walk along the left side of the house that leads to my door."

"Okay, side door it is."

"You'll be able to find me okay?"

"I'll find you. I promise."

Odd choice of words, I thought as I prepared to say good-bye.

"I look forward to seeing you Sunday night," I said. "And thank you for saying yes."

I heard Nancy exhale a smile and give up a tiny chuckle. "You're welcome. I'm looking forward to seeing you too."

And then she hung up.

For the second time that afternoon, I put my hands behind my head, leaned back in my chair and stared up at the ceiling. "Holy shit," I said out loud.

Got that right, said the voice softly from somewhere in my head.

"She said yes. I can't believe it. I can't believe I did that, and I can't believe she said yes."

Me neither, agreed the voice, harsh once again. *You realize you asked her out on a date, don't you?* the voice continued. *You realize, regardless of what you're telling yourself, this is a date. Your wife's not even dead two weeks, and you're going out on a date! Jesus Christ! I don't believe you! What are you thinking? Are you thinking at all? Why are you doing this, John?*

I had no ready answer. I hadn't planned on asking Nancy out to dinner, and I certainly had no intention of asking anyone out on a date. But I had to admit the voice was right. Dinner with Nancy Charlton certainly seemed like a date.

With difficulty, I shook off the disapproval I felt deep inside, brought my hands down from behind my head, leaned forward and tried to focus on the paperwork strewn across my desk.

Fifty

My father's fork noticeably slowed for an instant as he lifted it from his plate to his mouth. My mother stopped chewing and then swallowed with difficulty. Dinner continued, but the mood at the dining room table changed instantly.

"And what's her name?" my father asked without looking up from his plate.

"Nancy Charlton," I replied, feeling like a sixteen-year-old again.

"And how do you know her?"

"She's our next-door neighbors' daughter."

My mother carefully wiped her mouth, folded her napkin and placed it back in her lap. "When did you call her?" she asked.

"Today. From the office. I called her at work."

"How did you know where to reach her?" my father interjected.

"Her name was on a list of blood donors—potential blood donors, I should say—that I found last night while I was going through some paperwork."

He gave a nod to indicate he understood, but he said nothing. For a split second I wondered if his last question, taken in the context of the preceding one, signaled a darker rationale for the interrogation. But before I could give the thought any further consideration, my mother was asking me another question.

"What night did you ask her out for?"

"Sunday night. This coming Sunday night. But only if that's okay with you guys. If you've got other plans or anything like that, I'll just call her and cancel."

"No," my mother replied, "we don't have anything planned."

"So you don't mind if I go out? You don't mind watching the kids for me?"

"We never mind watching the children," my father answered, even though I had directed the question to my mother.

I noticed he hadn't answered the first half of my question. *But what can I expect?* I asked myself. *What would I think if my son asked a woman out to dinner eleven days after his wife died?*

"It's not a date," I volunteered, immediately regretting that I felt the need to explain. I looked first at my mother and then at my father. "I need someone to talk to. Someone who didn't know Peg. Someone who's not involved. Someone who's... not hurting like we are. Do you understand what I'm saying?"

My father put down his fork and took a sip of his wine before answering. "I can understand your needing to talk to someone, son. I truly can. What I can't understand is why you picked this Nancy Charlton to talk to. You just saw her name on some list, and you decided to call her. I'm sorry, but that makes no sense to me whatsoever." He sighed and then continued. "And I have to admit I don't like the idea of you taking someone out this soon after Peg's death. I know you need to talk to someone, but..." His voice trailed off.

"I'm not comfortable with the idea either," my mother said softly, "but I think we have to leave that decision up to John. He knows what he's feeling, and I'd like to think he knows what he's doing." She reached across the table and patted my hand.

"Well, I hope so," my father replied without much conviction. He started to pick up his fork, but changed his mind. "I have a suggestion," he said. "If you need someone to talk to, why don't you give Father Richardson a call? He called when he heard about Peg, and he told me he'd make himself available if you wanted to see him."

191

"That was nice of him, Pop, but he's not my priest, and I wouldn't feel right imposing on him like that."

"You're not imposing on him," my father pressed. "He offered to help if you thought he could."

"It's not the worst idea, I suppose. I mean, he is a priest, and who knows? Maybe he'll say something that'll help. Tell you what," I said after another moment of thought. "If you call him, I'll see him."

"I'll call him first thing in the morning. Should I try to get an appointment for tomorrow night?"

"No, I wouldn't do that. Tomorrow's Friday and the beginning of Labor Day weekend. I'm sure he's got better things to do than talk to me. Why not try for next week? Say Tuesday or Wednesday night?"

"Okay. That's what I'll do," my father said, nodding his head enthusiastically—happy, I could tell, to be charged with the task. Then he looked at me over the top of his glasses and lowered his head as if we were co-conspirators. "I don't suppose you'd hold off going out with this Nancy Charlton until after you've talked to Father Richardson, would you?"

I smiled, not surprised by his suggestion. "No, Pop. I won't do that. I think I can talk to both her and Father Richardson."

He gave a grunt and shook his head sadly. "I just hope you know what you're doing, son," he said as he picked up his fork. "I just hope you know what you're doing."

Fifty-one

Friday came and went, then Saturday, and then came Sunday, August 31st. Mercifully, my parents said nothing more about Nancy or our dinner plans for Sunday night. But they really didn't have to, given the war that was going on in my mind. A war between emotion and logic, between conventional right and unconventional wrong. A war between me and a harsh, persistent voice I was beginning to recognize as my conscience. A voice that, as one might expect, had been the cause of much pain over the last three days.

But in spite of the voice, here I was standing in the guest bathroom of my parents' home, staring at myself in the mirror, in the final minutes of getting ready to pick up Nancy.

"Why are you all dressed up, Daddy?" Jennie asked from the hall as she peered into the bathroom.

"Hi, sweetheart," I said while I retied my tie for the fourth time. "Daddy's going out for a little while tonight."

"Will you come back?" Jennie asked, her eyes wide with fear.

"Of course I will, silly." I knelt down to give her a reassuring hug, and my heart ached at the thought of what must have prompted that question. "I'll be back. I promise. And then tomorrow morning, you and I and John will have breakfast together. How does that sound?"

"Can I have pancakes?"

"You can if Grandma makes them. But you'll have to ask Grandma because Daddy doesn't know how to make pancakes."

"I'll ask Grandma then."

She gave me a hurried kiss before scampering down the hall calling "Grandma." I turned back to the mirror one last time.

I don't believe you're doing this, the voice suddenly said to me from the face in the mirror. *I really don't believe you're going out on a date!*

"This isn't a date. I'm just going out to dinner with someone."

That's bullshit. And we've already been there! You know damn well this is a date.

"I just want someone to talk to. That's all."

There were at least five hundred other names on that list. You could have called any one of them if all you wanted to do is talk.

"You know that's not true. I don't know most of those people."

You don't know Nancy Charlton either. At least not well enough to think you can talk to her.

"I think I can."

Yeah, right.

"What are you saying? Why do you think I called her?"

I don't know why you called her. But I do know you used to watch her go to work every morning. And I remember how she looked that day in her parents' backyard when her mother invited you over for a beer. Remember that, pal? The yellow bikini? And I remember how you and Dave and Frank Bennett used to talk about what a good-looking kid she was. Yeah, I remember that too. So... why do I think you called her? Beats me, but somehow I don't think it was just to talk.

"Now that's crap. For Christ's sake, my wife just died."

My point exactly.

"What kind of person do you think I am?"

You tell me, pal. You tell me.

I tried to think of a suitable response—one that would both satisfy the voice and stop the warring thoughts. But I couldn't.

"Well," I said to the face in the mirror, "I don't know if calling Nancy was right or wrong, but that doesn't matter at this point. I've got a date to take this lady out to dinner, and I'm sure as hell not going to break it."

You just said "date," the voice shot back.

"Yes, I did. Because this is a date. Just not that kind of date."

I decided to call this latest exchange with the voice a draw. It was time to pick up Nancy.

Fifty-two

Nancy stood in front of her closet in her bra and panties and pushed one outfit after another aside, trying to find something "appropriate" for a night like this. She characterized each outfit out loud to herself as she slid the hangers from right to left.

"Too somber."

"Too cheerful."

"Too sexy. God, I can't wear that!"

"Too frumpy."

"Too old."

Finally on the fourth pass through everything she owned, she settled on a maroon velvet dress.

"Not too cheerful but not too somber either," she said, holding the dress out in front of her. "A little sexy but not too sexy. And I look good in it."

She took the dress off the hanger, stepped into it and reached behind her to pull up the zipper. She turned around and looked at herself in the full-length mirror on the wall opposite the closet, smoothing out the material as she turned. She stood in front of the mirror for several seconds, and she liked what she saw.

I should have another Tom Collins, she thought. *He'll be here in twenty minutes.* Panic started to rise again in the pit of her stomach. *But if I do that, I'll be half in the bag when he gets here. But, God, I am so scared. What if I can't think of anything to say? What if I say the wrong thing? I wonder if it's okay to talk about what happened? Or should I wait until he brings it up? I better wait until he brings it up.*

The hell with it. I'm going to have another Tom Collins before he gets here.

She was on her way back from the kitchen, her drink in hand, when the telephone rang.

Don't tell me he's not coming, she thought as she picked up the receiver. *Not after all the worrying I've done.*

"Nan?"

She let out a sigh of relief. "Hi, Mom. How are you?"

"I'm calling to see if you're okay."

"I'm okay. Just a little nervous."

"I hope you know what you're doing, Nancy."

"Me too."

"I still can't believe he asked you out on a date."

"This isn't a date. He just needs someone to talk to."

"Yeah, right."

"Mom, he's going to be here any minute. I have to go."

"Be careful, will you? Promise me you'll be careful?"

"I will. I promise."

"Call me tomorrow, and let me know how everything went."

"I will. But now I gotta go."

"I just hope you know what you're doing."

"Gotta go, Mom. Bye."

Nancy hung up the receiver and rested her head against the wall for a few seconds with her eyes closed. She gave a sigh and went into the living room to put a James Taylor album on the stereo. She turned the volume down so her landlord wouldn't pound his cane on the floor upstairs, then walked back to the mirror one last time. Satisfied that she was ready, she sat down on the couch and took a sip of her drink.

Nothing to do now but wait.

Fifty-three

At two minutes to seven, I turned onto Elm Street. True to its name, large, old elm trees lined both sides of the street. A few were healthy and strong, but most were either dead or dying or badly damaged by lightning strikes and hurricanes. Most of the homes on the street were old and large as well, some brick, some clapboard, one of stucco, but a few were modest, middle-class split-level houses built in the fifties and sixties, probably on property that had once belonged to the owners of the larger, older homes.

Nancy lived in one of these split-levels. The owner lived on the second floor and had converted part of the ground floor into an apartment to supplement a retirement income. Nancy was his tenant. Her landlord's home, like most of the other homes on the street, was well kept. The lawn and shrubs did not appear to be professionally maintained, but were nevertheless well manicured. To the right of the steps leading up to the front door was a one-car garage, to the left a narrow concrete walk from the sidewalk to a ground level side entrance. According to Nancy's directions, that was the door to her apartment.

The house was on the left as I came down the street, so I turned into the driveway to turn the car around and park in front of the house. As I backed out, I noticed that a man cutting his lawn across the street was watching me, as was a woman watering some flowers next door. By the time I pulled up next to the curb behind Nancy's car, both had stopped what they were doing, and neither of them made any attempt to conceal their interest in me. I got out of my car and gave the man across the street a quick smile and a quicker nod, the attention I was getting reminding me that I didn't belong here. I pushed the thought aside and started up the walk to Nancy's apartment.

When I reached the side entrance, I found the inside door open, and through the outer screen door, I heard music coming from inside the apartment. I rang the doorbell, and the music stopped almost immediately, followed by the sound of high heels on a hard floor. And then Nancy appeared.

"Hi," she said as she pushed the screen door open and pulled the inside door closed behind her. She stepped out into the early evening light. "You're right on time."

I smiled and attempted to appear at ease. "I try to be," I answered. "Don't always succeed, but I try to be."

She turned away for a second, locked the inside door and let the screen door close by itself. Then she faced me.

I was momentarily speechless. To begin with, I was struck by how young she looked. She couldn't have been more than twenty-four, twenty-five at most. She was a kid compared to me. But I also couldn't believe how attractive she was. She was about five-four, had beautifully smooth tanned skin, deep green eyes set far apart, and soft, short brown hair tinged with gold from the sun. She wore a deep maroon velvet dress with a scoop neck and short sleeves, and black heels. She had broad shoulders and broad hips, and she was big-breasted. She wasn't thin, but she certainly wasn't fat. She was shapely, quite shapely, and she looked... soft. Wonderfully soft. But most of all, I was taken aback by how wonderful she smelled. Even though we were standing probably four feet apart, she exuded the smell of soap, shampoo and perfume. So for that first second or two, I just stood where I was and savored her smell.

"Did you have any trouble finding me?" Nancy asked.

"No, none whatsoever. Your directions were fine," I stammered, trying to regain my composure.

"So where are we going?"

"A place in Locust Valley called Caminari's," I answered. "I think you'll like it. If you like Italian food, that is."

"I do," she responded enthusiastically. "I'm part Italian."

"Then I guessed right. Shall we?"

Nancy said yes with her smile, and I followed her down the walk to my car.

As I opened the car door for her, I saw that my new friend across the street had not yet resumed cutting his lawn, but rather had watched everything Nancy and I had done up to that moment.

"Quite a watchdog you've got across the street," I said as I slid behind the steering wheel.

"What do you mean?" Nancy asked.

I indicated the guy with a nod of my head. "He stopped cutting his grass the minute I arrived, and he's been watching me ever since."

"I guess he's not used to seeing a man come to my apartment," Nancy suggested.

I looked over at her as I pulled away from the curb to see if she was serious, but she was staring straight ahead, so I couldn't tell for sure.

The scent of soap and shampoo and perfume filled the car while I waited for traffic to allow me to turn onto Roslyn Road. *This is crazy*, I thought. *Here I am, thirty-four years old, sitting next to a woman probably ten years younger than I am—admittedly a very lovely woman, but still probably ten years younger—and a perfect stranger, and I'm taking her out to dinner, and my wife died two weeks ago this morning. I must be out of my mind!*

I made my turn onto Roslyn Road and began to accelerate.

I don't believe I'm doing this. I really don't. But it's too late to worry about it . . . so I won't.

A quick look over at Nancy again, then back to the road and the traffic in front of us.

God, she smells good.

Fifty-four

Caminari's was the perfect spot for the type of evening I had planned—an upscale restaurant with thick carpet, heavy draperies, starched white tablecloths and soft lighting—known for good food, attentive service and, most importantly, the kind of quiet, subdued atmosphere that the locals demanded and that was ideal for conversation. Caminari's was located on the northeast corner of the only intersection in Locust Valley, a delightful little village where employees of the wealthy came to shop for their employers, and where the wealthy came to browse through its antique shops, dress shops or saddlery—or to eat at Caminari's.

This was a Sunday night, so the restaurant was even quieter than usual. The maitre d' showed us to a table for four in the far left corner with a window on either side looking out onto the streets that formed the intersection. He pulled out a chair for Nancy in front of one of the windows, and I took the chair in the corner. He unfolded our napkins for us, placed them in our laps, welcomed us to Caminari's and asked if we would like something to drink.

"What's your pleasure?" I asked Nancy.

"I don't know," she answered tentatively. "What are you going to have?"

"I'm going to have a scotch on the rocks," I replied.

She thought for a second, and then looked up at the maitre d'.

"I'd like a Tom Collins, please."

He turned to me.

"And a J & B on the rocks with a twist."

He gave a slight bow and was gone. We were alone.

I watched him walk across the dining room towards the bar and turned to Nancy. "So how long have you been living in Roslyn?" I asked.

"Four weeks as of yesterday."

"Oh, you just moved in," I said, immediately wondering why I had just stated the obvious. "And before that you were living at home, right?"

"Yes," Nancy replied.

"Then this is a whole new experience for you. Living on your own, I mean."

She nodded.

"Do you like it?"

"I do. Very much. Don't get me wrong. I love my parents, and I love our home, but I thought the time was right for me to be out on my own."

Neither of us said anything for a moment.

"I gather you work in Manhattan?" I asked, afraid to let the silence go on for too long.

"Yes," she answered with a smile that I took to be tinged with a little bit of pride. "For *National Geographic* magazine."

"What do you do there?"

"I'm the administrative assistant to the Eastern advertising manager. It's not what I expected to be doing with my life, but it's exciting, it's fun and it pays well. So I'm not complaining."

"What did you expect to be doing?"

"Well, I was a biology major in college. And my plan was to become a veterinarian. But I dropped out at the end of my sophomore year."

Nancy looked around the dining room for a moment, seeming to consider whether or not she should continue. "Then I went to Katharine Gibbs and enrolled in their executive secretarial program. The day after graduation I had my first interview—at *National Geographic*—and they hired me. And that's my story."

Something about the way she said "And that's my story" signaled that she was finished talking about her job and the path that had led her to it, so I decided to change the subject.

But before I could think of a new topic, Nancy started to speak. "My mother tells me you're a boater."

"Yeah. Have been most of my life, really."

"Do you have a boat now?" she asked.

"Yeah. A sailboat."

"That's cool," she said with a smile. "What kind? Not that I'd know what you're talking about, I guess. I don't know anything about sailboats. Our family has always had powerboats."

"Well, mine is a sloop, which means it has one mast. And it's an O'Day. Not the best or most expensive, but a good boat."

"How big?"

"Thirty feet."

"Wow, it's a real boat then. Not a Sunfish you sail off the beach."

I couldn't help smiling. "No, it's a real boat. With bunks, galley, dining area, head with shower. The whole nine yards."

"My family's been boating ever since I can remember," Nancy said, "and my childhood centered around the water and boats. In fact, my parents are still boaters. But I've never been on a sailboat."

"Well, maybe sometime I can take you out on mine," I said without thinking.

She looked at me, seemed to consider saying something, changed her mind and then nodded, barely noticeably. She seemed to pull back.

Now why did I say that? I thought. *Totally inappropriate. What the hell is the matter with me?*

Fortunately, before the silence could go on for too long, a waiter brought our drinks. Nancy pulled the wrapper off the top of the straw in her glass and was about to take a sip when I proposed a toast. I raised my glass to hers, and she hesitantly brought hers to mine.

"Thanks for saying yes to tonight," I said.

"You're welcome," she replied uneasily. Then, "So… how are you doing?"

I knew she was going to ask me that question at some point in the evening, and I had prepared a safe response—one that wouldn't be totally honest, but at the same time, one that wouldn't make me come apart in front of a complete stranger. Unfortunately, I forgot what I had planned to say.

"I don't know, to be perfectly honest," I said instead. "I know that sounds weird, but looking inside where I'd find the answer is too painful. So I don't. Look inside, I mean." I scanned the dining room slowly as I spoke. I knew if I made eye contact with Nancy, I'd lose my composure before I could answer her question.

"I go to work. I come home. I have dinner with my kids and my parents. I put my kids to bed. I look at TV with my parents. I go to bed. The next morning I get up and do it all over again. That's the way things have been since a week ago Thursday when I went back to work."

Nancy nodded in understanding. "May I ask you another question?" she said after a few seconds of silence.

"Sure. What?"

"Why did you call me?"

"Why did I call you in particular, or why did I ask you to join me for dinner?"

"Both."

I took another sip of my drink and watched the ice make tiny eddies in the amber liquor as I tried to think of an answer to her question.

"I don't know why I called you," I finally said, still staring into my glass. "I really don't. I just saw your name on that blood donor list…"
I looked up at her, and our eyes met. "…and something told me I should call you. I know that was totally inappropriate, not the right thing to do at all, but…"

Without intending to, I sighed.

"As to why I asked you to join me for dinner… the truth is, I didn't mean to. That wasn't my intent when I called you. Then I heard your voice, and the next thing I knew, I was asking you out. But that doesn't answer your question as to why, does it? I guess the answer is I needed… need… someone to talk to. Someone who isn't affected by my wife's death. Someone who's not emotionally involved. I can't talk to my folks because, quite frankly, they're wrecks. I can't talk to my friends because they're too caught up in the whole situation and have their own issues to deal with. And I can't talk to co-workers because I have none in the usual sense. I'm the boss's son." I waited a second before continuing. "I don't know why I thought I could talk to you. But I think I was right."

Nancy took a sip of her drink. "I almost cancelled," she said.

I smiled sadly. "I'm not surprised. Why?"

"A lot of reasons. First..." she hesitated before continuing. "First, your wife died two weeks ago. And I said to myself, this is just not right. I don't know why John Herbert is calling me or what he expects from me, but no one should be doing what he's doing. No one. And I certainly shouldn't be part of it. Then I thought about how much older you are. And I wondered how I could possibly talk to you." She shrugged and looked down at her drink. "I guess I didn't feel experienced enough or mature enough. I don't know. I was just terrified I'd sit here and not know what to say."

"Then why did you come?"

"Because I felt so bad for you. And because I knew you were a nice guy." She stopped and gave me a little smile. "And because something told me I should," she continued. "Like what you said. I knew this wasn't right, but something wouldn't let me cancel. Something told me this was... okay. Even if it didn't seem okay."

I started to take another sip of my drink but realized my glass was empty. "And what about now?" I asked. I looked at my watch. "I realize we've only been together for an hour, but what about now? Are you glad you came?"

Nancy looked at me thoughtfully before answering. "Yes," she finally said. "I'm glad I came. And I'm not terrified anymore."

We looked at each other, and as we did, different feelings washed over me, one after another, all in the space of those few seconds. Happiness first when I realized how much I was enjoying being with this woman, then contentment at how comfortable I felt with her even though I barely knew her, followed by guilt because I knew I shouldn't be feeling either of those things—and culminating in sadness, a deep, deep sadness, because the good feelings of a moment ago had just been shattered.

But I was experiencing something else, I realized. A sense of being out of place. A sense of inappropriateness, for lack of a better word. I didn't belong here tonight. I belonged home with my kids.

"Would you like another drink?" I asked, anxious to move away from where my thoughts were taking me.

"Please," Nancy replied, finishing the Tom Collins in front of her with two long swallows.

I caught our waiter's eye and signaled him to bring us another round.

Nancy leaned back in her chair with her hands in her lap. "You mentioned before you were the boss's son. What do you do?"

"I work in a family-owned manufacturing company called Herbert Products. We make equipment for the printing industry. Accessory equipment. I've worked there twelve years now."

"Is it a big company?"

"No. Not really. We employ seventy, seventy-five people."

"That's big. Big to me, anyway. What's your position there?"

"Well, my father's president of the firm; I'm executive vice president. I manage new product introductions, pricing, product design. I work with our sales force and our VP of sales. I handle our advertising, marketing, trade shows. And I get involved a lot with customer service."

"Do you like your job?"

"I do. Like you, I'm not doing what I thought I'd be doing with my life, but I enjoy my work."

"Now it's my turn to ask you," Nancy said. "What did you expect to be doing?"

"I was going to be a doctor. A surgeon. At least that was the plan when I went to college. But my grades weren't good enough to get me into medical school. So, when the last rejection came in from the last school, I resigned myself to the fact that I wasn't going to be a doctor and went to work for my father while I waited to be drafted and sent to Viet Nam. Which didn't happen, thank God, but that's another story."

"Tell me about your children. Jennie and…?"

"John."

"That's right. John. The Tom Collins must be hitting bottom."

"Well… what can I say? They're both great little kids, but completely different from one another. John's nine months old and always has this great big smile on his face. He's the happiest little guy you can imagine and needs almost no attention from anyone. Plop him down; he'll find something to amuse himself with. And Jennie…" I smiled at the thought of Jennie. "Jennie's the most beautiful little girl in the world. Everyone says that. And she's my angel. But she's very serious and very grown up, even though she just turned three. So on the one hand, I have my happy-go-lucky little guy; and on the other hand, I have my very serious, very grown-up china doll. Quite a combination."

I thought about the kids, at home tonight with their grandmother and grandfather, and that made me think again about where I was. I needed to change the topic.

"So, let's get back to you," I said more abruptly than I'd intended. "What made you leave college, if you don't mind my asking?"

"I don't mind. I'm just a little sensitive about not having finished."

"Why didn't you?" I pressed.

"A couple of reasons. I guess number one was that I was an A student in high school. I was on the honor roll all four years, in the Honor Society, graduated thirty-third in a class of six hundred ten. So I thought I was pretty smart. Then I went to Lebanon Valley College and started getting C's and D's for the first time in my life. In my major, no less. I felt like a total failure."

She stopped talking for a moment and looked past me, a faraway look in her eye. "Reason number two was… my family was in turmoil. My father had dreamed all his life of owning his own business, and when I was a junior in high school, he quit his job of thirty years as a salesman for a restaurant equipment manufacturer and used his life savings to buy a convenience store up in Swan Lake, New York. Near Liberty. Without ever telling my mother, I might add, until the night he came home to announce he was now in business for himself."

She shook her head sadly. "Looking back, it was the dumbest thing he ever could have done. Swan Lake, that whole area, is a vacation spot for orthodox Jews from New York City. And here was my dad, as Norwegian as Leif Erickson, trying to make a living running a kosher delicatessen serving orthodox Jews on their vacations. Anyway, he couldn't run it all by himself during the summer vacation months, so for four years my mother, my brother and I spent our summers working eighteen-hour days, trying to help him keep it afloat.

"But finally, after four years and a horrible fourth summer, he admitted defeat and gave up. Gave up, locked the door and came home to Huntington. Never tried to sell the business. Just emptied the shelves of everything we might be able to use at home and walked away. He lost every cent he paid for it—which was everything he had. So here I was, at home at the end of summer vacation, about to start my junior year, still feeling like a total academic failure, not sure I still wanted to be a veterinarian; and here my family was, almost broke, my father without a job. So I decided not to go back to college. Decided I needed to step back. Reassess my goals. I knew I hadn't been happy at Lebanon Valley, but I didn't know what other direction to follow.

"So I took out a loan—my parents were in no financial shape to help me anymore—and I enrolled at Katharine Gibbs as a kind of stepping stone. I figured at least I'd be able to find work while I tried to sort out what I wanted to do with my life. And things worked out. Even at the ripe old age of twenty, I knew happiness doesn't just come to you. You have to go out and find it."

"And you liked Katharine Gibbs?"

Nancy nodded enthusiastically and smiled. "Oh, yeah. I was a round peg in a round hole. I loved every minute, and what other girls struggled with, I breezed through. Effortlessly. I graduated number one in my class, and as I said before, I went into Manhattan for my first job interview—at *National Geographic*—the day after I graduated. When they saw my skill levels, they offered me the job right then and there and asked if I could start the next day. I'd already fallen in love with Manhattan, so I said yes. And I'm still there, and I still love it."

"That's great," I said. "I mean it. That's really cool. And I liked what you said about happiness not coming to you—that you have to go find it. A lot of truth in that."

Nancy didn't reply. She just twirled her straw in her drink and smiled. Sadly, I thought.

"I'm surprised you were free tonight," I said after a few moments of silence.

"What do you mean?" she asked.

I had intended my statement to be an indirect compliment, but something told me Nancy hadn't taken it that way.

"Well, you know. I called you Thursday afternoon, and this is a three-day weekend. I was just surprised you didn't already have a date for tonight."

"Why would that have surprised you?"

"I would have assumed you were involved with someone," I answered, knowing that wasn't the right thing to say either as soon as I said it.

"Why?" Nancy asked.

I chuckled, realizing I was getting in deeper with every word, and tried to figure out how to answer her without making things worse again.

"You're a very attractive young woman," I said, "and I would have thought there was someone special in your life."

"Well, there isn't," Nancy replied flatly.

"Kind of between involvements?"

"No. Not between involvements. More like I've never been involved. With anyone. Not seriously, at least."

"I find that hard to believe."

"Well, it's the truth. Every guy I've ever gone out with turned out to be a jerk before the evening was over. So I haven't had many opportunities to go out with someone more than once. Which means you're talking to someone who's never had a serious relationship with anyone and who, truth be known, has no experience with men whatsoever."

By the time Nancy had finished talking, she was almost whispering. She took another sip of her drink and looked over at me. "I don't believe I just told you that," she said shaking her head in embarrassment.

"Me neither," I replied.

We sat quietly for several seconds, both of us looking into our drinks, each of us wondering whether we should continue this line of conversation or drop it entirely. But before either of us could make up our minds, our waiter appeared to take our order for dinner.

We talked through our appetizers, our entrees and over espressos until Caminari's was empty, and it was time to take Nancy home. I asked for our check, and Nancy went to the ladies' room. While I waited for her, I found myself thinking about how surreal the evening had been. I felt married, but I wasn't. I had little kids to take care of, and I wanted to be home with them, but I wasn't. In one sense, I didn't want to be here at all, but I was. I couldn't deny the evening had been fun, but it had been wrong. Waiting for Nancy to come back to the table, I felt like I was seeing another woman. Like I was cheating on my wife. I felt guilty about that and guilty at the thought of how much I had enjoyed talking to Nancy and listening to her—guilty at the thought of how I had enjoyed being able to forget, if only for a few hours, what my life had become.

Fifty-five

We left Caminari's at nine forty-five. Hardly anyone else was on the road in spite of the relatively early hour, which made the ride back to Nancy's apartment strangely peaceful. Streetlights in this area were few and far between, usually appearing only at the occasional intersection, so most of the time we sat in darkness except for the light from the dashboard. Again, the interior of the car was filled with the smell of Nancy— the smell of soap and shampoo and perfume. She smelled wonderful. Intoxicating.

We were on a particularly dark stretch of road, one without any streetlights for over a mile, when I reached across the seat and took Nancy's hand. I had only intended to hold her hand, but as soon as I felt the warmth and softness of her skin, the need to be more intimate with her became irresistible. I could not sit in the dark with her like that, feeling her presence next to me, and not do something more. So without thinking I lifted her hand to my lips and kissed the tips of each of her fingers. Then I parted my lips and ran my tongue first around the tips of her fingers, then down the sides of her fingers and finally down to the web of skin between her fingers. I felt her body stiffen, and I felt her eyes on me. But she didn't pull back her hand, and I kept running my tongue up and down and between her fingers while I stared at the road ahead. As we approached a streetlight, I dried her fingers with a few kisses and brought her hand back down to the seat beside me.

Nancy stared at me as pale yellow light momentarily filled the interior of the car. "Well," she said. "That was quite something. Although I'm not sure what it was."

I glanced over at her in the fading light of the street lamp, now behind us. "I'm sorry. I don't know why I did that."

"No. No. That's... okay. I've just... never had that done to me before."

I looked over at her again, but now I could barely see her in the dark. "Funny thing is," I admitted, "I've never done that to anyone before."

Nancy said nothing, but she pulled her hand away, not abruptly but purposefully, and she turned to look at the road in front of us.

The lights of Northern Boulevard were just ahead. A right on Northern Boulevard and we'd be at Nancy's apartment in a few minutes.

Fifty-six

I turned onto Nancy's street, and just as I had done earlier in the evening, pulled into her landlord's driveway so I could turn the car around and park in front of the house. I stopped a few feet behind Nancy's car and turned off the ignition.

"Can I buy you a drink before you go home?" Nancy asked.

"Sure," I replied, surprised by the offer but pleased at the thought. "I'd like that."

I reached into the back seat to retrieve my jacket, got out of the car and joined Nancy on the sidewalk. But as I turned in the direction of her apartment, I saw that she was about to head down the street. I stopped, confused.

"Where are you going?" I asked. "I thought you were going to buy me a drink."

"I am."

"Why are you walking down the street then?" I asked.

Now Nancy was confused. "Because Ricky's is down the street. On Roslyn Road."

"Ricky's?"

"Yes, Ricky's. The restaurant at the end of the street. You can see it from here. I thought we'd have a drink there."

"So you were really going to buy me a drink."

"Of course I was. What did you think I meant?"

"I thought you were going to have me in for a drink. In your apartment."

"Oh no," Nancy said, without hesitation and with a gentle shake of her head. "I didn't mean I was inviting you back to my apartment for a drink. I meant that I wanted to buy you a drink. As in pay for it. At Ricky's."

"Ahh," I replied, embarrassed at the misunderstanding and suddenly feeling very clumsy. "I didn't realize that was what you meant. I'm sorry."

A moment of silence in the dark.

"Look, Ricky's is fine," I assured her, regaining my composure. "Come on. Let's go."

But Nancy didn't move, uncertain as to what to do. "Oh, I don't know," she said, looking first down the street in the direction of Ricky's and then up at the darkened second floor windows of her landlord's house. "It's silly to go there, I guess. I mean, we're here, so maybe you should come in."

"We can go to Ricky's if that's what you'd like."

"No. Really. Come in. Just ignore the mess. I'm still unpacking and trying to get organized."

"I promise I won't look."

Nancy gave me a quick smile and started up the walk to her apartment door. She had forgotten to leave the outside light on when she left the apartment, so the side yard between her landlord's house and the house next door was in almost total darkness. As a result, we couldn't see the walkway as we walked down the side of the house but rather had to feel for the pavement through our shoes—a soft step meant we were off the walk and on the grass.

"Here we are," she announced, and she opened the screen door.

I stood close behind her and held the screen door open as she rummaged through her pocketbook looking for her keys. The neighborhood was absolutely quiet—the only sound a slight rustling of leaves in the branches above us—and the quiet allowed me to think about how erotic, how illicit, how wrong it felt to be standing in the dark with this woman, waiting to be let into her apartment.

But my thoughts were interrupted by the sound of Nancy's key going into the lock and by the sound of the lock turning open. I stepped inside and followed Nancy down a short hall. We turned into an eat-in kitchen, walked through another short hall past a bathroom and a closet and into a large wood-paneled living room, lit for the moment only by the light from the kitchen.

I stopped a few steps into the living room and surveyed the room in front of me. To the right of the doorway was a large overstuffed arm-chair, and against the right-hand wall was a small shelf system for Nancy's stereo and records. Directly ahead was a large convertible sofa with an end table and lamp at either end and a cocktail table in front. To the left of the sofa a pair of sliding glass doors opened onto a patio and the back yard. In front of the sliding doors were potted plants of all different sizes and types, some on the floor, some on plant stands, others on folding snack tables. Against the wall to the left was a round dining table with four chairs. All in all, Nancy's apartment was simple, but warm and inviting. And there was no mess to forgive. Everything was in perfect order. Somehow I was not surprised.

Nancy switched on each of the end table lamps and pulled the drapes across the sliding glass doors. Then she turned to me and asked what I'd like to drink.

"What do you have?" I asked.

"Not a lot. White wine, beer, gin, vodka—I think—and a little bran-dy. Although I don't know how good the brandy is. But that's it, I'm afraid."

"I'll take vodka. With lots of ice, and a twist of lemon if you have it."

"Vodka with ice and lemon," Nancy repeated as she walked past me and over to the closet next to the bathroom. She pulled out a bottle of Smirnoff. "Is this okay?" she asked, holding the bottle up for me to see.

"That's fine," I replied, and I sat down on the sofa to wait for her.

She came back a few minutes later with a glass of white wine in one hand and a twelve-ounce highball glass in the other, filled to the top with ice cubes and vodka. She sat down on the sofa—close enough to show she felt comfortable with me, yet far enough away to be proper.

I touched my glass to hers. "Again, thank you for joining me to-night," I said, looking into those green eyes.

"And again, you're welcome," Nancy said, returning my look for only a second before turning away.

I took a sip of my drink and almost gagged. As I leaned forward to put my glass on the cocktail table, I saw the cause of the problem. Instead of using a twist of lemon skin, Nancy had cut a large wedge of lemon and squeezed it into the vodka and had then dropped the crushed wedge into the glass. The combination of lemon juice and vodka was ghastly and made the drink almost undrinkable.

"Is something wrong with your drink?" Nancy asked, noticing the look on my face.

"No. Not at all," I replied, too quickly. "It's fine."

"It isn't," she pressed. "I can tell something's wrong with it. You looked like you were going to choke." She paused. "Tell me what I did wrong. I've never made a drink like that, and I'll never learn how unless you tell me what's wrong with this one."

I couldn't believe she was so concerned about my drink, but she was. So in spite of not wanting to make a big deal of it, I did as she asked. "Well, first, the next time someone asks for something on the rocks," I started, "give them their drink in a rocks glass. You know, the short, stubby ones. Not a tall one like this. And only give them an ounce and a half or two ounces. I mean... I'll never be able to finish all this. And, second, a twist of lemon means you peel off a strip of the lemon's skin, just the skin, and then you give it a twist before you put it in the glass. That way you get just a hint of lemon and not lots of lemon juice."

She listened attentively to what I was saying, but the second I stopped, she was off the sofa and reaching for my glass. "Let me make you another drink," she said, holding out her hand.

"No. This is fine. Really. Sit. Besides," I said, holding up the glass and seeing what must have been seven ounces of vodka, "there's too much here to waste."

She stood in front of me for several seconds, seeming to debate whether she should wrestle the glass out of my hand, and then she sat down with a sigh. "Next time I'll do it right," she announced softly.

"Can there be a 'next time'?" I asked.

She looked at me, looked away, then turned back to me. "If you want... yes."

I smiled at her and took her hand. I ran my thumb over the back of her hand, feeling her skin, her bones, her sinews. Seconds passed. Neither of us spoke.

"Will you go back to your house soon," Nancy asked, "or will you move in with your parents?"

"I won't move in with my parents," I said pensively, watching my thumb go back and forth over her hand. "I'll go back to my house. Sometime within the next few weeks, I guess."

"What'll you do about your children? You know, in terms of child care while you're at work?"

"I don't know. I'll hire a housekeeper or a full-time babysitter or something. But right now... I just don't know."

Nancy looked at me sadly for several moments before she spoke again. "I can't stop thinking about your kids," she said. "Especially Jennie. She's so little, and yet she's old enough to know what's happened. Just not old enough to know why." She shook her head slowly. "Not that anyone knows why, I guess," she added.

I nodded in agreement, but I didn't respond. I knew if I did, the dark thoughts that had been my constant companions for the past two weeks, that had been just outside the edges of my mind tonight, would come rushing in, and I'd lose control. So I said nothing and tried to keep those terrible thoughts at bay, at least for a little while longer.

Nancy continued to look at me, staring intently into my eyes. I tried to hold her gaze, but I couldn't. Instead I looked at her hair, her forehead, her eyebrows, those deep green eyes, her mouth, her neck, her shoulders. And then without any forethought, without any preamble, I heard myself saying, "May I kiss you?"

Nancy smiled for the first time in several minutes. Her smile was a nervous smile, an uncertain smile, but I took the smile as a yes.

She was sitting at an angle to me, one leg up on the sofa curled under the other. I wrapped an arm around her shoulder to bring her closer to me. Ever so gently. My fingertips felt the warmth of the exposed skin of her arm. I leaned forward and downward to her upraised face. Her eyes were already closed, her lips barely together.

We kissed. An ever so soft, barely touching kind of a kiss. Just enough to let me feel the velvet touch of her lips and the heat of her breath, tinged with Chardonnay.

I drew back, but Nancy's eyes were still closed. I kissed her again, this time harder, feeling her lips give way to mine, feeling them part slightly more. We kissed again and again and again. Each time her smell, her warmth, her softness enveloped me.

I slid closer to her, then next to her, then tight against her. I kissed her ear, then the side of her neck, then her throat. *Too low. Too soon*, I thought. I kissed the side of her neck again and then her throat, again too low, far too low.

"God, you taste good," I whispered. I stopped kissing her and looked at her face. I could feel the flush on my cheeks and hands. She opened her eyes and gave me a very tentative smile.

"May I take off your dress?" I asked in a voice that didn't sound like mine. I hadn't thought about what I was saying. I just said it because it seemed like a perfectly natural thing to ask. And because at that moment, more than anything, I wanted to pull down the zipper of her dress and watch it fall to the floor.

Nancy sat back and slowly, deliberately, pushed herself away from me and out of my arms. She gave a nervous laugh and looked at me. "I don't think so," she replied, pulling the left shoulder of her dress back up where it belonged.

I muttered an apology and sat back, trying to calm down, knowing I shouldn't have asked, yet not at all sorry I had. I had never done that before in all my years of dating. I had never been so bold, so forthright. I had simply never had the nerve. So what had made me behave like this tonight with Nancy, so easily, so naturally, so quickly? I didn't know, and I didn't care. All I knew was that the dark thoughts were far away.

Nancy looked at her watch. "You should go home," she said softly. "It's late."

It was almost midnight. Not late, really, but given what had just happened, time to go. "You're right," I agreed. "I should be getting home."

"I hope I didn't upset you," I said as we walked towards the kitchen. "I don't know what I was thinking. I've never done that before either. I mean, never so bluntly. So quickly. With someone I've only just met."

Nancy looked up at me in the nicest, softest way. "It's okay. I'm not upset." She paused. "I just kept my dress on."

"Yeah, you did, damn it," I said with a laugh.

Nancy laughed too, a genuine, comfortable laugh, and led the way down the hall. When we reached the door, she turned on the porch light and gave me a quick peck on the cheek.

"Get home safely. And thank you for a wonderful evening. I enjoyed being with you."

"You're welcome. And thank you. Again."

I pushed open the screen door and stepped out into the silent August night.

Fifty-seven

Elm Street was deserted. The surrounding houses were dark. The neighborhood was silent. Surprising for the Sunday night of Labor Day weekend. When I reached the car I stood in the street and felt the solitude and the stillness and the darkness press in on me. I was alone. Again. I hadn't been for almost five hours, but now I was. I looked up and down the street, wondering if anyone was watching me. I decided I didn't care. It was time to go home.

I unlocked the car, threw my jacket across the back seat and got in. I was about to put the key into the ignition when I realized the car still smelled of Nancy. I sat back in the seat for a second and took a deep breath of what was left of her. Then I leaned forward, started the car and headed down Elm Street to Roslyn Road.

My mind was surprisingly devoid of thought for the first four or five minutes after I pulled away from Nancy's apartment. Maybe from fatigue. Maybe from the need to concentrate, given the amount I'd had to drink. Maybe because Roslyn Road was a four-lane road that should have been a two-lane road. Or maybe some thoughts just take a while to come to the surface. Regardless, by the time I turned east on Northern Boulevard, the war in my mind between me and me was beginning to rage.

"That was fun," I said to myself. "She's a nice girl. Fun to talk to. Fun to be with. And attractive. Very attractive."

But before I could take even a moment's pleasure in these thoughts, I heard that voice from somewhere deep inside.

Do you have any idea what you did tonight? the voice asked, harsh as ever. *Do you realize you went out on a date tonight? Two weeks after your wife died? What the hell is the matter with you? Why did you do that? How could you do that? Do you have any idea how bad this looks? Can you imagine what your friends are going to say when they find out? What your family will think when they find out? Can you imagine what the folks are already thinking? Christ Almighty, John, your father worshipped Peg. What the hell must he think? What must Peg think if she's looking down on you now?*

The voice paused. I could imagine its nameless, shapeless source shaking its head in disbelief and disgust.

And to make matters worse, you kiss her. And you enjoy it. I mean you really enjoy it. And then you ask if you can take her dress off. Unbelievable! Absolutely unbelievable! If I didn't know better, I'd swear you never loved Peg at all.

"That's not true," I said, my eyes now filled with tears. "That's just not true. I loved Peg more than anything else in the world. You know that! And I miss her. Terribly. You know that too. I don't know why I called Nancy or why I did any of the things I did tonight. And I know what people are going to say. But I also know when I saw Nancy's name on that damned list, I had to call her. I knew somehow she was the only way I was going to be able to feel anything other than this ache, even if only for a few hours. And I was right."

You may have been "right," pal, the voice answered, *but this has got to stop. And it has to stop now. What you're doing isn't done. Your wife died. You're a widower. You're supposed to be in mourning. For what? A year? You can't start dating a woman two weeks after your wife died. You just can't do it! There are rules, you know. Rules you're supposed to follow. And if you don't, mark my words, you'll pay. I don't know how, but you will.*

I snorted before responding. I could feel anger and frustration starting to rise. "You know what?" I said to the voice. "The last thing I'm worried about is what'll happen to me if I break the goddamn rules. Maybe because I can't imagine paying a higher price than losing Peg. Maybe because I don't care what everybody else thinks because they're not in my shoes. Maybe I just don't give a shit. Period! I don't know. What I do know is I felt good tonight. For the first time since Peg died.

And if that pisses everybody off, well, maybe I should say 'so be it.' I'm the one who lost my wife. No one else. So maybe I'm the one who should decide how to behave."

I slowed down for a red light at the intersection of Wolver Hollow Road and Northern Boulevard and came to a stop. I waited for a response from the voice, but none came.

The light changed to green, and I turned left onto Wolver Hollow Road. Within a few minutes, I was on the same part of the road where I had started to kiss Nancy's fingers, and I found myself smiling at the recollection.

The voice remained silent, but it would return. I knew I could count on that.

Fifty-eight

Nancy had just finished blow-drying her hair when the telephone rang at twenty minutes after five on September 1st, Labor Day afternoon. She wrapped the bath towel around her and walked from the bathroom into the kitchen, answering the phone on the fourth ring.

"Hello?" she answered, cradling the phone in the crook of her neck as she tried to tighten the towel around her.

"Nan?" said the voice on the other end.

"Yep, it's me, Mom," she replied, letting the receiver slide down into her hand, the towel now secure.

"Where've you been? I've been calling you all day."

"I went to Jones Beach."

"All by yourself?"

Nancy looked up at the ceiling. "Yes, Mom, all by myself."

"So how was last night?"

Nancy tucked the towel under her and sat down on one of the kitchen chairs. This was not going to be a short call. "Last night was good. He's a very nice guy."

"You don't sound overly enthused. What aren't you telling me?"

Nancy picked at a fingernail with her thumb. "I'm not 'not telling' you anything, Mom. We had a very nice evening."

"So what's the problem? What am I missing here?"

"You know what the problem is. The problem is his wife died. The problem is she died only two weeks ago. The problem is he never should have asked me out, and I never should have said yes."

"So? I still must be missing something. Everything you just told me, you already knew. Why is any of this a problem now when it wasn't last week when he called?"

Nancy stopped fiddling with her fingernail, put her feet up on the opposite chair and looked around the kitchen as if in search of help. "It's a problem now because I've found out what a nice person he is. I mean he is really nice, Mom. And he's intelligent, sensitive, confident. A perfect gentleman. He's everything I've ever wanted. All my life I've looked for someone who was cool but not conceited. Sure of himself but not full of himself. Good looking but without an attitude. Gentle but not soft." She smiled at the next thought. "Someone whose hands are warm and dry, not cold and clammy. Whose fingernails are clean. Who smells clean. All my life I hoped I'd find someone like that, and now I have; and I can't have him."

Nancy stopped, collected her thoughts and then continued. "I went out with him out of sympathy. Nothing more. I got wrapped up in the tragedy of what happened and wanted to help him. I said that to you, when I first heard his wife had died. That I wished there was something I could do to help this man. So I go out with him, and what happens? He turns out to be the nicest man I've ever met. Except he can never be mine. Because he's just lost his wife, and he still loves her... as he should. Oh shit," Nancy concluded with a sigh. "I wish I'd never met him."

"Well, at least now I know why you're upset," Shirley said. "But you know... in a sense you really don't have a problem, because neither you nor John has a choice in what you do next. You both do nothing. Simple as that. He can't get involved with someone this soon after losing his wife, and you can't let yourself get involved with him.

"There are conventions, Nan," Shirley continued, "customs, rules— whatever you want to call them—which people adhere to. Have to adhere to. Whether they agree with them or not. Not to mention the fact that you're a young girl. The last thing in the world you need to do is get involved with a man this much older than you with two children. That's foolish in the best of circumstances, but plain crazy and asking for trouble when his wife's only been dead a few weeks. And you know what? I'll bet John knows this as well as I do. He's not going to call you again. And nothing's going to happen between the two of you. Because it can't."

"You're right," Nancy agreed reluctantly. "But if he does call me and asks me out again, I'm going to tell him no, and I'm going to ask him not to call me anymore. Because I don't need this."

"Sounds harsh, Nan, but that's what you have to be ready to do. Some rules you don't break and not get hurt."

Nancy glanced at the kitchen clock. It was almost five thirty-five. "Well, I appreciate the advice, Mom. I really do. But right now, I think I should say good-bye. I still have to get dressed—I'm sitting here in a towel —I want to straighten up the apartment, and I have to make dinner. And… tomorrow's a workday, so I'd like to get to bed early."

"Okay. Maybe we'll see you next weekend?"

"Yeah, maybe. I'd like that."

"Good. Call and let me know."

"I will."

"And Nan?"

"What, Mom?"

"Remember what I said."

"I will."

Nancy swung her feet off the chair in front of her, got up slowly and hung up the receiver. She walked back into the bathroom, hung up her towel and struggled to fend off a growing sense of sadness and loneliness.

"Why did this have to happen?" she said aloud to her herself. "Why am I always in the wrong place at the wrong time?"

Fifty-nine

Nancy was taking the vacuum out of the hall closet when the phone rang again at five forty-five. *Wonder what she forgot to tell me?* she thought as she put the vacuum down in the middle of the hall and stepped over it to get to the phone.

"Hello?" she answered.

"Hi, Nan. It's John."

Her heart leaped. "Hi. How are you?" she asked, excited but frightened. Terribly frightened, she quickly realized.

"I'm good. How about you?"

"I'm okay."

"I just... wanted to tell you again that I really enjoyed being with you and talking to you last night."

"I enjoyed being with you too."

"Well, I'm glad to hear that," I said, struggling to find the words I wanted to say next. "I really am."

A few seconds of awkward silence passed while Nancy waited for me to speak.

"I, uh... the reason for my call is... and I hope you don't mind my asking this... but I was wondering if maybe we could get together next Saturday night. I know this is completely unorthodox, and I know I shouldn't be asking you to spend any more time with me. But I am. And hopefully, you'll say yes. So the question is... are you free next Saturday night? Maybe go to a movie?"

Nancy's mind started to race. *My God*, she thought. *I can't believe this is happening. I don't want to tell him no, but I have to. Now. Before it's too late. Before things get out of hand.*

"You still there?" I asked.

I thought I heard a little chuckle. "Yes, I'm still here. And yes, I'm free next Saturday night."

"Great. That's great. Same time? Seven o'clock?"

"That'll be fine."

"Good. I'll see you then."

"Okay," Nancy answered. "Have a good week."

"You too."

Nancy stared at the phone for several seconds after hanging up. *Looks like rules are about to be broken*, she said to herself with a resigned sigh. Then she bent down to plug in the vacuum.

Sixty

My appointment with Father Richardson was at seven o'clock on Tuesday evening, September 2nd. I pulled into the church parking lot about five minutes before seven, parked under a huge old tulip tree and headed across the street to St. John's of Lattington Episcopal Church.

As I approached the church, I was struck by the incongruity that such a small, relatively unimposing structure could be the church that the wealthiest people on Long Island, the "old money," the aristocracy, so to speak, called theirs. In addition to having a relatively small footprint, the church was not a high structure and hadn't been given a high steeple. Instead, the roof had a relatively low pitch, which reduced the overall height of the roof line; and the bell tower, if one could call it a tower, was a squat rectangular affair affixed to one corner of the church and extended only five or six feet above the roof peak.

But what the church lacked in size and height was made up for in quality of construction. The walls were built from blocks of pale gray stone, each three feet long, two feet high and two feet thick. The headers and sills above and below each stained glass window and above and below the heavy double oak doors at the back of the church were rough chiseled granite, and the roof was covered with thick slate shingles. The gutters, downspouts and flashing which accented each corner of the building and the roof were all heavy gauge copper, now blackish-green with age.

The oak doors at the back of the church opened onto broad granite steps and a large flagstone courtyard. A flagstone walk ran along one side of the church from the courtyard to a single oak door, which was the entrance to the church offices. Four ancient oaks towered overhead, and the shadows they cast belied the hour as I headed towards the side door.

When I reached the door, I lifted the wrought iron ring below a small leaded glass window and let it fall twice against the striker plate. I waited, but no one came to the door. I was about to lift the ring a third time when I heard an old lock set turn with a metallic clank. A second later and the door swung outward.

"John," Father Richardson said, his hand extended to me in greeting, "it's good to see you. It's been a long time."

"It has been, Father," I agreed. "I think the last time we spoke was Christmas Eve—three, maybe four years ago."

"Come in. Come in," Father Richardson said, holding the door open with one hand and waving me inside with the other. "We'll go upstairs to my study."

I stepped inside and followed him down a narrow hall towards an even narrower staircase. "Has it been that long?" he asked as he started up the stairs. "I thought I saw you last Christmas Eve."

"I think you're right, Father," I replied after a moment of thought. "Your memory's better than mine. We were here last Christmas Eve."

He turned left at the top of the stairs and walked down another narrow hall. We passed several small offices and then turned into the last office at the end of the hall.

"Let's sit over here," Father Richardson suggested as we entered his study. He indicated an area in the corner with two wing chairs and a pair of small candle tables. "Less formal, don't you think? Can I get you anything? Coffee? Tea?"

"No thanks, Father. I'm fine. I literally just got up from dinner."

"You're sure?"

"I'm sure. Really. But thank you anyway."

Father Richardson settled into his chair, crossed one leg over the other and clasped his hands together in his lap.

"So what can I do for you?" he began.

I gave an uncomfortable little laugh. "I'm not sure."

Father Richardson smiled, but he made no reply.

"I guess you're aware that my wife died two weeks ago," I started hesitantly. "Actually, two weeks ago this past Sunday."

"Yes, I know. I was so saddened to hear that. Saddened and shocked. Such a young woman. Such a nice person."

"She was, Father," I agreed with a heavy sigh. "She was. Anyway," I continued, "as my father probably told you when he called, I don't have anyone I can talk to about Peggy's death or about what I'm feeling. What I'm thinking. I can't talk to my folks because they're already upset enough. I mean, they're barely able to hold themselves together, let alone help me. And I can't talk to friends for pretty much the same reason. They're having their own problems coping. And I don't have anyone at work I can talk to. So that kind of leaves me alone, and my father thought you might be able to help me deal with some of the things I'm wrestling with."

"Do you think I can?"

"Maybe."

"How are you holding up?"

"Well, needless to say, these last two weeks have been pretty tough. But I'm all right as long as I don't let myself think about what's happened. As long as I stay focused on other things. But if I start to think about Peg... I come apart at the seams."

"Tell me why," Father Richardson asked softly.

"It's not just that she's dead, Father, or that I miss her. Sure, that's part of it. A huge part of it. But it's more than that. More than just the pain of losing her. It's the fear, the terror really, of having to live life without her. Peg was everything to me, Father. She was my anchor. My best friend. She showed me beauty in so many things. Things I took for granted until I met her. She was my sense of humor. The one who made people our friends. I just came along for the ride. She was my adviser. My lover. Mother of my children. Pride and joy of my folks. She was everything to me and for me. And now she's gone, and I don't know what I'm going to do. I can't help wondering if my life's over. And if it is, then I wonder what I'm supposed to do next. If anything."

I stopped for a moment.

"I've never felt so alone in my entire life, Father. And that's the most frightening part, I think. Being totally alone."

"But you're not alone," Father Richardson replied. "You have two beautiful children. You have your parents. Not to mention your friends."

I shook my head. "It's not the same, Father. You know that. Sure, my children love me. But they're not company to me like Peg was. I'll never be able to talk to them like I was able to talk to her. I can't look to them for support. And the same thing's true with my parents and my friends. They can't take the place of my wife. And because they can't, I'm alone. So alone I'm scared to death."

Father Richardson looked at me for several seconds before saying anything. "Well," he began finally, "let me try to tell you a few of the things I've learned about the death of a husband or wife." He leaned forward in his chair and rested his elbows on his knees.

"First, your life isn't over. Not even close. It may seem that way today and tomorrow and next week, maybe even next year, but your life isn't over. They say time heals all wounds, and most of the time that's true. As time passes, so too will the pain of losing Peggy. That doesn't mean you'll forget her, because you won't. But someday the memory of her won't be painful.

"Second, even though you find it hard to accept, you're not alone. You have your children, and believe me, as time goes on, they'll be a tremendous source of joy and comfort to you. You have your parents, and although they can't take the place of your wife, they can still be a deep source of love and support if you let them. And you have the friends you and Peggy made over the years. Peggy's death doesn't mean your relationships with these people have to end. They can continue to exist just as strongly, just as deeply, as when Peggy was alive. The relationships will be different without Peggy here, that's for certain, but they can and should continue.

"Third, and this is the most difficult thing to believe, I'm sure..."
He took a deep breath and held it to emphasize the importance of what he was about to say. "Unless you want to be alone for the rest of your

life, you don't need to be. In time, if you let it happen, chances are you'll meet someone, fall in love with her and start a whole new life with her."

"How could I ever do that, Father?" I asked. "How could I replace her with someone else?"

"I didn't say this someone new would replace Peggy, John. No one will ever 'replace' Peggy, nor should they. If someone new comes into your life, they come in on their own terms as their own person. They don't take Peggy's place. They create their own place."

Father Richardson looked down at his hands and then up at me. "You honored Peggy in life by being a faithful, loving husband. You do her no disservice now by living your life as God intended—with love at its center. Love of life, and if the opportunity presents itself, love for someone new. I like to think of our lives as a story, with each major event in our lives the chapters. Your marriage to Peggy was one of the chapters in your life story. That chapter's over now, and there's nothing wrong with you starting a new chapter when the time to do so is right."

"And when is the time right, Father? One year? Two years? Five years? I know that seems like a silly question, but how do I know when it's okay to start that new chapter? Assuming I have the chance to."

"You'll know when the time is right," Father Richardson said with a smile. "Believe me. You won't need anyone to tell you."

I thought about what he had said, and a question—perhaps more a challenge—came to mind.

"What would you say, Father," I said slowly, not really certain I should continue, "if I told you I took a woman out to dinner Sunday night?"

"I'd say that's a little unusual, but I'd also say you know in your heart whether it was the right thing or wrong thing to do."

"And what if I told you I really enjoyed being with her, talking to her? What if I said being with her made the pain of losing Peg go away for a few hours?"

"I'd say that's a little unusual, but I'd also say you know in your heart whether it was the right thing or wrong thing to do." He paused. "Contrary to what you may believe, John, there are no hard and fast rules where love is involved. Either love lost or love found. My advice to you is to do what your heart tells you to do. You're a good person, John. You know what's right in God's eyes. And God's eyes are all that matter."

I looked at Father Richardson and nodded in understanding. He smiled in acknowledgement and sat back. "Follow your heart, John. It won't lead you astray."

"Thank you, Father. For the wise words... and for the reassurance."

"I'm glad I was able to be of help. Give my best to your mom and dad, will you?"

He rose from his chair, and I followed him down the hall and down the staircase. When we reached the side entrance, he pushed the heavy oak door open and extended his hand.

"Good night," he said. "And good luck."

Sixty-one

Saturday, September 7th, was warm but dreary. It had started to drizzle intermittently around one in the afternoon, but by the time I pulled up in front of Nancy's apartment at seven o'clock, the rain was falling steadily. I got out of the car and quickly pulled on my raincoat. As I did, I looked over my shoulder at the house across the street and then at the house to the right of Nancy's, curious to see if my arrival had been noticed by anyone from last week's welcoming committee. No one was in sight.

I started up the walk to Nancy's apartment, hunching my shoulders in a futile attempt to repel the rain. When I reached the side door, I saw that the inside door was open. Just as it had been on Sunday night. And again I heard music coming from inside the apartment. I rang the bell, and within seconds Nancy appeared.

"Hi," she said as she pushed open the screen door. "You're right on time. Again."

"I told you I try," I replied, taking a step into the hall.

"Yes, you did. I just didn't know whether to believe you." She looked outside. "It's raining hard now."

"Yeah. Started to come down pretty steady as I was leaving the house."

Nancy watched the rain for a second, and then she closed and locked the inside door. For some reason I was unnerved by her closing and locking the door.

She turned to face me. "Let me take that," she said, her arms outstretched for my raincoat. She watched me as I took the raincoat off, and that unnerved me too.

"Kind of wet, I'm afraid," I said as I handed it to her.

"I'll hang it in the bathroom. So how are you?" she asked over her shoulder as I followed her down the hall and into the kitchen.

"I'm good. You?"

"I'm good," she answered lightly from the bathroom.

I stood in the middle of the kitchen, feeling awkward and out of place.

"Did you pick a movie for us to see?" Nancy asked when she reappeared a moment later.

"I was going to leave that up to you. I meant to bring a paper so we could see what was playing, but I forgot. So hopefully you have a *Newsday* or a *Daily News*?"

Nancy shook her head no.

"Well, that's not a problem if I can use your phone. I'll call a few theaters, see what's playing, get some times. Okay?"

"Sure. Help yourself," she answered with a smile, gesturing towards the phone on the wall.

I started to walk towards the phone, but as I did, a flash of lightning lit up the side yard outside Nancy's kitchen window. Less than a second later, a crash of thunder made us both wince and was followed by the sound of torrents of rain water hitting the aluminum canopy over her side door.

"Wow," I exclaimed as the thunder subsided. "That was close. You sure you want to go out tonight?"

"What do you mean?" Nancy asked. "You're already here."

"I meant outside. Are you sure you want to go to a movie?"

"Well, if we don't go to a movie, what'll we do?" I detected a note of concern in her voice.

"Can we stay here? Until the rain stops?"

Nancy gave an uneasy chuckle. "Stay here? You want to stay here?"

"Only if you're comfortable with that."

235

She looked at me for a long time before responding. "We can stay here, I guess," she said unenthusiastically. "At least until the rain stops. But then we should go to our movie."

Nancy looked around the kitchen at nothing in particular. Then she shook her head and rolled her eyes, probably in disbelief at what she had just agreed to. "Can I get you something to drink?" she asked.

I gave a laugh, remembering last Sunday's drink. "I'll have vodka on the rocks with a twist."

"My way or your way?" she asked as she opened the closet door and took out her bottle of Smirnoff.

I laughed again and sat down at the kitchen table. I watched her take a rocks glass down from a cabinet over the stove, fill it with ice and then carefully pour two ounces of vodka into a glass jigger. And I couldn't help smiling when, after pouring the vodka into my glass, she took a lemon out of her refrigerator, deftly peeled off a strip of its skin, gave it a firm twist and dropped it into my drink.

Unbeknown to me, however, while I was watching Nancy make my drink, Nancy was in the process of scolding herself for what she perceived to be a lapse in good judgment. *What have I done now?* Nancy was asking herself. *We were supposed to go to a movie, not stay here. I am really not comfortable with this at all. I mean, here we are again—alone in my apartment. What'll I do if he starts kissing my fingers again? Or worse yet, asks me to take off my dress again? Damn it! I can't believe I let this happen.*

Well, he's here, and that's that. Nothing I can do about it now. But I need to keep him talking. I need to ask him questions. Have to avoid long silences.

"Here," she said as she handed me my drink. "I think you'll like this one better than the last one." She gave me a little smirk, poured herself a glass of Chardonnay, and drinks in hand, we went into the living room.

"Looks like you're pretty well settled in," I observed, noticing that the cardboard boxes I had seen Sunday night were gone.

"I am. I still have stuff I want to get, but I'm all unpacked at least."

"Still like living alone?"

Nancy smiled. "Yeah, I do," she admitted almost sheepishly.

"Your folks okay with it?"

"I think they're getting there. My dad wasn't the problem. My mother was. She couldn't understand why I didn't want to keep living at home. She saw no reason for me to move out and thought it was a big waste of money. I think at one point, while I was looking at apartments, she even started to take it as a personal affront. You know, like suddenly her house wasn't good enough for me anymore. And that really concerned me, because my mom and I are close. I mean we're more like friends than mother and daughter, and I didn't want to do anything that would destroy that relationship."

"But you moved out anyway."

"Yeah. I thought it was the right thing to do. I'm twenty-five, for God's sake."

"Ancient," I teased.

"No, really…"

"I'm just kidding. So how does your mother feel now?"

"I think she's kind of in a state of transition. She's gone from anger to hurt to resignation. Hopefully, pretty soon she'll hit acceptance."

"Well, you've got a great place here, and some day you'll look back on the time you lived here, and you'll have great memories."

Nancy smiled again. "I hope so," she replied. "Good memories are a wonderful thing."

Almost instantly, her face clouded over. *Damn*, she thought. *Why did I say that? Questions. I need to ask questions.*

She forced a smile and changed the subject. "You said Sunday night you'd been a boater all your life. Have you really been boating all your life?"

"Most of it. According to my father, I was boating before I was born—he and my mother used to go canoeing all the time while she was pregnant with me."

"Did your family always have sailboats?"

"No. No sailboats back then. Just small powerboats."

"Like what?"

"Well, let's see. When I was four or five, my folks had a sixteen-foot outboard runabout. And when I was eight, my father had a twenty-four-foot cabin cruiser named *Escape*."

"Did you ever have a boat of your own? Before your sailboat, I mean?"

"Yeah, I did," I answered, marveling to myself at how clear some memories still were. *I can't remember what Peg's voice sounded like,* I thought, *but I can remember the boat I had twenty-five years ago like it was yesterday. Why is that?*

I shook off the darkness and focused on Nancy's question. "Around the time my father bought *Escape*, my grandfather built me an eight-foot dinghy, a wooden pram. You know, the kind with the flat bow? Then when I was ten, I bought a five-horsepower engine for it with my snow shoveling money, and my father fitted the dinghy with a little mahogany front deck, a steering wheel and a remote throttle. So instead of a three-person dinghy, I wound up with a one-person speedboat. At least that's how I looked at it. I tell you, that little thing moved. And then, when I started to make money with my band, I bought a seventeen-foot Commodore. A beautiful wooden lap strake runabout with a fifty horse-power Evinrude. Which was a lot of power in those days. That was a beautiful boat! My pride and joy."

"Do you like the smell of gasoline?" Nancy asked suddenly.

Her question took me totally by surprise. For a second I had no idea what she was talking about, and then I knew. "Yes! Yes! I do. I love the smell of gasoline, and when I smell gasoline I think of boats. Weird, but I do. You too?"

"Me too," Nancy replied. "I love the smell of gasoline. And creosote. And the smell of a wooden boat on a hot summer day. That combination of paint, caulking, oil, gasoline and… wood. And the smell of salty air. I love it all. The best times I ever had growing up," Nancy continued, "were on my parents' and grandparents' boats. I can still remember waking up in my bunk to the smell of coffee brewing on the alcohol stove. And the morning dew on the decks and in the cockpit and how glass smooth the water was early in the morning before any breeze came up. And how my job was to sweep the companionway and the main salon every morning after breakfast. I remember swimming all day, coming out of the water only for lunch and dinner. And waiting that hour before I was allowed back in so I wouldn't get a cramp. I had so much fun fishing in my grandfather's dinghy with my brother, clamming at low tide, eating whatever we caught for dinner. What wonderful times."

"You got that right," I agreed, equally deep in reverie.

Nancy interrupted my thoughts with another question. "You said you bought one of your boats with money you earned with your band?"

"That's right."

"What instrument did you play?"

"Drums. I was the drummer in a rock and roll band called 'The Majestics.'" I couldn't help grinning at the thought of The Majestics and the stream of memories the name brought to the surface.

"How big a group?"

"There were five of us—lead guitar, rhythm guitar, bass and electric organ. And me on the drums."

"Were you good?"

"Yeah, we were. I have to say we were. We started out playing at church youth group functions, then at class dances and proms at local high schools, and then at beach clubs and bars. Made a lot of money and had some unbelievable experiences. The band also gave me a chance to be somebody—to stop feeling like a loser."

"What do you mean?" Nancy asked, confused by my admission.

I let out a little sigh. I hadn't really intended to go down this road, but I was committed now. "When I was a little kid, I was always picked on. Don't know why. Maybe because I was soft. Maybe because I wore glasses. Who knows? But picked on I was. Things were so bad at one point while I was in grade school that my mother drove me to and from school every day. Otherwise the kids would push me through the hedges of a house on the way to school and throw my books all over the street."

I gave a cynical snort at the thought of my pain back then. "Anyway, humiliation and low self-esteem were very much a part of my life. I remember one day in the third grade, the gym teacher, Mr. Elliot... God,

I remember this like it was yesterday… picked Bobby Goodman and Peter Erland as team captains for kickball and told them to pick their team members. So Bobby and Peter, little shits that they were, with great ceremony picked their teams one by one until finally they'd selected everyone but a short, hopelessly fat kid and me. And there I stood for what seemed like an eternity, in the middle of the gymnasium, with all my classmates standing along the walls of the gym watching, waiting, giggling, while Bobby and Peter negotiated between themselves as to who would get the fat kid and who would get me."

"What a nightmare," Nancy exclaimed, shaking her head in disbelief.

"When it was time for me to go into seventh grade," I continued, "my folks sent me to St. Paul's School for Boys in Garden City. And nothing changed. My first year there I spent the second half of every lunch hour—the time when we were allowed outside before afternoon classes—hunkered down underneath the bleachers out by the football field, hiding until the second bell so no one would beat me up.

"Then two things happened. First, I started to lift weights in eighth grade. So by the time I started ninth grade, I'd lost the baby fat and gained some muscle. And the bullies left me alone. And second—this is where the band comes in—some of the kids on the sophomore class dance committee knew about The Majestics, and they asked us to play for the dance. Which we did.

"And let me tell you, my classmates were amazed at how good The Majestics were and at how good I was on the drums. That night literally changed the rest of my high school experience. So… a long story, but the band gave me a new lease on life when I very badly needed one."

I took a long sip of my drink, the first in several minutes. "I didn't mean to keep going on like that," I apologized. "Sometimes the answer to a question just leads to other things, I guess. I'm sorry for talking so much."

"Don't be silly," Nancy replied. "If I didn't want you to talk, I wouldn't have asked the questions."

"What surprises me," I said, "is that you've only asked me about my distant past, so to speak. You know what I mean. No questions about my being married. No questions about my wife. No questions about her death. No questions about stuff like that. Even though I know you must have them."

"I thought if you wanted to talk about those things, you'd bring them up," Nancy said. "I shouldn't because I don't know if you want to talk about them or not."

"You're right," I agreed, "but don't be afraid to ask those questions if you ever want to."

"Do you mean that?"

"I do."

"Well, maybe I can ask you something now?"

"Sure. Fire away."

"Maybe I shouldn't ask you this," Nancy started hesitantly, "but I need to. So my question is, what about Peg? Do you think about her? And about what happened?"

"What do you mean?" I asked, genuinely confused. "I don't understand what you're asking."

"I guess what I'm saying is… we're sitting here talking about fun things, fun memories, and you seem perfectly okay. But I can't believe you are. So I'm wondering if you think about Peg. That's my question. You have to be. She must be right below the surface, and yet you don't show it. And I'm wondering how that's possible."

I took a deep breath and exhaled slowly. "Wow, that is a question," I said. I pulled at an eyebrow, buying myself time.

"You don't have to answer. I probably shouldn't have asked."

"No. No, it's all right. I'm glad you did." I took another deep breath, this one shakier than the first, and my eyes started to fill. "She is right below the surface, as you put it, Nancy. She's there all the time. Even now as we sit here. But I can't let myself think about her, because when I do, this is what happens." I wiped my eyes with the heel of my hand.

"So most of the time, when I'm in the office, when I'm with a customer, with the kids, with you tonight, I don't think about her. I don't let myself think about her. Because I know if I do, I'll start behaving like this." I shuddered and wiped my eyes again.

241

"I miss her so much I can't think about her or talk about her without coming apart. She was the most important thing in the world to me. And when I realize I'll never see her again for as long as I live…"

I stopped talking and reached for my handkerchief. "Sorry," I said. "Didn't mean to expose you to this."

"Why not?"

"You don't need this, and I don't need this."

"I knew I shouldn't have asked," Nancy said, visibly annoyed with herself.

"No, no. I'm not saying that. Not at all."

"What are you saying then?"

"I'm saying you don't need to watch a guy you hardly know cry. And I'm saying, trying to say… Let me put it this way. When I was with you Sunday night… I was running away. And tonight, sitting here with you… I'm running away again. I know that's wrong, but it's just so good to forget all the stuff that's happened. If only for a little while. Is that so terrible?"

"No, that's not so terrible. But you should talk about Peg to someone. Because you need to. To feel better. To be happy again. To be able to face the rest of your life. And if you want to talk to me about her—if you think that'll help you—I don't mind. I'd like to hear about her. And I don't mind if you cry. Honest."

Nancy watched me wipe my eyes with my handkerchief. She watched me blow my nose one last time, and she watched me carefully fold the handkerchief before stuffing it back into my pocket. She watched me shudder again and heave a deep sigh. And as she watched me, she thought about herself and what she was doing.

This is absolutely crazy, she thought. *Why am I doing this? Why am I telling you to talk to me about your wife? About something so terribly personal and painful? Why am I letting you use me like that? I guess because you're in pain, and you need help. And because something tells me you're special. Maybe very special. So I'll let you run away to me. At least for now.*

Sixty-two

I started to tell Nancy about Peg that night. She asked how we met, and I told her about Sarah O'Connell and New Year's Eve and the umbrella stand.

"Did Peg live in the city while you were going out with her?" Nancy asked.

"Yeah. She had an apartment."

"Where?"

"East 67th street. 220 East 67th Street. On the 8th floor. A really nice apartment too. Big living room, separate kitchen, dining alcove, two bedrooms. Hardwood floors. Even had a small balcony overlooking 67th Street."

"Wow. That's quite a place for one person."

"Oh, no. I didn't mean to imply that. She shared it with Sarah, who was her roommate, and two other girls."

"Still, that's quite a place. Especially in the city."

"You're right. It was. And because her apartment was on the East Side, she was in the middle of everything. We went out every weekend to really great spots for drinks, dinner, whatever. Romantic 'New York' type of places, if you know what I mean. We went to shows. On Broadway. Off Broadway. Concerts. You name it. We did it."

I realized I was looking past Nancy, not at her, as I got caught up in the memories of Saturday nights in another life. I purposefully shifted my gaze back to her.

243

"We had a lot of fun," I continued. "And sometimes all of her roommates would go home for the weekend or go away with their boyfriends and we'd have the whole apartment to ourselves. That was really neat."

"What was Peggy's maiden name?"

Another question from left field. "Reilly. Her full name was Margaret Ellen Reilly."

"So she was Irish?"

I smiled. "Oh, yes, she was Irish. Very much the Irish colleen, as my father used to call her."

"Was she born in Ireland?"

"No. She was born here. Her parents were born in Ireland, though. Both her mother and her father. Her mother, Maureen—her maiden name was Casey, I think—came to the States when she was in her late twenties and worked as a hotel maid. Her father was a sailor and came here when he was about forty. He met Maureen somehow somewhere in New York, married her and moved to Englewood, New Jersey."

"Was Peg their only child?"

"No. They had four daughters. Peg was the oldest. Then there was Kathleen, then Megan, then Erin."

Nancy reached for her glass of Chardonnay and took a sip. "Did Peggy go to college?" she asked as she sat back again.

"She did. She went to Douglass College for Women in New Brunswick, New Jersey—I think it's part of Rutgers—and she majored in English."

"I take it she graduated?"

"Yes. But she almost didn't because she almost didn't go to college."

"Why?"

"While she was a senior in high school, her father died of complications from gall bladder surgery, which left her mother with no income except for a small police officer's pension. So Peg thought she wouldn't be able to afford to go to college. But an old-line women's club of some sort in Englewood learned of her situation and asked her to meet with them. She did, and they gave her a full scholarship to Douglass. She really lucked out."

"I'll say. Did she move into the apartment right after she graduated?"

"No. When she graduated, she moved back home with her mother and commuted from Englewood to a job in the city for about a year. And then, like you, she decided it was time to move out and get a place of her own. Which is how she ended up in the apartment on 67th Street."

"Is that when you met her? After she moved into the city, I mean?"

"No," I said with an apparently suspicious-looking smile. "She was still living at home when I met her."

"Why are you smiling like that?" Nancy asked.

"Boy, you don't miss much, do you?"

"I try not to," Nancy answered, a bit smugly.

"I was just remembering the first time I picked Peg up at her house. On our second date. Our first date, you'll recall, was on New Year's Eve, and I picked her up at my cousin's house. Anyway, I ring the doorbell, and Peg answers the door, says hello or whatever and asks me to come in so she can introduce me to her mother. I come inside, and I find myself face to face with a little, wiry, blue-haired old lady who's sitting on the sofa, with crochet work or needlepoint or something in her lap. And she's looking up at me through horn-rimmed glasses with these incredibly piercing blue eyes. My first reaction is, 'My God, what a nasty old bitch.' I'm almost scared of her as I stand there saying hello, trying to be charming. Turns out she wasn't like that at all, but that was my first impression. The funny thing is, looking back years later, I realized I was probably her worst nightmare come true. She was undoubtedly hoping someday Peggy would marry a Michael or a Sean or a Patsy, and here I was, a dyed-in-the-wool WASP. That's why I smiled."

"How long did the two of you date?"

"Before I asked her to marry me?"

"Yes."

"Let's see. Our first date was New Year's Eve in 1968. And I asked her to marry me in October of 1970. So that would make it almost two years. Which reminds me of a funny story."

I leaned forward, picked up my glass from the cocktail table and took a quick sip. "The night I proposed to Peg, I made reservations at a really nice place on Central Park South called Harry's New York Bar. To me, Harry's New York Bar was the perfect place to ask someone to marry you—dark mahogany paneling, thick carpets, starched tablecloths, waiters in tuxedos, really subdued lighting, quiet even when the place was full. A really cool place.

"I made reservations for eight o'clock, but I went to Harry's around seven-thirty before I picked up Peg. I wanted to tell the maitre d' what I was going to do, and I wanted to leave Peg's engagement ring with him so she wouldn't see the lump in my jacket pocket from the ring box or feel it and ask what it was. So I go there, I tell the maitre d' my plan, give him the ring, and then I take a cab over to Peg's apartment. But as I'm riding over to her place, it suddenly dawns on me that I've just given a total stranger a $4,000 ring. I don't know his name. I don't have a receipt. I don't even have something to prove I went there. So I'm sweating bullets all the way over to Peggy's and all the way back to Harry's. Well, to make a long story short, I get her seated at our table, I go up to the maitre d', and I ask him for my ring box…"

I paused for a second to add to the suspense.

"…which he instantly retrieves from his desk and hands to me… with a huge smile… a pat on the back… and a really nice 'Good luck, son.'"

"That's a great story. Was she surprised?"

"Yes, she was," I replied as my eyes started to fill with tears. "And very happy. She loved me very much and wanted to spend the rest of her life with me. And she did. Just not for as long as either of us thought."

Nancy put her hand on my arm, but she said nothing. She just listened, and I kept talking. About Jennie and John and what we'd gone through to have them. About the trips we'd taken. About our house and how we'd made it our own room by room. About how my parents had loved Peg like the daughter they never had. About the beautiful, seemingly charmed life we had led. About how we learned Peg was sick and what we did, step by step, day by day, until she died. About how much I loved Peg and how much I missed her.

I told Nancy how grateful I was to be able to talk to her about things like these. How much I appreciated her listening, and how she always seemed to know what to say. I told Nancy many things that night.

We never did make it to the movie.

Sixty-three

I hadn't yet pulled away from the curb in front of Nancy's apartment before the voice started to grumble. *Do you mind telling me what that was all about?*

"What do you mean?" I asked. I really wasn't enthused about another encounter with me.

What do I mean? Well, let's start at the top. First of all, tonight was a date. I think we can agree on that. Reprehensible though that may be. And given tonight was a date, why the hell did you spend most of the evening talking about Peg? You barely know this woman, and yet you tell her all about your dead wife and how much you love her and miss her. Why would you do that? I'm sorry, but something's wrong here, and I don't get it.

"What's to get?" I replied reluctantly. "I needed someone to talk to, and for whatever reason, I can talk to Nancy."

But why are you talking about Peg when that's so painful for you? And why are you talking to Nancy about her?

"Maybe talking about Peg," I said after several moments of thought, "is a way of keeping her here—with me—a little longer. Maybe it's a way of not letting her slip away. Maybe, if she can hear me, it's a way of telling her I love her. I don't know. You tell me."

Can't help you there, pal, the voice retorted. *Only you know the answer.*

I slowed down for an upcoming red light. "As for why I talked to Nancy about Peg… I have no idea. I only know I was able to. About Peg.

248

About everything. We really connected. I think maybe we're a lot alike. Kindred spirits, sort of."

Oh, gimme a break, will you? the voice shot back, exasperated by this last speculation. *You just met this woman, and suddenly she's so special? I don't think so, John.*

The light changed to green. The voice said nothing more.

Sixty-four

I saw Nancy the following Saturday night and the one after that. Both times the same thing happened. We made a drink before we left the apartment, then we sat down on the couch to talk, and we kept talking until the evening was half over, and it was too late to do what we had originally planned.

But on our fifth date, Saturday, September 27th, we were determined not to let that happen again. We had resolved earlier in the week that we wouldn't have a drink before we went out, that we wouldn't even sit down. But our resolution didn't help at all, because instead we stood in the middle of the kitchen and talked. Finally Nancy realized if we didn't stop, it would once again be too late for us to go out.

"We really should be leaving if we're going to go," she reminded me.

"I know," I replied, but I didn't move from where I'd been standing for the last twenty-five minutes.

"Don't you want to go out for dinner?" she asked.

"I do. I was just enjoying talking to you. But I can do that over dinner."

"Well, we don't have to go, you know. If you want to stay here, that's fine with me. I've got crackers and cheese we can have with our drinks and frozen pizza we can have for dinner if that's what you want to do."

"No, no, I'd like to go out for dinner. Assuming you do."

250

"I do. I'm ready."

"Then why aren't you moving?" I asked.

Nancy smiled. "Because I'm waiting for you to. You really don't want to go, do you?" she added a second later.

"I want to if you want to."

She smiled again. "I'd rather stay here," she admitted.

"Me too."

"Does this mean we can sit down now?" Nancy asked.

I started to laugh. "I think so."

"And I can get out of these high heels and into something comfortable?"

"That too."

"Good. Then take off your jacket and tie and make yourself something to drink. I'll be with you in a minute."

She opened the closet, took something off a hanger and went into the bathroom, closing the door behind her. I laid my jacket and tie over the back of the armchair and stood in the living room doorway, uncertain as to whether I should start rummaging through Nancy's closet for something to drink or wait for her. After a second of deliberation, I decided to wait and went over to the couch to sit down.

A minute later, Nancy emerged from the bathroom with her dress and slip over her arm. She pulled a hanger out of the closet for the dress and hung her slip on a hook. Then she turned and came into the living room.

The transformation was startling. Instead of a black cocktail dress and black high heels, she now wore a faded denim work shirt, probably her father's or her brother's, and many sizes too big for her. The shoulders came a third of the way down to her elbows, and the shirttails came almost to her knees. She had left the top two buttons undone, and she was barefoot. She looked... undressed. Yet she wasn't. The shirt and bare feet gave her a totally relaxed look, but her make-up and hair were just as they were before and added an elegant dimension to her appearance.

"You look beautiful," I said to her softly as she walked over to the couch. "Absolutely beautiful."

"Yeah, right," Nancy replied, oblivious to the effect she was having on me. "Don't you want something to drink?"

"I do. I was just waiting for you to get dressed. Or undressed. I'm not sure which you did."

"Is this okay?" Nancy asked, suddenly serious. She held out the side of the shirt between a thumb and forefinger. "I can put something else on if you want."

"No, you don't have to change," I said, shaking my head and smiling at her obvious concern. "I meant it when I said you look beautiful. You really do. It's just that you also look... sexy. Very sexy, as a matter of fact. That's all I was trying to say."

Nancy looked hard at me for a few seconds and then started to head back into the kitchen. "I'm going to pour myself a Chardonnay. What can I get for you?"

"I'll have some Chardonnay too if you have enough."

"Oh, I have enough. Not much for dinner, but lots of Chardonnay."

She came back a few minutes later, a glass of wine in each hand, and sat down next to me. We touched glasses and took a sip.

"This is good," I said after the first swallow. "And this is good."

"What's good?"

"The wine and being here. With you. Just the two of us. Not having to sit up and behave in a restaurant."

"Sit up and behave? What do you mean?"

"Oh, that's just an expression my folks used when I was little and started to get fidgety at the dinner table. I'd be told to 'Sit up and behave.' In no uncertain terms, I might add. So I think of going to a restaurant as meaning I have to sit up and behave."

"Well, you don't have to sit up and behave here."

"I don't have to behave?"

"That's not what I meant," Nancy replied, and she gave me a gentle push away from her.

"Can I ask you something?" I said.

"Sure. What?"

"I don't mean to pry, but you're such an attractive girl, a beautiful girl. And so much fun to be with. I just don't understand why you're not already taken. Why you're not involved with someone. Maybe not married or engaged, but at least going out with someone seriously. I would've thought someone would've scoffed you up in a minute. And yet, here you are with me."

"I told you why the first night we went out. Every guy I've ever dated turned out to be a disappointment in one way or another. Usually even before the first date was over."

"Is it possible you expect too much from people?"

"I don't think so. I don't think so at all, as a matter of fact. I know what I want in a man, and it shouldn't be that hard to find. Although it has been so far," she added wistfully.

"What are you looking for? If you don't mind telling me."

"Funny you should ask, because my mother and I had a conversation along the same lines just a few weeks ago."

Nancy turned the stem of her wine glass slowly between her fingers, searching for the right words to describe very personal feelings. "I'm looking for someone," she began slowly, "who makes me feel good about myself. Someone who respects me. Who treats me like a lady. Someone I'm attracted to. Mentally and physically. Someone I'm not intimidated by. Someone I can talk to. And someone who will listen to me when I do."

"That's it?" I asked, feigning incredulity.

"That's it," Nancy replied with a shrug of her shoulders and a toss of her head. "That's the man I'm hoping to find someday."

"Well, I'm sure you will. You just have to be patient. Who knows? Maybe he'll find you."

"Maybe. But sometimes I wonder if things would work out even if he did come along."

"Why would you wonder something like that? You're attractive. You're smart. Funny. Why wouldn't things work out if you found the right person?"

"I told you already."

"Tell me again."

253

"Because I don't have a lot of experience with men. As a matter of fact…"

Nancy looked at me and stared directly into my eyes. She seemed to be trying to decide whether or not to continue. She was still looking directly into my eyes when she started to speak again.

"You are looking at a twenty-five-year-old woman who is still a virgin—hard though that may be to believe in this day and age."

She took a deep breath. Her face was flushed.

"I kind of assumed that from some of the things you've said," I replied.

"I've actually wondered at times," she continued, "if something's wrong with me. Not because I'm still a virgin, but because I need to find the right person first. There are times when I almost feel like a freak or something. All of my friends have had sex, and they all know what it's like. But I haven't, and I don't. At the same time something—call it my moral compass if you want—won't let me get involved with someone that way if I know he's not the person I'm looking for. Waiting for. Does any of this make any sense at all?"

"What you're saying makes perfect sense," I said, amazed by her candor. "And what's so terrible about still being a virgin? Sure, kind of rare these days for someone your age, but as far as I'm concerned, a beautiful thing. You're saving yourself for the right person. That's all. And that's good. Nothing to be ashamed of. Something to be proud of. Nothing wrong with you if that's the position you take. Someday that special person will come along, the time will be right, and… you'll want to give him that gift. Believe me. Just be patient."

Nancy nodded and looked away. We sat perfectly still, Nancy staring at a spot on the opposite wall, me staring at Nancy, thinking how beautiful she was. She was sitting at an angle to me, one bare leg tucked up under the other. The top two buttons of her shirt were open, exposing her throat and upper chest, but the shirt added an element of mystery by revealing nothing else. I was certain that in her mind she was adequately dressed—and she was. But I couldn't get past the thought that she was wearing only a shirt. And that bothered me. I shook my head in an attempt to get rid of that thought and broke what had become a silence of more than a minute.

"What are you thinking?" I asked.

She turned towards me. "At that moment I was thinking about our ride home from Caminari's. About what you did to my fingers."

"And?"

"I was thinking about how terrified I was. How I didn't know if it was right or wrong to let you do that. Part of me said it was wrong. But it was so tender, I couldn't pull my hand away. I was afraid to let you keep doing it, but I was more afraid to ask you to stop." Nancy shivered. "Why did you do that?" she asked very seriously. "I mean, wasn't that a very intimate thing to do?"

"It was. And totally inappropriate. I apologize. Really, I do."

I took a sip of wine and returned Nancy's steady gaze. Her eyes were searching my face for something, and I wondered what she was looking for.

"What are you trying to tell me?" I asked.

"Nothing."

"You are."

"I'm not."

"May I kiss you?"

"Yes."

She closed her eyes, and I kissed her softly. Her lips were warm and dry. I drew away. Her eyes remained closed. I kissed her again. Harder. I ran my fingers through her hair and buried my face in it and smelled her shampoo and her skin. I kissed her ear, behind her ear, the side of her neck, under her chin, her lips again. A harder, wetter kiss.

I stopped. Nancy opened her eyes, and she looked deeply into mine. So deeply.

I kissed her forehead, her throat, then the base of her throat, as low as the denim shirt allowed. I reached for the top button of the denim shirt and unbuttoned it.

Nancy held me tighter. She kissed the side of my face once, twice, three times.

I buried my face between the denim folds and felt Nancy's skin against my lips. The smell of soap and perfume and Nancy enveloped me once again. I unbuttoned the next button. Slowly. Painfully slowly. The folds of the denim shirt began to part.

Nancy looked at me with a strange look. Was it a look of sadness? Desire? Or was it a look of having finally arrived somewhere?

"Are you sure this is okay?" I asked softly.

"Yes," she whispered, her breath hot in my ear. "I'm sure."

Sixty-five

I started my drive home from Nancy's apartment shortly after two-thirty Sunday morning. I drove in silence, the only sounds the low hum of the engine, the higher-pitched hum of the tires on concrete, and the rhythmic clunk as they crossed expansion joints in the road surface. I'd been tempted to turn on the radio when I left Nancy's, thinking music would ease the monotony of the drive home and help me stay awake, but I opted for silence instead. I knew the voice would come sooner or later, and I knew silence would enable its arrival, and I reasoned that the sooner it came, the sooner it would leave.

I shook my head in amazement at what had transpired over the last few hours. *I wonder if Nancy's all right. If she's happy tonight happened. Or if she's crying hysterically right now, promising herself she'll never see me again? I wonder why tonight happened in the first place. Does she think I'm the guy she's been waiting for?*

I slowed for a red light, came to a complete stop and waited. I looked to my right, then to my left, then straight ahead. Not another car was in sight. I was waiting for traffic to pass that didn't exist.

"Nothing to say about tonight?" I said out loud to the voice.

I braced for an answer, but none came.

"Wonder what that means."

The light changed to green, and I came up to speed slowly, deep in thought.

257

"Four weeks ago, you went crazy because I asked Nancy out to dinner. And because I kissed her. And asked if I could take off her dress. And tonight, nothing? Tonight of all nights? Why is that?"

I pondered my question as I drove past darkened homes, one after another. I wondered for a moment if anybody anywhere was still awake. Half a minute later high beams dropping to low beams from a westbound sedan as it rushed by assured me there was.

"Because tonight was so special? Is that it?" I asked. "Or are you in shock and still trying to figure out what to say? Or was tonight so wrong you've simply given up on me?"

I shook my head impatiently—impatient with myself, impatient with the voice.

"Or because tonight was so incredibly beautiful? Because nothing so beautiful, so tender could be wrong?"

I nodded in silent acknowledgement of that thought as I slowed for another red light and then accelerated when the light turned green before I reached the intersection.

"Is that it?"

Again no answer.

I was getting exasperated. I felt foolish talking to myself—the voice —like this, but I needed to know what the voice thought—what I thought.

"You know," I said with an air of finality, "if you have something to say, you better say it now, because pretty soon I'm gonna be done listening."

The road surface changed from concrete to macadam, and the hum of the tires dropped to a lower pitch. The clunk of the tires hitting expansion joints disappeared, and the hum of the engine seemed to get louder.

Suddenly the voice filled my head. *I've given up on you, pal. Simple as that! Because you're not listening.*

"I always listen," I replied. "I just don't always do what you tell me to do."

You got that right, the voice agreed.

"That's it?" I asked, desperately wishing I weren't so intent on introspection.

Oh, there's more. Lots more. If you think you can handle it. Can you?

I didn't answer.

I'll take that for a yes, the voice said harshly. *I got three points to make,* it said after several seconds, *and then I'm done.*

First, I find it hard to believe you allowed tonight to happen. What were you thinking? Do you have any idea what you've done? Do you have any idea how much you're going to end up hurting this girl?

Second, talk about taking advantage of someone! You take the cake, my friend. You're thirty-four. She's just turned twenty-five. You've been married nine years. She's never been with a man before. Not until tonight at least. You're a goddamned walking tragedy, and she feels sorry for you. And you let this happen. Unbelievable! You tell yourself tonight was beautiful? Tender? Maybe for you, my friend, but what about Nancy? How's she going to feel tomorrow morning? How's she going to feel after giving herself to you when you get your head straight and move on? Did you think about that? Did you? You know you didn't.

And third, again I ask—what about Peg? How could you let tonight happen when Peg hasn't been dead for two months yet? Unbelievable, John. Unbelievable.

Anyway, you wanted to hear from me, and now you have. And now you can ignore everything I've said.

"I will," I answered angrily. "You know I will."

Yeah, the voice replied, with what I took to be a sigh. *I know you will.*

Book
Four

Sixty-six

I moved back into our house on Wednesday, October 1st, six weeks and three days from the day Peg died. I had wanted to move back sooner, but first I had to find someone to take care of Jennie and John.

I placed an ad in the *New York Times* on Sunday, September 7th, that read "Recently widowed 34-year-old man seeks today's equivalent of Mary Poppins to care for 3-year-old girl and 8-month-old boy in delightful home in old section of Huntington, Long Island. The children are beautiful and well-behaved and desperately need a special someone to take care of them. Are you that someone? If you think you might be, please send resume, references and salary requirements to *NYT* Box No. 11278."

I thought the ad was great. But either the ad wasn't as good as I thought or the demand for nannies was greater than I knew, because I received no replies that week or the following week or the week after that. A different approach was obviously needed. So on Sunday, September 28th, I pored through the Help Wanted section of the *Times*, highlighting employment agency ads, my plan being to contact these agencies on Monday morning.

But my calls Monday morning produced nothing for a multitude of reasons.

"I'm sorry, Mr. Herbert, but we only place people in homes here in Manhattan."

Or, "I'm sorry, Mr. Herbert, but no one is going to want to assume responsibility for an eight-month-old. He's simply too young."

Or, "Have you worked with us before, Mr. Herbert? I see. Well, I'm sorry, but we limit our placements to families with whom we've worked in the past."

Or, "And where is Mrs. Herbert? Oh, I'm so sorry. Well, unfortunately, we have a policy that prevents us from placing anyone in a home occupied by a single male. I do hope you understand."

Or, "I'm sorry, but our ad was an attempt to find people. We don't have anyone to send you now and haven't had anyone for several weeks. There's a very strong demand for nannies, you know."

And on it went until my last call, to London Personnel. An Elaine Weisman took my call and listened to my story. "I'm so sorry, Mr. Herbert. Both for you and your children." She paused. "When did Mrs. Herbert pass away?"

"August 17th," I replied.

"And who's been taking care of the children since then?"

"My parents. The children and I are living with my parents until I can find someone to take care of them."

"I see. Well, maybe we can help. Which is saying something in this market. Anyway, I learned this morning that a woman we placed in a home about two years ago under similar circumstances—the wife died, and the husband needed someone to care for their little boy—has just been let go because the husband has remarried and no longer requires her services. She's a Jamaican woman, 55, refined, very clean. Honest. Reliable. Very good with children. Has three of her own. Grown up now, of course. We've placed her in several homes over the last ten years, and our clients have always found her to be a wonderful addition to their families. Her name is Loretta Roberts. Would you like to meet her?"

"Yes!" I answered. "Absolutely. How... how do we do this?"

"You're in Huntington now, I presume?"

"No, actually. I'm in Westbury right now. Where I work. I'm calling from my office."

"I see. Well, is there a train station nearby? Because if there is and if I'm able to get in touch with Loretta, I can ask her to take a train out to you this afternoon from Brooklyn—where she lives—so you can meet her. And then, if you like her, you can introduce her to the children, show her the house, etc."

"Today?"

"She's available today, Mr. Herbert, but she won't be for long, I assure you. If I were you, I'd meet with Loretta this afternoon and hire her immediately if you like her."

"Wow. Well, there's a Long Island Railroad station here in Westbury."

"Wonderful! Would you be able to meet her at the station?"

"Of course. I just need to know what train she'll be on."

"Let me call you back after I reach Loretta, and I'll give you her arrival time in Westbury then, okay?"

"That's fine."

"Where can I reach you the rest of today?"

"At my office number. 516-334-6500."

"Good. Now, Mr. Herbert, we haven't talked about Loretta's salary or about our fee structure yet, so let me take a moment on that. Loretta was making $325 a week at her last position, and I'm certain she's asking for that now. Is that a problem?"

"No. That won't be a problem."

"Our fee is four weeks salary, $1,300 in this case, payable after Loretta' first full week of employment. But the fee is fully refundable if for any reason you're not satisfied with her performance during her first four weeks with you. Is that satisfactory?"

"Yes, that's satisfactory," I answered, not caring what Loretta cost if she allowed the kids and me to take even one small step in the direction of normalcy.

"Excellent. Then I'll talk to you again as soon as I've reached Loretta. Good-bye, Mr. Herbert."

Sixty-seven

At two-forty that afternoon I was standing in front of my car, watching an eastbound train leave the Westbury station. As the last car rolled out, ten or eleven people came out of the doors below the passenger platform. Several of them were men in suits who had probably taken the afternoon off to enjoy this beautiful September day. Four were white women, three in business suits, one in some sort of uniform. The last two people out of the doors were both black women, but one, not as well-dressed as the other, immediately got into a waiting taxi. The better-dressed woman stood to the right of the doors, unsure as to where to go next.

She was about five foot three. Her skin was a very dark brown, and she looked quite trim in a brown skirt, black turtleneck sweater and low heels. She wore her hair in a close-cut Afro and was beginning to show a little gray at the temples. She was attractive and well-groomed.

I crossed the street from the parking lot where I'd been waiting and approached her slowly to give her a chance to get her bearings and move on if she were not Loretta Roberts. But she stood where she was and when she saw me walking towards her, she smiled.

"Mrs. Roberts?" I asked.

"Mr. Herbert?" she replied.

We shook hands, and her grip was strong. She had an accent that was a combination of Jamaican and English that transformed "Mr. Herbert" into "Meestah Erbert." It sounded nice.

266

"It's a pleasure to meet you, Loretta," I began. "Was your train ride okay?"

"Oh, it was fine," she said with a warm laugh. "Very fine."

"My car's parked across the street," I said as I started to lead her away from the station house doors. "I thought we'd drive out to Huntington first, which is where I live, so you can see our house. Is that all right?"

"I'd certainly like to do that before I go back to the city tonight, Mr. Herbert," Loretta answered softly, "but perhaps I could meet the children first?"

I smiled, and I tried not to jump to any conclusions, but I couldn't ignore the fact that Loretta was more interested in meeting my children than in seeing where she might be living.

"That's fine with me, Loretta," I replied. "We'll go over to my parents' house first—that's where the children and I are staying—and I'll introduce you to Jennie and John. Then, when you're ready, we'll go out to Huntington, and I'll show you our house."

We got into my car, and I pulled out of the parking lot, turned right onto Railroad Avenue and continued up Railroad to Post Avenue, reaching Post just as the light turned red. As I waited for traffic to allow me to make a right turn, I asked Loretta how long she'd been out of work.

"Really only today," she replied. "Yesterday was my last day with the family I've been with for the last two years."

"You didn't waste any time looking for a new position, did you? Not even one day off."

"I'm not a wealthy person, Mr. Herbert. If I don't work, I can't afford my rent. And if I can't afford my rent, I lose my apartment, which is really all I have."

"I see. I gather you live alone?"

"I do, yes."

The light changed to green, and I turned onto Post heading north through the village of Westbury.

"But you're married, yes?" I asked.

Loretta laughed. "Oh, yes, I'm married. I just don't live with my husband anymore."

"Where does your husband live?"

"He's in Jamaica. Where he's been ever since I left over thirty years ago to go to England to make a better life for my children and me. He was quite happy with the life we had, and he made it clear to me that if I had the notion to go to England, I would have to go without him. So I did." She gave a sigh and lifted her head slightly higher, as if in defiance of the man she'd left behind so long ago.

"So you were born in Jamaica and then left Jamaica for England," I repeated. "How long did you live in England?"

"Almost twenty years."

"Well, that explains your English accent, doesn't it?"

"Yes, I suppose it does."

"Did you work as a nanny all that time?"

"Yes. And now for ten years in the United States."

"Elaine said you have three children. Is that right?"

"Yes. One daughter and two sons. But they're all grown up now. One of my sons is married and has two children of his own."

"Where do your children live?"

"They live in Jamaica with their daddy. When I came to the United States, they decided to move back to Jamaica to live with him."

"Do you ever see them?"

"My daughter, Jane, yes. She comes to see me once a year. But my two sons are like their father, and they don't want to leave Jamaica. Not even to visit their mama." I saw her swallow hard out of the corner of my eye.

"I'm sorry to hear that," I replied, hoping I hadn't been too inquisitive.

"Oh no, it's all right," she said quietly. "This happens all the time all over the world. You raise them, and sometimes then you lose them. That's just the way things are."

"Now, tell me about your children," she said after a moment of silence.

"Well, Jennie just turned three in August, and she's quite the little lady. She loves to get all dressed up, and she loves to talk. Constantly.

John's only nine months old—ten months old as of tomorrow—so he doesn't have a lot to say yet, but he's a happy little guy, always smiling, always giggling. Truly a joy to be around."

And on I went, with Loretta listening intently, until we turned into my parents' driveway. I pulled up to the back of the house and parked next to the hemlock hedge that shielded the pool area.

"Ready?" I asked as we got out of the car.

"Yes, I am," Loretta answered, with what appeared to be completely calm confidence.

We headed towards the walk leading to the pool deck and heard the sounds of children squealing and splashing. As we came around the hedge, I saw my mother sitting on the edge of the pool with John on her knee. Jennie paddled in front of her, inflatable water wings on each arm.

Jennie saw us first. "Daddy. Watch me swim! Watch me swim!"

And with that, she stretched out face down in the water and proceeded to splash furiously... and futilely.

"That's great, sweetheart," I yelled. "Just keep at it. You'll be swimming in no time."

My mother watched us as we crossed the pool deck.

"Mom, this is Loretta Roberts, the lady I told you about this morning."

"Hello, Loretta," my mother said, extending her hand up to Loretta. "It's nice to meet you."

"It's nice to meet you, Mrs. Herbert," Loretta replied. She took my mother's hand, and then she bent down to get closer to John.

"And this little man must be John," she said, tickling him under the chin. John giggled and started swinging his feet in the pool, splashing water on himself and my mother.

"And I'm Jennie," Jennie piped up from the base of the pool steps, the swimming demonstration over. "I'm his big sister."

"I can see that," said Loretta. "And what a beautiful little girl you are. Your daddy must be very proud of you."

"Our mommy died," said Jennie, getting right to the heart of the matter.

"I know," answered Loretta. "That must make you very sad sometimes."

"It does," Jennie said, as she climbed out of the pool to stand next to me. "Are you going to take care of us?"

"Well, that depends," said Loretta. She straightened up and looked intently at both children, who, in turn, looked up equally intently at her.

"That's what my grandma said," Jennie continued.

"Well, we'll see, sweetheart," I interjected, taking Loretta off the hook. "If Mrs. Roberts likes us, maybe she'll start taking care of us real soon."

"I hope so, because I want to go home."

"Home is where everyone wants to be, child," said Loretta.

An awkward silence followed for several seconds as my mother looked at Jennie, then down at John, then up at me and finally up at Loretta.

"They're wonderful children, Loretta. If you and Mr. Herbert come to terms, I hope you'll take good care of my kids."

"If I'm given the chance to, I will, Mrs. Herbert. You can be sure of that."

Again an awkward silence.

"Let me take you out to the house, Loretta," I suggested, "and we'll see how you like it."

"I'm certain I'm going to like your house, Mr. Herbert," Loretta replied, looking not at me but at the children. "I'm certain I'll like it very much. Lord, those are beautiful children," she then added, shaking her head in mild disbelief.

"They are. But thank you for saying so. Mom, I'll see you in a few hours. Okay?"

My mother nodded, and Jennie stepped back into the pool. I gave my mother a little wave and followed Loretta around the hedge to the car.

Sixty-eight

We arrived at my house a few minutes before four o'clock. As I turned into the driveway, I was struck by how foreign our home had become, even though the house looked the same as when Peg and I had lived there just a few short weeks ago. I was coming back to a place I had known and loved for years, and yet I felt as if I were arriving at a place that I didn't know at all.

I drove to the back of the house and parked in front of the garage. The two of us walked up the steps to the back porch, and I unlocked the door. I stood to one side to let Loretta go in first and then followed her inside.

The house smelled like it had been closed up for weeks, which of course it had been. The smell was a combination of old house, dust, a hint of stale cooking odor, and dead flowers, thanks to a drooping floral arrangement left on the dinette table weeks ago. Not an unpleasant smell, but a strange, sad one. Not the way the house used to smell.

Loretta took a few steps into the back hall and then stopped and waited for me while I hooked the screen door. I stepped around her and quickly led her past the kitchen and the dinette, suddenly anxious to end the tour before we'd even begun.

"Obviously, the kitchen. With a little dinette area, as you can see," I said over my shoulder without giving her any time to inspect either room.

Loretta followed me down the center hall and into the front foyer.

"Dining room's on your left. Living room and sunroom on your right. There's a large family room off the sunroom where we watch TV." A wry smile crept across my face. "Where we used to watch TV, I guess I should say."

I waited while Loretta looked into each room, and then I started up the stairs to the second floor to show her the children's rooms and the room that would be hers.

"And this is Jennie's room," I said, turning on the ceiling light.

"My goodness," Loretta exclaimed. "How pretty. And so bright and colorful with all the greens and oranges. But look at all those animals in the wallpaper. Tigers and elephants and giraffes and monkeys! Don't they scare her?"

"No, not a bit. She loves them all and has a name for every one of them, I think."

We stood just inside the doorway while Loretta looked around Jennie's room, taking in the furniture, the bedspread, the throw pillows, the circus lamp on her dresser, the lime green carpet, the matching plaid drapes and wallpaper, shaking her head with a smile.

When she was done, I turned off the light and led her down the hall to John's room. It was much smaller than Jennie's and contained only his crib and a dresser with a changing table on top of it. But the room was papered in bold blue vertical stripes with matching curtains, and with its blue woodwork and blue ceiling, the room looked every bit like the little man's room it was.

"So pretty," Loretta murmured, shaking her head again. "And what room is that?" she asked, pointing to her left as we started back towards the stairs.

"That was our bedroom," I replied. I felt a sharp pang in my chest. "My wife's and mine. Well... I guess it's still my bedroom, isn't it?"

Loretta gave half a nod, but she made no response.

"The bathroom's to your left," I said when we reached the head of the stairs. "We only have the one full bath, unfortunately. The bathroom downstairs doesn't have a tub or shower."

I started down the stairs, crossed the mid-flight landing and opened the door to a fourth bedroom snuggled under the roof over the east end of the house. I turned on the light and took a few steps into the room.

"And this is where you'll be if you come to live with us," I said.

Loretta came into the room tentatively and looked around carefully. She opened the closet door and peered into the closet, and then she looked out the window on the north side that offered a full view of the back yard.

"Oh, this is so very nice, Mr. Herbert. And so close to the children. Almost like I'm part of the family."

"You like it?"

"Yes. Yes, I do. Very much."

I waited while Loretta continued to inspect the room, and then we headed downstairs. When we reached the base of the stairs, I looked at my watch.

"You know, it's twenty after four. Instead of fighting rush hour traffic on the way back to the Westbury station, why don't I take you to the Huntington station? It's only a few minutes away, and it's on the same line as Westbury. Depending on the train schedules, you could be home that much quicker, and I'll be back at my parents' house that much sooner."

"That will be fine," Loretta answered. "I bought a round trip ticket for Westbury, but I'm certain the conductor can make the necessary adjustment."

I nodded in agreement and led Loretta down the hall to the back door.

"Your home is beautiful, Mr. Herbert," Loretta said as I backed out of the driveway. "Mrs. Herbert had wonderful taste."

Again I felt that sharp pang in my chest. I waited for a car to pass before backing out into the street and tried to clear the lump in my throat.

"It was a wonderful house to live in, Loretta," I said finally. "And yes, Mrs. Herbert did have wonderful taste."

Within five minutes we were pulling into the parking area for the Huntington Railroad Station. I found a spot to park just past the main entrance to the station house, and realizing the moment of truth had arrived, I turned in my seat so I could face Loretta.

"So what do you think, Loretta?" I began. "Would you like to come and live with my children and me?"

"I would like that very much, Mr. Herbert. Very much indeed."

"We didn't talk about this, but I need you to do the cooking and the laundry for the children and me, as well as general housecleaning. Is that all right with you?"

"Of course. That's part of the position."

"Great. And your work week is…?"

"I work six days a week, preferably with Sundays as my day off. I try to leave for Brooklyn between four and five Saturday afternoon, and I return Sunday afternoon around the same time."

"I assume you have a driver's license?"

Loretta's face fell. "No, I'm afraid I don't."

"I see. Well, we can work around that. Do you have references I can contact?"

"I do," Loretta confirmed, and she reached into her pocketbook. "I can give you their names and telephone numbers."

I waved my hand in dismissal of her offer. "No, that's okay. I asked because I know I'm supposed to. I also know I should call these people, but…" I pulled at my ear, wondering if I were doing the right thing. "I like you, and something tells me you'll take good care of my children. And, quite frankly, I don't want to risk losing you."

"Thank you for saying that," Loretta said, as she slid her address book back into her pocketbook. "That's very nice to hear."

"When could you start?" I asked.

"When do you want me to start?"

"Well… today's Monday. Would Wednesday, October 1st, be too soon?"

"Wednesday would be fine. I'll take a train out from Brooklyn Wednesday morning and take a taxi to the house. I should be at the house by nine-thirty latest. Would that be all right?"

"That'd be perfect, Loretta."

"Thank you, Mr. Herbert. I hope you'll be satisfied with me."

"I'm sure I will be, Loretta. And thank you."

She extended her hand.

The children had a nanny, I had a housekeeper, and soon we'd be home.

Sixty-nine

Coming home sounded wonderful that Monday as I pulled away from the Huntington train station, and in many ways it was. But I quickly learned coming home meant coming back to a world entirely different from the one I had known before.

Now that I was home, in the house I had once shared with Peg, the memory of Peg and our life together surrounded me like a blanket, and at times I felt like the blanket would suffocate me. Pain came from everywhere and everything.

From Jennie as I knelt beside her on our first night home when she asked if Mommy could hear her prayers.

"Of course she can," I answered without thinking.

"Does that mean she'll come home if I ask her to in my prayers?" Jennie asked.

"No, sweetheart," I said, realizing I was on dangerous ground. "Mommy has to stay in heaven with God."

"Why, Daddy? Doesn't God know we need her here?"

"Yes, Jen. God knows that, but..."

I stopped mid-sentence, and my eyes filled. I had asked the same question, but I had no answer for her.

"Hey, you," I said instead. "It's late, and you still haven't said your prayers. So let's get started. Okay?"

She nodded and clasped her hands tight against her forehead. "Our Father, who art in heaven..."

Pain came from John—from just looking at him. He was now ten months old and happy as any baby could be. But when I looked at him, I didn't see a happy, healthy baby. I saw instead a little boy who would never know the woman who had given him life and who had loved him so much for so short a time. I saw a little boy who would only know his mother through pictures and stories, and I wondered if he would think about her when he grew up, or would he not miss that which he'd never had.

Pain came from every corner of the house. From Peg's needlepoints on the walls. From her books in the living room bookcases, from her sewing box, from a salt and pepper shaker she'd bought in Austria. From the pictures and mementos of trips we'd taken, things we'd done. From her closet, still filled with her clothes just as it had been the night she left for the hospital. From the smell of her perfume that clung to her dresses and blouses and suits.

Pain came from the mail almost every day. From a bill addressed to Peg. Or from a needlepoint catalog she had ordered. Or from her issue of *Better Homes and Gardens*. Or, worst of all, from a letter to her from someone who didn't know she had died.

Pain came from Loretta because she was there and Peg wasn't. Every morning when I came downstairs and saw her standing at the stove. Every night when I rounded the turn in the driveway and saw her standing at the sink through the kitchen window.

Pain came every night when the children and Loretta were in bed. When I sat at my desk alone in the family room and listened to the silence of a house asleep.

Pain came from Peg's garden, now overgrown, and from her roses, now stalky, with petals pale from lack of food and ragged from hungry insects. From the circus lamp in Jennie's room that Peg had assembled herself and painted shortly before giving birth to Jen. From the entries in our check register, so many of which reflected an outlook forward-looking and full of hope and yet so ignorant of what was to come. From her cookbooks, her crepe pan, her crystal, her makeup.

Pain came from everywhere, it seemed. No matter where I looked, I was reminded of Peg. She was everywhere but nowhere.

So whenever I could, I escaped. I ran away. Somewhere. Anywhere.

Seventy

"John, an Elaine Weisman from London Personnel is on 2," my secretary announced.

I was surprised to be hearing from Elaine, and I was immediately concerned. Loretta had started working for me on October 1st. Today was October 15th. Elaine Weisman's call, I reasoned, could only mean bad news—either Loretta didn't like some aspect of living with us, or she wanted substantially more money. Or, God forbid, she wanted to quit. I punched 2 and picked up the receiver with more than a little apprehension.

"Hi, Elaine," I began in my most cheerful voice. "How are you doing this morning?"

"I'm fine, Mr. Herbert. How about you?"

"I'm good. But then it's still early."

Elaine laughed. A nice laugh.

"What can I do for you?" I asked.

"Well, first of all, I called to see how things are going with Loretta. I wanted to find out if you like her and if she's working out for you and the children."

I inwardly breathed a sigh of relief. "She's great, Elaine. Very conscientious. Very interested in doing her job well. Very concerned that I might not be happy with her. So far things couldn't be better, but I appreciate your follow-up."

"I'm just doing my job," Elaine replied. "Now assuming everything continues to go smoothly, Loretta's fourth week with you will end on October 28th."

"Correct."

"Please remember our fee is fully refundable until the 28th if for any reason you're not satisfied with Loretta's performance. But only until the 28th. Not any time after that. So if you decide you're not happy with Loretta over the next two weeks, you must let me know right away."

"I will, Elaine, but fortunately I don't think we have to worry about that."

"Well, that's great, Mr. Herbert." She hesitated a moment before continuing. "May I call you John?"

"Of course," I answered, momentarily taken aback by the question. "Just don't call me late for dinner."

Elaine laughed again. "I probably shouldn't say what I'm about to, but… oh, this is embarrassing… you have a very nice voice over the phone, and I can't help but think that you must be a very nice man."

"Umm… thank you," I stammered. "That's… very nice of you to say." I suddenly realized I was smiling.

"Anyway," Elaine continued, "I was wondering if by any chance you might like to come into the city some night and have a drink with me."

"Uh… wow… I don't know what to say."

"Say yes."

I shook my head in amazement at what was transpiring. "Okay. I mean, yes. I'd like that. Uh… when? Where?"

"What are you doing tomorrow night?"

"Nothing, really. Tomorrow night will work."

"Great. There's a cocktail lounge on Lexington and 38th called the Quiet Corner. It's a really nice little spot. Why don't I meet you there at, say, six? Is that all right?"

"That's fine," I said, my mind swirling. "I'll see you tomorrow night at six then."

"Great. Bye."

I hung up and found myself wondering what the hell had just happened. Apparently a woman I didn't know, except for having had a few telephone conversations with her, had just asked me out on a date.

"Unbelievable," I muttered to myself, as I tried to remember what I was doing before Elaine's call. "Absolutely unbelievable!"

Seventy-one

Traffic through the Queens Midtown Tunnel was heavier going into the city than I had expected, and finding a parking garage took longer than I had expected, so I didn't arrive at the Quiet Corner until five minutes after six. No one was standing out front, so I assumed Elaine had either not yet arrived or was already inside.

I pulled the Quiet Corner's heavy wood door towards me and stepped out of the late afternoon sunlight into almost total darkness. Before my eyes could adjust to the lack of lighting, a voice to my left addressed me.

"Good evening, sir. Welcome to the Quiet Corner. Will you be sitting at the bar or would you like a booth?"

"I'm not really sure," I replied, still barely able to see. "I'm supposed to meet someone here, but I don't know what she looks like."

"Ah," the maitre d' answered, as if he'd had a revelation of sorts. "You must be Mr. Herbert."

"That's me."

"Right this way, Mr. Herbert. The lady is waiting for you."

He flicked on a little pencil light which he held at his side, and I followed the tiny circle of light next to his foot down a narrow hallway. On either side, I was now able to discern what appeared to be booths, each one separated from the next by floor-to-ceiling partitions with floor-length beaded curtains across the open side to provide privacy from intruding eyes. We walked past five or six of these booths before the maitre d' stopped and pulled back a beaded curtain to reveal a U-shaped banquette and a large table. A woman sat in the back of the booth facing me. With his free hand the maitre d' indicated that I should enter.

"Mr. Herbert has arrived, ma'am," he said.

"Elaine?" I asked.

"Yes. Hi."

"It's nice to meet you."

"Nice to meet you face-to-face," Elaine replied.

I extended my hand and sat down. "This is quite the place," I said, hoping my discomfort with the Quiet Corner wasn't apparent.

"It is a little over the top," Elaine admitted, "but it's a great place to have a quiet drink without having to put up with blaring TV's or loud drunks."

I noticed Elaine didn't have a drink in front of her. "Have you ordered anything yet?" I asked.

"No. I was waiting for you. If you know what you want, just pull that string over your shoulder. That turns on a little light outside the booth and lets them know you want service."

I reached up, pulled the string, and then looked at Elaine. She was in her early thirties, I guessed, probably Jewish, had short black hair and impeccable makeup. She was quite attractive. A waiter arrived, and Elaine ordered a daiquiri. I ordered a scotch and soda.

We talked a little about Peg and the kids at first, then a lot about what I did for a living and her different experiences living in the city. I was nervous—nervous about being with her, and nervous about the Quiet Corner—so the first scotch and soda went down very quickly. As did the second and the third. By the time my fourth drink arrived, I had breezed past relaxed and was well on my way to whatever they call the next level of intoxication. We stopped talking as the waiter placed my drink in front of me, but as he withdrew Elaine looked at me and smiled.

We were now sitting right next to each other and, not surprisingly, Elaine had become much more attractive since the first scotch and soda. I gently pried her fingers off the stem of her glass and brought her hand to my lips. I kissed each of her fingertips for a moment or two and then after running my tongue up and down the sides of her fingers, I began to suck on her fingertips, one by one. Elaine watched me intently with wide-eyed amazement.

Suddenly the voice broke through the haze of scotch.

What the hell do you think you're doing? it asked. *Trying for a repeat? It was sexy with Nancy, so why not see what happens with this one? Is that it? Jesus Christ, John. What's the matter with you? Is nothing sacred? Special? Knock this shit off, will you?*

I stopped kissing Elaine's fingers and slowly placed her hand back in front of her.

"My God!" Elaine exclaimed. "That was sexy."

"Sorry," I said with a sigh. "Shouldn't have done that."

"No, to the contrary. You can do that any time you want," said Elaine. She slid closer and began to run her fingers through my hair just above my ear. "Know what we should do?" she asked.

I shook my head.

"We should get a check, and you should come back to my apartment with me—it's in Brooklyn, but it's just a few subway stops away—and I'll make us dinner. We'll have some wine… and we can make an evening of this. What do you say?"

I sighed again, the voice's words lingering in my mind. "I'd love to, Elaine. I really would. But I should get home. Tomorrow's a work day, and I've already had too much to drink. But thank you for the invitation. I really appreciate it."

Elaine looked down at her empty glass and then at me. "Well… you don't know what you're missing. And I'm a great cook. But I understand. Let me give you my number, though, so you can call me. Okay?"

"That'd be great," I said, at this point anxious to leave.

She fished in her pocketbook for a pen, wrote her number on a cocktail napkin and handed the napkin to me. "Call me," she said. "Promise me you'll call."

"I will. I promise."

I paid the check, and we left the beaded booth. A minute later we stepped out onto the sidewalk and into the bright lights of Lexington

Avenue. I extended my hand, but Elaine gave me a light kiss on the cheek instead.

"Call me," she said, and she began to walk to her subway stop.

I nodded, gave her a wave and started to walk in the opposite direction down Lexington Avenue to my car. And as my head cleared, I thought of Nancy and her fingers, and I felt ashamed.

Seventy-two

S. Anne Burnett was Dave Clayton's contribution to my new life as a single man. Sally Evans was Beth's.

S. Anne Burnett came first, the result of a conversation with Dave one Saturday afternoon. He knew I had taken Nancy out several times and asked if I were still seeing her. When I told him I was, he volunteered the opinion that if I were going to date, I shouldn't be dating just one person but rather should "see what's out there," as he put it. He then proceeded to tell me about a woman in his office, single, attractive, who might like to go out with me if I were interested. I wasn't, but I must not have made that sufficiently clear, because Dave called Monday night to say he'd spoken with the woman, and she was expecting to hear from me. So I called S. Anne Burnett and invited her out to dinner on Friday, October 24th.

S. Anne Burnett, I soon learned, came from money. Big money. The kind of money most of us only dream of. The kind of money that paid for an apartment on the forty-first floor of a brand new building in midtown Manhattan. A building with a doorman who brought me to the concierge, who escorted me to the elevator and, with his key, selected Miss Burnett's floor for me. The kind of money that paid for a Spanish maid who greeted me at the door to the apartment and ushered me into the living room to wait while Miss Burnett finished getting ready.

S. Anne Burnett came out of her bedroom and into the living room twenty minutes later. She was tall, blond and slender, and although her facial features were plain, her stature, clothes and overall demeanor made her look regal. Shortly after we walked into the very elegant, very over-priced French restaurant I had selected for dinner, however, I realized S. Anne Burnett was out of my league. She did her best to disguise the fact, but I could tell she was bored. We ate dinner, I brought her back to her doorman, and I went home, wishing I had spent the evening with Nancy instead. I never did learn what the "S" stood for.

On Friday, November 7th, I went out with Sally Evans, a co-worker of Beth's, who was Beth's attempt to remedy Dave's lack of matchmaking skills. Sally was thirty-three years old, single and lived at home with her parents in Armonk up in Westchester County. She was about five seven, with light brown hair not quite to her shoulders. She had a nice figure and was reasonably attractive. When I met her at her front door, my first impression was one of propriety. Or maybe, I thought an instant later, she was just old before her time, with her functional low-heeled black pumps, black skirt, grey mohair sweater buttoned all the way to her neck, and short string of white pearls.

But Sally was nice, and she was pleasant to talk to, her conversation intelligent, her questions sensitive, her answers thoughtful. We had dinner at a small café she had selected at my request, and we talked animatedly the whole time. When dinner was over, our waiter asked if we'd like any-thing else—an after-dinner drink perhaps—and to my surprise, Sally said she'd like a brandy. So we had a brandy. And then a second.

We left the café shortly after eleven and headed back to Sally's house. As we drove down her street, Sally asked me if I'd like to come in for a drink, and I accepted her invitation. I parked my car in the driveway as she suggested and followed her up the walk to her front door. I waited while she found her house keys and then followed her inside. The house was completely dark, so I assumed that her parents had already gone to bed.

"Just give me a minute to put some lights on and to freshen up," Sally said in a voice I thought too loud, given her parents were asleep.

"Don't wake your folks," I whispered.

"No need to worry," she said with a soft smile. "They're not here."

"Ah," I replied, thinking I understood the situation. "On vacation?"

She stood motionless, looking at me. "No. They're spending the night with friends here in town."

I nodded as if this made perfect sense. "Well, that's smart," I said. "If you don't have to drive after a party, don't."

"They didn't go to a party. They're just spending the night there."

I nodded again, not certain what to say next.

Sally took a step towards me. She looked directly at me, her eyes unwavering. "They knew I was going out with you tonight... and they thought maybe... we'd like to have the house to ourselves."

"I see," was all I could manage to say.

And I did. Suddenly I saw everything. All too clearly. I saw Sally, a truly nice person, but already in her thirties, living with her parents, very much aware she was running out of time. And I saw her parents, conservative as they probably were, ready to help her obtain the husband she wanted... any way they could. But exploitation was never something I did well.

"Wow, Sally... uh... I don't know what to say. Uh... I just don't. I do know that... although it's not really late, I've got sixty-five, seventy miles to do before I get home, so... I probably shouldn't stay."

She smiled sadly.

"I hope you understand," I added. "Maybe a rain check?"

"Of course. Some other time. You have my number."

"I do. And... I'll call you. In the meantime, thanks for a wonderful evening. I really enjoyed meeting you. I mean that."

Sally nodded and walked me to the front door. "Get home safely," she said.

I stepped out into the cool November night. Dry leaves crackled under my feet as I walked to my car. The basic part of my brain, the crude male part, was wondering what the hell was the matter with me, but the other part, the part where the voice lived, was pleased.

I started the car and backed out of the driveway. *Lots of lonely people in the world,* I thought as I drove down Sally's street. I stopped at a stop sign and made a right turn. *I'm sure glad I've got Nancy.*

Yet you're here, the voice said from somewhere in the dark recesses of my mind. *Why is that?*

"Don't know," I answered. "Don't know."

Seventy-three

Word gets around fast about some things. My date with Sally was on Friday, November 7th, and on Saturday, November 8th, Amy Bennett, the woman who lived behind me, called to ask if I remembered her husband's cousin, Kate McPherson.

"Yeah, I think so," I replied. "I met her at your Christmas party last year, right? Tall redhead? Very attractive, as I recall."

"You recall right," Amy said with a laugh. "Well, anyway, Beth told me you went out with a woman she knows from work, and I was wondering if you might want to go out with Kate. I know she's not seeing anyone, and who knows? Maybe the two of you'll hit it off."

"Oh, I don't know, Amy. We hardly know each other. And it's been almost a year since we met. She probably won't even remember who I am."

"I'll bet she does. But let me call, and we'll find out."

"She was very nice," I admitted, recalling that evening which now seemed so long ago.

"So can I call her?"

"You want an answer now?"

"Why not?"

"No reason, I guess. Except I'm not completely comfortable with the idea. But supposing I say yes. What's your plan?"

"I'll give her a call sometime this weekend. See if she's interested. If she is, the rest is up to you. How's that sound?"

"Sounds simple."

"Good. I'll talk to you soon. Bye."

I started to ask her to say hello to her husband for me, but she'd already hung up. Preoccupied by troubling thoughts, I went back down to the basement, where I'd been painting storm windows.

I wonder what's going on? I said to myself as I dipped my brush into a can of exterior white. *Why am I such a hot commodity all of a sudden? Why are all these people trying to fix me up with someone? Are they that interested in my well-being? Or...* I stopped painting for a moment. *...are they just trying to get me away from Nancy?*

I shook my head in frustration.

No way to tell, John. No way to tell.

Seventy-four

Kate McPherson remembered me and told Amy Bennett she'd "love" to hear from me. So Monday night, November 10th, before I called Nancy, I called Kate, and after several minutes of pleasant conversation, I asked her out for the evening of Friday, November 21st.

Her apartment was on West 73rd Street, she said. Apartment 3B. I told her I wasn't familiar with the west side of Manhattan and asked if she would mind making dinner reservations for us. She assured me that wasn't a problem. A new restaurant had opened a few weeks ago around the corner from her apartment, and she'd been anxious to try it out. We could go there if that was all right with me. I told her that was fine.

The buildings on Kate's end of West 73rd Street were all five- and six-story turn-of-the-century brownstones, ranging from exquisite to neglected, each with high ceilings, tall windows and a flight of steps leading up to the front door. Kate's apartment was in one of the better ones.

I arrived promptly at seven-thirty, climbed the steps to a set of wood and glass double doors, and stepped into a small vestibule. I pressed the buzzer for Apartment 3B and heard Kate's voice on the speaker. She'd be down in a minute, she said. She'd ask me up, but two of her roommates were still getting dressed and, well, I understood, she was sure.

A minute later, Kate McPherson stepped out of the elevator.

Kate was different. I think she was a year or two older than I was, and she was a big woman, solidly built and at least five-ten in her heels.

She worked as a personal shopper for wealthy women at one of New York's leading department stores, and as a result she was high fashion—very stylishly dressed, very well made up. With shoulder-length, deep red hair, she was stunning.

Kate was different, and so was our evening. We had dinner at the new restaurant, a dark, quiet establishment that did as nice a job on the food as they did with the atmosphere. After dinner, Kate suggested we have a drink at a lounge around the corner, and for the next hour and a half, we sat bathed in soft blue neon light, drinking Grand Marnier, listening to a jazz trio. When the trio took their second break, Kate said she had a surprise for me.

We walked five blocks south and then turned onto a side street. Midway down the street Kate went up to a steel door belonging to what I thought was a warehouse. She slapped hard on the door twice, and an imposing fellow pushed the door open. Kate said something to him, and within seconds we were walking down a long flight of stairs to a huge basement, easily the size of a basketball court, jammed with people dancing to a live hard rock band playing at ear-splitting volume. We had a drink and danced to a couple of numbers as best we could, given the crush of people, until I signaled to Kate that I wanted to leave. We climbed back up to street level and stepped out into the quiet darkness.

"I hope you don't mind," I apologized, "but that was a little too loud and a little too crowded for me."

"No, that's all right," Kate said, taking my arm. "It's not that bad normally. I don't know what the deal was tonight."

We headed for the lights of 9th Avenue and then started to walk uptown towards Kate's apartment.

"I hope you enjoyed tonight," Kate said.

"I did. Very much. Tonight was the kind of night a guy like me from the suburbs could never pull off on his own. This was cool." I gave a little bow. "And I thank you."

"You are most welcome," Kate replied, returning the bow in exaggerated fashion. "Now, on to more important things. Can I buy you a drink when we get back to my apartment?"

"Are your roommates dressed yet?"

Kate laughed. "They're dressed and out for the rest of tonight, I'm sure. They're stewardesses, so they're not around much, but when they are, they really try to pack everything in they can."

I looked at my watch. "God, I can't believe it's almost one-thirty."

"Is that a no to the drink?"

"No, it's not," I said, feeling quite relaxed and happy at that moment. "Yes to the drink. To hell with the hour."

We reached Kate's building within a few minutes, and I followed her into the elevator. She punched 3, and a moment later we stepped out into a short, tiled hallway. She unlocked the door to her apartment, and I followed her inside.

From where I stood, I could see a living room and a hall onto which several doors opened, presumably from the bedrooms, the kitchen and the bathroom. The living room was sparsely furnished, with only a sofa along one wall and a bookcase and two armchairs along the other. Floor-to-ceiling windows at one end of the room afforded a view of the street below.

"If you need to use the bathroom, it's the first door on your left," Kate said, as she took off her coat. "Make yourself at home while I get comfortable, okay?"

"Will do," I replied.

I took off my coat and jacket and looked around for someplace to hang them. Finding none, I laid them on one of the armchairs.

I walked down the hall to the door Kate had pointed to, opened it tentatively and confirmed it was in fact the bathroom. I quietly locked the door, lifted the toilet seat and took in the room around me. Shampoo bottles, hair spray cans, lipsticks, toothbrushes, toothpaste tubes, hairbrushes, combs, and every other imaginable beauty product or hygiene product occupied every available horizontal surface. I was putting the toilet seat down when I noticed a red rubber bag hanging over the bathtub faucet and connected to a long rubber tube with a nozzle of some sort on the end.

"What the hell is that?" I wondered as I washed my hands. "A hot water bottle? Or...? No. Can't be that... but I'll bet it is."

I shook my head and unlocked the bathroom door, feeling like I'd led a very sheltered life. Had I been sober, I probably would have felt less than comfortable.

I walked over to one of the living room windows and parted the curtains. I was peering down into the street when I heard a door close down the hall. I turned around, and a second later Kate walked into the living room—naked.

I knew my mouth was open, but I was powerless to close it and unable to say a word. So I just stared at her—first at her face, then at the rest of her—while Kate stood where she was in the middle of the room, hands on her hips, enjoying my reaction thoroughly.

Finally words came. "Jesus Christ, Kate," I stammered. "What the hell are you doing?"

"I told you I was going to get comfortable," Kate replied, smiling.

"Yeah, but... I mean you're... you've got nothing on, Kate. And I feel a little weird standing here like this... looking at you."

"Of course you do, silly. That's because you still have your clothes on. Get undressed."

I started to say something, but Kate had already turned away from me and was starting to take the cushions off of the sofa.

"What are you doing now?" I asked.

"I'm pulling out the sofa bed," she said over her shoulder. "My bedroom's a total disaster. I can't bring you back there."

She stood up and faced me, a cushion in one hand. "Are you going to get undressed," she asked, "or do I need to help you?"

I felt like I was in another world, like this really wasn't happening. But it was, so I started to undress. By the time I was down to my shorts, Kate had finished pulling out the sofa bed and was lying on her side, her head propped up on one elbow, watching me. As I put my shorts on the armchair, now piled with my clothes, she eyed me from head to toe, smiled and patted the bed next to her.

"Come here," she said in a throaty whisper.

I lay down next to her and kissed her. She immediately wrapped an arm around my neck and returned the kiss hungrily, almost urgently. She kissed me once, twice, three times—deep, wet kisses—pressed her body against mine and draped one leg over my thigh.

But suddenly I was repulsed—by Kate's nakedness, by her kisses, the smell of her perfume, the feel of her hair tumbling into my face, even by the weight of her leg on mine.

I disentangled myself from her and sat up quickly. "I'm sorry, Kate," I heard myself saying, "but I can't do this. It's not right."

"Don't be silly," she replied, sweeping her hair away from her eyes. "Of course it's right."

"No, it isn't. But I can't expect you to understand that."

"I think I do, though. What you don't understand is you're not married anymore, which is what makes this okay."

I exhaled sharply as I got up off the bed and walked over to the chair where I'd hung my clothes. "This isn't about my wife, Kate," I said, pulling on my shorts. "Should be, but isn't."

Kate sat up and tucked one leg under the other. "Well, if this isn't about her, then what is this about? Have I done something wrong? Is something wrong with me?"

"No, nothing's wrong with you. And you haven't done anything wrong. Other than shock the hell out of me."

"Then why are you leaving? Why won't you make love to me?"

"I told you, Kate. I can't make love to you because… this doesn't feel right. I don't know why, but it doesn't."

I buttoned my pants and pulled up my fly.

"You can't be serious," Kate said incredulously.

"I'm afraid I am."

I tucked in my undershirt. Kate looked down at one of her hands for a second before looking up at me again.

"I guess this is where I'm supposed to say I understand," she said quietly.

"I think so, but then... I really don't know what the rules are any more. I thought I knew how to behave in different situations, but I'm finding out that I don't."

I tucked my shirt into my pants and sat down on the now-empty chair to put on my shoes and socks. Kate sat on the bed watching me, making no attempt to cover herself.

I stood up, put on my jacket and draped my coat over my arm. "I... uh... gotta go," I said, gesturing in the direction of the door.

Kate sat perfectly still.

"I didn't mean to put you in this position," I said. "I really didn't."

"What position did you put me in?"

"Well... you know... this." I indicated her nudity with my free hand. "Without anything happening, I mean."

"Hey, that's life, I guess," Kate said with a shrug.

"Yeah. Well... I... uh... don't know whether to shake hands or give you a kiss or what."

"Let's just shake hands," Kate replied flatly, and she extended her hand up to me.

Three minutes later, I reached the sidewalk in front of Kate's building and started the two-block walk to my car. As I walked down the empty sidewalk, I tried to understand what had made me leave Kate. My adolescent fantasy could have come true tonight, I realized, but I'd run away. I wondered why, but the answer eluded me. Instead I found myself wondering where Nancy was at that moment.

Seventy-five

Dave was wrong. Four dates with four very different women convinced me of that. Maybe he had been right in theory when he said I
shouldn't be seeing only one person, but I wasn't living in theory. I was
living in the shadow of Peg's memory. Whenever I thought of her or
looked at my children or at the woman who now managed my home,
first sadness, then loneliness, then terror swept over me, and I felt an
irresistible urge to run away, away from all the things that were not as
they were supposed to be.

So I did. I ran away. But only to Nancy. Because only with Nancy
could I forget. Theory be damned.

And some nights, even with Nancy, I couldn't forget. The memories
would be too much to handle; the tears would start, and they wouldn't
stop. Nancy would hold my hand or stroke my head, and she'd listen and
let me cry. When I was finished crying, she'd tell me that she understood
and that everything was going to be all right. And the storm would be
over. For the moment.

But escape was essential. Escape from a world turned upside down.
From a world of what had been but was no more. Escape to a place of
warmth, understanding and safety.

Escape was non-negotiable. I had to be with Nancy to survive. I
found that I could live in my new world, with all its darkness, but only,
only, if I were able to rise to the surface now and then for a breath of the
fresh air and a glimpse of the light that Nancy brought me.

Foolishly, I never thought about the effect my behavior was having on Nancy. I never reflected on how difficult it was for her to see me cry over the memory of a woman I still loved. I never wondered how long she'd be able to listen to me talk about Peg before she decided she couldn't listen anymore. I never noticed she stopped asking questions about Peg, and I never saw how she looked at me sometimes. I never realized how deeply involved with me she was getting, which meant I didn't worry about what might happen to her if things didn't work out. I was like a drowning man—so terrified at the prospect of losing his own life that he endangers the life of the person who swims out to save him. I only knew I wanted to survive, and Nancy was making that possible.

But Nancy was no fool. She knew she was exposing herself to heartache, and she knew the emotional investment she was making would probably be for naught. But she ignored her concerns and fears. Instead she took our relationship and its risks one day at a time. She tried not to worry about the future and endeavored to enjoy the time we had together —for however long that turned out to be.

Nancy and I saw one another through November. We spent most of our time together alone, insulated. No one took notice of us. No one demanded either an explanation from us for our actions or retribution from us for having dared to ignore their conventions. Everyone—family and friends—simply left us alone—uncriticized, unaccountable—expecting me eventually to behave properly and us to go our separate ways.

But then came December, and December is different. December is a time for celebration. A time for parties. Christmas parties. New Year's parties. A time of lights and carols and candles and presents. A time to eat and drink. A time to be with people celebrating a wonderfully religious time of year or a wonderfully sentimental time of year or both. A time to be with people celebrating the end of the year just past and the promise of the new year about to begin. December is not a time to be insulated or withdrawn. It's a time for inclusion. A time to embrace the people you love and the people you like and even the people you just know in passing.

So in December, Nancy and I emerged and allowed ourselves to be drawn into the rhythm of the season. Friends extended holiday party invitations to us, and we accepted. First to Amy and Frank Bennett's for a Christmas party the Saturday night before Christmas. Then to Bob and Audrey Weber's for a cocktail party the Saturday night after Christmas. And then out to dinner with Beth and Dave Clayton on New Year's Eve, to put 1980 behind us and step forward into 1981.

But emergence brought visibility. And visibility brought examination. And examination brought criticism. And criticism brought guilt… and pain. Much of the pain was caused by others. Sometimes intentionally. Sometimes not. Some of the pain we created ourselves. The pain that each month brought—from January through the following December—took its toll on us, punished us and threatened to break us apart.

Seventy-six

We sat across from one another in a booth at a diner a mile or so from Nancy's apartment. Although it was only ten-thirty New Year's Day morning, the diner was filled to capacity, and we had gotten the last table.

"You don't look too good this morning," I said to Nancy.

"I feel like hell. I was up all night crying. I didn't sleep at all."

"That explains your eyes then. They're all swollen and bloodshot. If I didn't know better, I'd swear you really tied one on."

"I wish I had. Maybe then everything that happened last night wouldn't hurt so much."

I reached across the table to take one of Nancy's hands in mine, but she pulled her hand away and looked around the diner. She shook her head and sighed deeply.

"Last night with Dave and Beth was so bad… I can't believe it. And then our conversation when we got back to the apartment… What a terrible New Year's Eve." She looked at me sadly. "Do you really have to go to lunch with your parents this afternoon? Can't we spend the day together?"

"Nan, we talked about this last night. Do I have to go? No. Do I want to go? Not really. But my folks asked me to go with them, and I said yes—I probably shouldn't have, but I did—and I can't back out now."

"But they asked you to go so these friends of theirs can introduce you to their daughter. That's why your parents asked you, and that's why you're going, and that's what really hurts me."

301

"I know, but I'll only be there for a few hours, and I'm sure as hell not going to get involved with this woman."

"That's not the point," Nancy said. "The point is you're not going to be with me today because you're spending the afternoon with another woman you haven't even met."

"Why are you getting so upset, Nan? You know I've seen other people over the past few months. What's the big deal about this, other than we won't be together this afternoon?"

"How would you feel if I went out with someone else? You wouldn't like that one bit, would you? That's the big deal."

"Nan, I never said you couldn't go out with other people. You just haven't."

"Are you saying you don't care if I do?"

"I'm not saying I don't care. All I'm saying is I wouldn't get upset if you did. Not like you're getting upset now. Sure, I'd prefer you didn't go out with anyone else, but... I'd understand if you did."

Nancy looked at me for several seconds and then stared at the open menu in front of her for half a minute before closing it.

"Let's go," she said, tears welling up in her eyes. "This isn't getting either of us anywhere, and if I'm going to cry, I'd rather do it in my apartment. Alone."

"You don't want breakfast?"

She shook her head.

"Not even coffee?"

"I want to leave, and I want to be alone. Can we go now?"

I closed my menu and followed Nancy out to my car.

1981 was not starting out particularly well.

Seventy-seven

Snow was falling steadily on Tuesday night, January 6th, as we tra-veled west from the Cleveland airport on our way to Toledo. We'd been on the road for forty-five minutes, but thanks to poor visibility and lower than normal speed on I-90, we'd gone less than forty miles, which meant we wouldn't arrive at our hotel until well after midnight.

I was traveling with Larry Thomas, our district sales manager for Ohio, Kentucky, Indiana and Pennsylvania, and we were on our way to Toledo for two days of sales calls. Larry had met my flight from New York, and our conversation had been lively for the first thirty minutes of our drive. But as the snow continued to fall and our speed continued to drop, Larry fell silent—undoubtedly in part because he was driving and sensed the need for extra diligence, but also probably because, like me, he was beginning to realize this was going to be a long night.

The white flakes racing into our headlight beams were giving me a headache, so I turned away from the windshield to look out the passen-ger side window. Every few minutes I was able to make out the lights of a farmhouse or a barn or a car on a distant country road, but otherwise the snow obscured what little there was to be seen. The view through the window was one of snowflakes hurtling past me and featureless black-ness. Mile after mile, Larry and I sat in silence except for the rhythmic slap of the windshield wipers and the muffled roar of the defroster. The silence inside the car coupled with the impenetrable blackness outside made me feel uneasy.

Wonder what Nancy's doing tonight, I thought as I watched a rivulet of melting snow run down the window. *Probably waiting for me to call her. Which isn't going to happen. Not tonight anyway.*

Miss her? the voice asked suddenly.

I was surprised at the voice's appearance. I hadn't heard the voice in almost two months, and I'd assumed it was gone and wouldn't return. But here it was, clear and strong as ever.

"Yeah, I do," I replied. "I always do."

Why? the voice asked, probing, prying, same as before.

I sighed, knowing the answer but not wanting to acknowledge it. "Because when I'm not with her, I'm scared."

Scared? What are you scared of?

"Lots of things."

Like what? the voice pressed, persistent in its quest for answers.

"I'm scared of living alone for the rest of my life. I'm scared of everything that means."

I turned away from the window and stared through the windshield, squinting at the brightness of the snow in our headlights.

"I'm scared for my kids. Scared about the kind of childhood they'll have without a mother. Scared about how they'll turn out. I'm scared something might happen to me. What happens to Jennie and John then? Hell, I could die tonight in this goddamned snowstorm.

"I'm scared there's something wrong with me. Because I haven't grieved for Peg the way I was supposed to. The way I should have. I found Nancy, and I ran away from everything to her."

You're not scared when you're with Nancy? the voice asked.

"No, I'm not."

Why?

"Because when I'm with her, I don't worry about the rest of my life; I just think about today and how good today is. And…because I love her."

You what?

"I love her," I repeated.

How can you say that? the voice asked, its tone harsher now, more critical.

"Why shouldn't I say it? It's true."

I thought I heard a familiar sigh. *John, John, John,* the voice began condescendingly. *We've been over this before. How many times do we need to have the same conversation before you get it into your head? You lost Peg only four and a half months ago. You started going out with Nancy two weeks after Peg died. And you've been going out with her ever since—two, three times a week. You're a hurtin' puppy, my friend, and although you don't know it, you're not capable of loving Nancy. Not really loving her. Needing her? Sure. Loving her? No way. Sorry, pal, but you're making a huge mistake if you think you love this kid. You're confusing need with love, and there's a big difference between the two. Big difference. So please... don't tell me you love Nancy, because you don't. You can't. And for God's sake, don't make matters worse by telling Nancy you love her. Don't do that, whatever you do.*

"You want to listen to something on the radio?" Larry asked.

"Sure, if you want to," I replied distractedly, startled at the sudden intrusion into my most personal thoughts.

A disc jockey announced a song by Hank Williams. I looked out at the snow swirling all around us.

"You're wrong," I said to the voice. "I do love her. I know I do."

Seventy-eight

I caught a three-forty flight out of Cleveland on Friday afternoon, January 9th. By seven-twenty I was at Nancy's apartment. We both felt like having Chinese food, so I suggested Long's in Hicksville—a thirty-minute drive, but worth the effort.

We arrived at Long's a few minutes after eight and were shown to a table immediately, a pleasant surprise for a Friday night at that hour. We ordered drinks and had just started to look at our menus when our waiter returned barely a minute later.

"So except for the weather, I gather your trip this week was good," Nancy said, taking a sip of her Tom Collins.

"Yeah, it was. I think Larry and I made some real progress on a couple of big potential orders."

I gave the lemon skin in my vodka an extra twist and savored a long swallow, grateful that my four days on the road were behind me.

"How was your week?" I asked.

"All right," Nancy replied. "Really quiet at the office, though. Post holiday doldrums in the advertising world, I guess."

"Did I tell you I tried to call you Tuesday night?"

"No, you didn't."

"Well, I did. I didn't get into my room until after midnight because of the snow, but I figured I'd give you a quick call anyway just to say hello. When you didn't answer, I thought maybe you'd decided not to, given the hour."

Nancy took another sip of her drink and looked across the table at me. "I wasn't home Tuesday night."

"At that hour? Where were you?"

"At my parents'."

"Ah. You spent the night there?"

"No. I came home. After you called, I guess."

"Must have been quite a visit," I joked.

Nancy didn't smile. "Actually, it was quite a visit," she said. "My dad was out of town on business, so I had dinner with my mother... and then I called a guy I knew before I met you... and invited him over for a drink."

"You're kidding. You invited this guy over for a drink with you and your mother?"

"My mother went to bed a few minutes after he got there."

I waited for Nancy to tell me more, but she didn't.

"So... who was this guy?" I asked, trying not to sound too interested.

"Our next-door neighbor's son. I had a monumental crush on him for years."

"So what did you two do all evening?"

"We talked."

"About what?"

"About how we were once and how we are now... how we've each changed."

"Sounds heavy. Did he behave?"

"What do you mean?"

"Well, did he try to kiss you or anything like that?"

"Yes. Yes he did."

"Did you let him?"

"Yes."

I looked across the table at Nancy, but our eyes met for only a second before she looked away.

"There's something you're not telling me, Nan," I said, suddenly afraid of where we were going. "Did he do more than kiss you?"

"Yes."

"Wow. Well… what did he do, if you don't mind my asking? You didn't sleep with him, did you?"

"Yes, I did."

"What? How is that possible? Is this some kind of joke, Nan? How could you sleep with him? You were in your parents' house, for God's sake."

"If it really matters to you, we made love in the family room. On the floor. Satisfied?"

Tears filled my eyes. Two waiters a few tables away watched us warily—wondering, I could tell, if our exchange would intensify and if they were going to have to intervene.

"Jesus, Nan. Why? What the hell were you thinking? Why would you do that? Why would you ever do that with someone other than me? Why, Nan?"

"Didn't you tell me New Year's Day you wouldn't mind if I went out with someone else? That you wouldn't be upset? Didn't you say that?"

"Yeah, but…"

"And you've gone out with other women since you met me, haven't you?"

"Yeah, a few, but…"

"So I figured… if you didn't care enough about me not to go out with other people… and if you didn't care if I went out with someone else … then why would you care if I slept with someone else? And for the record, he's not just anyone. I've wanted to go to bed with him since I was eighteen, nineteen years old, but I never did because… well, you know why."

"I can't believe you had sex with him," I stammered, still trying to come to grips with what I was hearing.

"You didn't sleep with any of those women you took out?" Nancy asked accusingly.

"No, Nan. I didn't," I said, trying hard to keep my voice low so the two waiters couldn't hear what I was saying. "Had the chance to. Make no mistake about that. But I didn't. Because of you."

Nancy sat perfectly still and started to bite her lower lip. Then she started to cry.

"I don't believe this," I said, shaking my head in despair. "I just don't believe this."

"I didn't think you'd care."

"Well... I do."

We sat in silence for close to five minutes, me staring into my vodka, Nancy slowly stirring her Tom Collins with her straw, both of us crying.

"Tell you what," I said finally. "I'll make you a deal. There's no way I can handle you seeing anyone else. I just can't do that. I can't! So... I will promise you tonight I will never see anyone else as long as we're together if you'll make the same promise to me. Does that sound like a good deal?"

Nancy started to speak, but her words were cut off by a sob. "Yes," she replied when she caught her breath. "That sounds like a good deal. Sounds like a wonderful deal, as a matter of fact."

I reached for her hand and squeezed it hard.

Seventy-nine

The five-ten train out of Penn Station had been late. Again. The
night sky was pitch black without its moon, and the temperature was
falling rapidly as Nancy trudged home from the Roslyn train station the
evening of Monday, January 26th. A brisk breeze out of the northwest
rattled the few leaves still clinging to the trees. Nancy was cold. She was
lonely. She was depressed.

Snow that had turned to slush in the afternoon sun was now frozen
and crunched under her leather boots as she struggled to find footing on
an unshoveled section of sidewalk. "I'm going to break my neck if I'm
not careful," she muttered to herself, recovering from a sideways slip into
a frozen footprint. She reached the end of the unshoveled property after a
few more careful steps and found herself once again on bare concrete.

She hated this walk, especially in the winter. She hated it because in
the dark and in the cold, the windows of the houses she passed glowed
yellow and warm, and the air carried the smell of wood smoke. As she
walked the three blocks to her apartment, she imagined husbands and
wives and children behind those warm yellow windows. She imagined
couples sitting in front of crackling fireplaces, glasses of wine in hand, and
families at the kitchen table ready to share a meal and exchange stories
about one another's day. In her mind each house was filled with warmth,
laughter and love.

Then she thought of her apartment, now only a block away, empty
and dark, with dinner, which she would eat alone, only a thought in her

mind. And that led her to think about John and how alive the apartment became whenever he was there. Which led her to think about how she felt about him.

"I love you, John," she said out loud as she walked down her street, head down, shoulders hunched against the cold.

The sound of her voice surprised her, but not as much as her words. She realized what she had just said was a declaration to herself, an acknowledgement of feelings she'd been resisting for months now.

She frequently talked to herself when she was alone in her apartment, but never outside in public like tonight. However, a glance ahead and a glance behind confirmed no one was in sight, and the sound of her own voice comforted her and made her feel less alone.

"But who am I kidding?" she continued. "You love Peg, not me. You're running away from what happened, and you're running away to me. I'm getting you on the rebound, that's all. I know you care for me, but I don't know how much, and I don't know how you'll feel about me when the pain of losing Peg starts to disappear. That's what makes this so risky. I could be making a complete fool out of myself and could wind up getting hurt really badly. And that scares me. A lot. If we'd met two years from now, everything might be different. But we didn't."

She shivered convulsively as a gust of wind cut through her coat. She tried to pull her collar tighter around her neck, to no avail.

"So what do I do? I can't leave you. I love you too much. And I can't tell you how I feel because if I do, I'm afraid I'll scare you away. Or worse, you'll stay because you feel sorry for me."

She turned onto the walkway that led to the side door of her apartment.

"Ironic, isn't it?" she said as she unlocked the door. "You know my most intimate secrets, but I can't share this with you. I can't tell you I love you."

Eighty

I saw Nancy every Friday and Saturday night and every Wednesday night that I was in town. Fortunately, child care wasn't an issue because Loretta watched the children on Wednesday and Friday nights, and either my folks or Peg's mother took care of the children on alternate Saturday nights when Loretta was off.

In addition to seeing Nancy three times a week, I called her every night we weren't together. I always called around nine o'clock because by then she had settled in for the evening, and I had been able to play with the kids for a while before putting them to bed. So my call on Monday night, January 26th, should have been more or less routine.

"Hello?" Nancy answered.

I smiled at the sound of her voice, soft and low and warm. I loved the sound of it. "Hi. It's me."

"I knew it was you," she said.

"How was your day?"

"Okay," she answered. "Train was late. As usual. And the walk home from the station was colder than hell. But other than that, okay. How about yours?"

"Okay too, I guess. A lot of crazy stuff going on at the office, but what else is new."

"Kids in bed?"

"Yeah. Just put out Jennie's light and just finished getting the bobby pins out of my hair."

"What?"

"It's Jen's newest way to delay going to bed. She knows I love getting my hair combed, so she makes me sit on the floor with my back against her bed, and she stands next to me combing away. Then when she's all done, she holds her handiwork in place with bobby pins and giggles at how silly I look. But she enjoys it."

"And you don't?"

"I do. The bobby pins, though, I could do without. Oh, before I forget," I continued, "Dave called a little while ago and asked if we had any plans for Saturday night. I told him we didn't, and he asked if we'd like to get together with them. Maybe go out for dinner someplace. Would you like that?"

Nancy didn't respond for several seconds. "No, I wouldn't," she answered finally. "In all honesty, I can't think of anything I'd rather not do."

"You don't want to go out for dinner, or you don't want to get together with them at all?"

"I don't want to go out with them at all. Not after New Year's Eve. I don't think I could handle another evening like that."

"It was that bad?"

"Oh God, John. How can you ask that?"

"Well, I know the evening had some rough spots, but..."

I heard Nancy exhale sharply in frustration and pictured her shaking her head. "Do you remember what happened during dinner, John? Do you remember Beth breaking down in tears? Do you remember what she said?"

"I remember her starting to cry at the table, yes. And I remember the gist of what she said—not word for word, but generally."

"Well, I remember every word. She said, and I quote, 'I'm sorry for behaving like this, but I just can't get used to the fact that we're sitting here together on New Year's Eve making like nothing has happened. But something has happened. Something terrible. Peg is dead, and she's not here. Instead, John, you're here with Nancy. Which I'm having trouble with. I'm sorry, but you can't plug Nancy into your life and expect every-

313

one to behave like everything's okay. Because it isn't, and it never will be. Maybe Dave can do it, but I can't. I won't.' "

Nancy stopped for a moment to let her words sink in. "Do you remember her saying that?" she asked.

"Yes."

"Do you remember how upset I was on the way home that night? How I cried for hours after we got back to the apartment? Do you remember how bad I felt?"

"Yes, I remember that too."

"Then how can you ask me to spend another evening with Beth and Dave knowing that's how she feels?"

"I guess I chose to think she didn't mean what she said, that she was just being emotional because it was New Year's Eve. They're my best friends, Nancy. You know that. I only wanted to give Beth the benefit of the doubt."

"But that's not fair to me, is it?" Nancy asked.

"No, it isn't, and I'm being selfish to expect you to pretend nothing happened. I'm sorry. Forget about Saturday night. I'll make up some sort of excuse."

Neither of us spoke for probably half a minute.

"But you know…" Nancy said, "the funny thing is, Beth's right. In a sense, you are making believe nothing has changed. For nine years, you and Peg were a couple, and you did things together, as a couple, with Beth and Dave. Then Peg dies, you meet me, and suddenly you and I are doing things with Beth and Dave. Like nothing happened. Beth resents that, John, and she has every right to. We're not a couple to her. You're you and I'm some kind of plug-in module that's supposed to replace Peg."

"What are you saying, Nan? We'll never go out with Beth and Dave again?"

"I'm not saying that, but things aren't that simple. Because the problem's not just with Beth and Dave. You know that, don't you?"

"Yeah, I do."

"When we were at Amy and Frank Bennett's house, at their cocktail party just before Christmas, no one, and I mean no one, talked to us. Oh sure, they came up to us and said hello, but more out of obligation than anything else, as far as I could tell. That or curiosity to see what kind of a woman starts dating a guy two weeks after his wife dies. But really, no one talked to us. No one spent any time with us."

"Except Beth and Dave."

"Except Beth and Dave. I'll grant you that. But all Amy Bennett talked about for the few minutes she was with us was what a good friend Peg was. What a wonderful mother Peg was. What a great person Peg was. How smart Peg was. All of which was true, I'm sure. But why tell me? Didn't she realize how much that hurt me? And what about Bob and Audrey Weber's party? Do you remember what that was like? Again, all Audrey and the other women could talk about was Peg and how much she loved her children and how good a mother she was and how good at juggling job and family she was and how beautiful her home was. Meanwhile the husbands are looking at me like I'm some kind of slut they'd jump on in a minute if their wives weren't there. So I've been asking myself why they would treat me like that. Know what I came up with?"

"No. What?"

"It's their way, consciously or unconsciously, I don't know which, of telling me that I don't belong with you and of telling you that you've behaved badly by going out with me so soon after Peg died. Basically, they're telling us we broke the rules by becoming involved with one another the way we did. I don't know what else it could be, John. I think I'm a nice person. Up until now, people have always liked me. Why else would your friends treat me like this?"

An overwhelming sadness started to wash over me. "Maybe you're right, Nan, and maybe they're right too. Maybe we have behaved badly, and maybe the time's come when we have to start paying for how we've behaved. I don't know. The real question is, what do we do?"

"I don't have the answer to that," Nancy said, "but I know I don't like to feel the way I felt with Beth and Dave and at the Bennetts' and the Webers'. I don't ever want to feel that way again. I'm me, John. Not Peg's replacement, but me. Your friends have to know that, and they have to accept me for who I am."

"I understand, and I agree with you. If they can't accept you on your own merits, and if they can't accept us as us, with all that means, well… the hell with them. I don't want to lose all my friends, Nan, in addition to Peg—make no mistake about that—but I'm not going to let them come between you and me; and I'm not going to let them hurt you. I don't blame them if they can't accept what we've done, but if they can't, we go forward alone. That's all we can do."

"You know I'm not asking you to turn your back on your friends."

"I know you're not, but what choice do I have?"

I stopped, wondering if I should continue; then I knew I had to.

"I love you, Nancy. Hopelessly. And I can't let anything get in the way of that."

"You love me?" Nancy asked quietly, incredulously.

"Yes. Very, very much."

"Wow."

"Anyway, we'll be okay," I assured her, "even if it's just the two of us. I promise."

"Are you sure you love me?" Nancy asked, so quietly I could barely hear her.

"I'm sure. Trust me."

"I'll try."

Her response wasn't at all what I'd expected or hoped for, and several seconds of silence didn't help.

"Well… I should say good night," I said. "I'll talk to you tomorrow night."

"I'll be here," Nancy replied softly.

I hung up the phone and leaned back in my chair. The curled leaves of a rhododendron outside the window rattled in the bitter cold January wind and tapped out a ragged rhythm against one of the window panes.

I was comfortable with everything I had said, and I'd meant every word, but somehow I felt like a swimmer who looks back at the shore he's left behind and is suddenly surprised and frightened to see how far away it is.

Eighty-one

I sat at my desk and stared at the telephone. "I told her I loved her," I said out loud, "and all she said was 'wow' and 'are you sure?' What's that mean? She doesn't love me? Or she does and she's just afraid to tell me?"

Probably means she doesn't love you, John. Why should she? She's only known you for a few months, and let's face it—this hasn't exactly been a typical courtship.

Nancy sat at her kitchen table, a can of diet soda in front of her, and nibbled on the side of her thumb as she stared at the telephone on the wall.

"John said he loved me," she said in disbelief. "He said he loved me, and all I said was 'wow.' Why didn't I tell him I love him too? What's the matter with me? What must he think?"

I continued to stare at the telephone as if it held the answers to my questions. "Why did I tell her I love her? Damn! I shouldn't have done that. Stupid!" I shook my head several times in anger. "Tonight wasn't the time for me to say that. I should have waited a few more months. Maybe a year. Who knows? But tonight was too soon."

Nancy shook her head in amazement, but also in concern.

"Does he really love me?" she asked herself, "or does he just need me and doesn't know the difference? He said he loved me. Hopelessly. That's what he said. I didn't ask him if he did. He said it on his own. He said he had no choice. Because he loved me. Hopelessly. And I just said 'wow.' I can't believe I did that."

Nancy brushed away a tear and stared at the telephone on the wall.

I leaned forward in my chair.

"Well, what's done is done," I said to myself sadly. "I can't unsay what I've said, and I can't make Nancy love me if she doesn't. End of discussion, John."

I looked at the papers strewn across my desk without seeing them.

Nancy's finger trembled as she pressed the keys of her phone, slowly, deliberately.

The first ring startled me. I looked at my watch. It was nine thirty-five.

The phone rang again. I wondered who could be calling at this hour, and then I realized I didn't care.

A third ring. "Maybe it's the folks," I thought with sudden apprehension. I picked up the receiver. "Hello?" I answered.

"Hi. It's me," Nancy said.

"Hi. What's up?"

"I love you too."

"You what?"

"I love you."

"You do?" I asked.

"I do. With all my heart. I have ever since that first night we went out."

"Thank you," I stammered. "Thank you for telling me. And thank you for loving me."

"Loving you is easy," Nancy replied. "You're everything I ever wanted."

I thought I heard a sniffle. "Will you call me tomorrow night?" she asked.

"What do you think?"

"I think yes."

We said good night, and I was reminded once again of the difference a minute or two can make in one's life.

Eighty-two

Nancy's phone was ringing when she came back into her office after a meeting with her boss on Monday morning, February 9th. She quickly walked over to her desk, picked up the receiver and punched the flashing button. "*National Geographic*. Nancy Charlton speaking."

"Hi, Nan. It's Mom."

The way her mother's voice dropped on the word "Mom" telegraphed concern.

"Hi, Mom," Nancy replied, grateful for a momentary respite from what had been a very hectic morning. "How are you?"

"I'm fine, but more important, how are you?"

"I'm okay. Shouldn't I be?" Nancy pulled her chair out from her desk and sat down with a sigh.

"Well, I imagine that would depend on how your dinner went. When I didn't hear from you over the weekend, I got concerned and thought I'd better call."

"What dinner are we talking about, Mom?" Nancy knew the answer, but for some reason she felt compelled to ask anyway.

"Your dinner with John's parents," her mother replied.

"I don't have time to get into all the details now, Mom. It's not even nine-thirty yet, and Brian's already given me a hundred things to do for an ad directors' luncheon on Friday. I'm swamped. Can I call you tonight?"

"Sure, but in a word, tell me how it went. Good? Bad? Hard to tell?"

Nancy needed to talk to someone about Friday night, but she knew she shouldn't take the time now. The steno pad in front of her contained page after page of instructions, with most of the items marked "urgent" or "do today." Still… she needed to talk, and her mother was prepared to listen. She decided *National Geographic* could wait for a couple of minutes.

"Bad," Nancy said. "In a word… bad."

"Why? Weren't John's parents nice?"

"They were nice. They weren't nasty or rude or anything. They just made me feel really uncomfortable with some of the things they said. And didn't say."

"Like what?"

"Well, for starters, they asked me what college I went to, and I told them Lebanon Valley. They said they'd never heard of it. Then Mr. Herbert asked me what major I had gotten my degree in. What could I do? Make believe I'd graduated? So I told them I didn't graduate. That I left at the end of my sophomore year. When I told them that, they kind of …You know how people sometimes raise their eyebrows a little and raise their chin a little but say nothing? Well, that's what they did.

"Then they asked me what my father did for a living, and I told them he was a salesman for Vollrath selling restaurant equipment. Mr. Herbert asked me how long Dad had been working for Vollrath, and again I didn't know what to say. So I told him he had just gone back to Vollrath after leaving to start his own business. Mr. Herbert asked what kind of business, and then he asked why Dad left it to go back to Vollrath. That led to the whole Swan Lake story and how Dad walked away from the place and lost everything."

"What did Mr. Herbert say to that?"

"Nothing. Nothing at all. He just sat there. They both just sat there. Almost as if what Dad had done was so inconceivable to them—that failure like his was so not part of their experience—that they didn't know what to say. And the funny thing is, all of this happened *before* things started to go downhill."

"It got worse?"

"Oh, yeah, it got worse. Like I said, it was a bad evening. Mrs. Herbert asked me if I liked to read. Again, what am I going to say? That I love to read and then not be able to tell her the name of the last book I read? So I told her I don't read a lot. That I don't really have the time, what with work and commuting and all. And that's when Peggy came up for the first time. When Mrs. Herbert told me that Peggy read all the time. On the train in the morning. On the train at night. Whenever she had the chance. According to her, Peggy read ketchup bottle labels at the dinette table if that's all there was to read.

"Needless to say, that made me feel less than great, especially after the college discussion. So I decide maybe a little sympathy for Nancy is in order. I tell Mr. and Mrs. Herbert about the parties John and I went to over the holidays and how uncomfortable I was because of everyone telling me what a great person Peggy was and what a great homemaker she was and what a great mother she was and all that. Anyway, want to guess what Mrs. Herbert's response was? 'Well, you have to understand, Nancy, how much everyone loved Peggy. She was a wonderful, wonderful person, you know. And of course it is rather soon for my son to be getting involved with someone.' I felt like she'd thrown a bucket of cold water at me, Mom."

"Well, I can certainly understand why you'd feel like that," her mother replied, "but in a way she's right, isn't she, Nan? About it being too soon for John to be getting involved with you?"

"Yes, she's right," Nancy agreed reluctantly, a painful ache starting to develop in the pit of her stomach. "You know that, and I know that. But she didn't have to say what she said, did she? She could have tried to understand how difficult things are for John and me. She could have tried to be a little warmer, a little more supportive, a little more encouraging, couldn't she?"

"Yes, she could have, Nan, but that's not the way people are. Not with a situation like this."

Nancy watched one of the sales reps walk past her open office door and wondered if anyone in the outer office was listening to all of this.

"Did John's father say anything?" her mother asked.

"What do you mean?"

"Did he say anything after Mrs. Herbert's comment?"

"Yes. About everyone loving Peggy. He said, and I quote, 'I certainly loved her. Peggy wasn't just my daughter-in-law. She was my sweetheart … the daughter we never had.'"

"How sad."

"Look, Mom, I gotta go. I've got to get back to work."

"What are you going to do?" her mother asked, ignoring Nancy's attempt to end the conversation.

"About what?"

"About John's parents. About the way the evening turned out?"

"There's nothing I can do, Mom. They obviously weren't impressed with me, but what can I do about that? If they like me, that's great. If they don't, that's not a problem I can solve. I just have to hope they give me a chance and try to see the good in me. What else can I do?"

"Nothing, I guess."

Nancy waited a moment before trying again to end the conversation. "Well, thanks for calling, Mom. I appreciate your concern. I really do. I'm glad we were able to talk."

"I wish there were something I could do, Nan."

"Me too," Nancy admitted as a tear rolled down her cheek. "But there isn't anything you or anybody else can do. I have to sort this out on my own as best I can. Anyway, I'll talk to you later in the week. Goodbye."

Nancy hung up without waiting for a response.

Eighty-three

"Good evening, ladies and gentlemen," a deep male voice intoned. "You have been listening to WPAT, 96.3 FM on your dial, coming to you this Thursday morning, February 12th, from Patterson, New Jersey. The time at the tone is 1:00 A.M." A soft chime sounded, and the voice returned. "We now return you to another hour of uninterrupted music for your listening pleasure."

I opened my eyes and looked up at the ceiling, barely visible in the dim light of Nancy's living room. Nancy was lying on her side snuggled up tight against me with her head on my chest and an arm draped across my stomach. In the second or two before the music began again, I could hear her breathing softly as she slept beside me in her convertible sofa bed.

God. One o'clock already, I thought. *I should go home. I gotta be in the office early tomorrow morning. No*, I thought to myself wryly a moment later, *you have to be in the office early this morning.*

But I didn't move for fear of disturbing Nancy. Instead I listened to the music and the intermittent creak of the living room's baseboard heaters as the thermostat called for more hot water to combat the cold of this February night. I was just starting to drift off when the ring of Nancy's telephone shattered the peacefulness of the warm darkness. Between the second and third ring, Nancy began to wake up. Without moving away from me, she stretched, lifted her head slightly and then laid her head back on my chest. "What time is it?" she asked sleepily.

"A little after one."

The telephone rang again. "Do you want me to answer that?" I asked.

"Who could be calling at this hour?" Nancy mumbled.

Another ring. "I don't know, but someone is. Do you want me to answer it?"

"Mmmmmmm," Nancy answered sleepily. "Please."

I lifted her arm off my stomach, gently lowered her head onto the pillow and rolled back the covers just enough to allow me to get up. I reached the phone on the seventh ring.

"Hello?" I answered, holding the receiver in one hand and rubbing my eyes with the other.

"John, it's Dave."

I stifled the beginning of a yawn and tried to shake off the cobwebs in my brain. "Dave. What's up? It's late. What are you doing still up?"

"I'm over at your house. With Loretta."

In an instant the cobwebs disappeared, and I was wide awake. "What's wrong, Dave? What's happened?"

"Nothing. Everything's okay except Jennie has a fever. Loretta thought she looked flushed tonight when she put her to bed, and Jennie woke up a little while ago, crying. Loretta took her temperature, but she couldn't read the thermometer. So she called me."

"Dave, I'm sorry."

"No, no, don't worry about it. Anyway, Jennie's temperature is 102.8. She's got some kind of bug, I guess, and I thought you should know. That's why I called. I also wanted to know if it was all right for Loretta to give her a couple of baby Tylenol."

I leaned on Nancy's kitchen wall for several seconds, my head on my forearm, before I said anything.

"You still there?" Dave asked.

"Yeah," I said with a heavy sigh. "I'm still here."

"So can Loretta give Jennie the Tylenol?"

"Sure. Tell her it's okay."

"Will do. Then I'm out of here."

"Dave, I don't know what to say. Other than thanks."

"Don't have to say anything," Dave replied, cutting me short.

"Yes, I do. I should've been there with Jennie. I know that. Supposing you hadn't been able to come over?"

"Well, I was, so there's no problem."

"Yeah, right."

"Look, I gotta get back to bed. I'll see you over the weekend."

"Sure. Hey… thanks again."

I waited for a reply, but I heard a dial tone instead. I hung up the phone and walked back into the living room. Nancy was awake by now, lying on her side, her chin in her hand. "Who was that?" she asked.

"That was Dave. Jennie's sick and has a temperature of 102.8. So I better get home. I'm sorry."

"Don't be silly," Nancy said. "But why did Dave call you? Why didn't Loretta call you?"

I snorted and shook my head in frustration as I started to get dressed. "Dave called me because Loretta called him. She thought Jennie had a fever and took her temperature, but she couldn't read the thermometer. So she called Dave over to read the damn thing, and Dave called me. Is that not something?" I shook my head again and rubbed my forehead. "If this doesn't tell you how screwed up my life has become, I don't know what does. My little girl gets sick, and my best friend has to get up in the middle of the night and come over to my house to read a thermometer for my housekeeper because I'm not there."

Nancy reached out and took my hands in hers. "You didn't know Jennie was sick when you came over tonight, did you?"

"No, of course not."

"Then you didn't do anything wrong."

I disengaged my hands from Nancy's and began to button my shirt. "I just feel like a really lousy father, Nan."

"You're not a lousy father. You're a wonderful father who's caught in the middle of a lousy situation. But things will work out. You just have to be patient."

"I should've been home with the kids tonight, but I had to come here. You know that. So either way I lose. Either I see my kids and don't see you, or I see you and don't see my kids. That's the choice I'm faced with, and that's a choice I can't make."

Nancy reached out again, pulled one of my hands down to her lips and kissed the back of it. "You don't have to make a choice," she said between kisses. "You see your children, and you see me. Maybe not as much as you'd like in either case, but that's all right. The children will survive, and I'll survive. Like I said, just be patient."

I put on my ski jacket and then bent down to kiss her good night. "I'm trying, Nan," I said as I straightened up. "Believe me, I'm trying."

I gave a little wave, and a moment later I stepped out into the cold, silent night.

Eighty-four

My parents and I had just finished lunch and were sitting at the dinette table on Sunday, March 16th, when my father asked me an odd question. "Have you ever seen Center Island?"

"No. Why?" I replied.

"No reason, really," he said. "Kind of surprising, though, when you realize we've lived in Mill Neck for seventeen years, and Center Island's only four miles away."

"I suppose so. Never thought about it."

"We should go there after lunch. Today's a beautiful day, it's a nice drive, and the area's like another world. The wealth of the people who live there is unbelievable."

"Isn't it gated?" I asked.

"Yeah, but they'll let us in. We'll tell the guard we're from Mill Neck and that we just want to drive around the island. Leave that to me."

He turned to my mother before I could reply. "Do you mind if we leave the kids with you for a little bit?"

"Not at all," she said, pushing back her chair. "Just give me a hand clearing the table, and I'll take care of the dishes while you're gone."

Within minutes our chores were done, and I found myself leaving for what I thought was an impromptu Sunday afternoon drive. We arrived at the gatehouse guarding the entrance to Center Island less than fifteen minutes later and slowed to a stop in front of the white wooden barrier gate blocking our lane. A uniformed guard stepped out, clipboard in hand, and came up to the driver's side of the car.

"Good afternoon, sir," he said cheerily. "May I ask who you're visiting?"

"Well, actually, no one," my father responded, equally cheerily. "I've been promising myself for months to take a drive around the island, and I thought today would be a great day for it. Is that possible?"

"I'm afraid not, sir," the guard replied, genuinely apologetic. "No one's allowed on the island unless they're a resident or the expected guest of a resident. In which case we enter their name in our approved visitor's log." He held up the clipboard in his hand for us to see.

"I understand," my father said, "but could we maybe make just one loop around the island and then come right back out? I live over in Mill Neck, and I wanted to show my son the area. Shouldn't take very long."

The guard looked over the roof of the car for a few seconds and then leaned down so he could look into the car and over at me. "How long would you need, sir?"

"Ten minutes," my father replied with his warmest smile. "Fifteen at most."

"Tell you what. I'll take down your license number so I know who you are, and you take your loop around the island. But you need to be back here in no more than fifteen minutes. Okay?"

"Not a problem. Thanks very much."

We waited while the guard went to the rear of the car and recorded the license number. When he was done, he gave us a wave and went back into the gatehouse to raise the barrier gate.

"Nicely done," I commented as we passed under the raised gate.

"All depends on the presentation," my father answered, feeling quite happy with himself.

Center Island, it turned out, was not an island at all, but rather a small peninsula joined at its northwest corner to the north shore of Long Island. Its southernmost end protruded into Oyster Bay Cove, with Cold Spring Harbor on its eastern shore, Oyster Bay on its western shore and Long Island Sound on its northern flank.

As we drove along on the narrow, two-lane road that made a meandering loop around the peninsula, I was disappointed to see that many of the homes were hidden from view, the only evidence of them being driveways that disappeared into woods and mailboxes at the end of those driveways. But every half mile or so we came upon a house visible from the road, typically nestled deep within a veritable forest of oak, black walnut and hickory and surrounded by acres of grass already green. Each house was more magnificent than the next—Tudors with stone turrets and leaded glass windows, center-hall brick colonials with slate roofs, and ultra modern concoctions of concrete, stainless steel and glass—each of them enclosing thousands of square feet of living space for the pleasure and egos of their invisible owners.

I was admiring one particularly huge Tudor, wondering what someone who could afford such a home did for a living, when my father's voice broke into my thoughts.

"You seem to be getting pretty involved with Nancy, son."

"What?" I asked, not certain I'd heard him correctly.

"I said you seem to be getting pretty involved with Nancy."

"What makes you say that?"

"You see her three nights a week. You must be getting pretty involved with her."

I shrugged my shoulders and looked out the side window, trying to decide how honest to be. "As a matter of fact," I said, turning back toward him after a moment of deliberation, "I am getting involved with Nancy. Very involved. Why?"

I waited for his answer, not sure what to expect, but he didn't respond for several seconds as he maneuvered the twists and turns of the road. I could tell he was thinking, though, choosing his words carefully.

"It's none of my business," he said finally, "and I hope you'll forgive me for asking you this, but aren't you concerned about getting serious with someone so soon after losing Peg? I mean, Peg's only been dead for seven months. Isn't it possible you're getting involved with Nancy on the rebound?"

"Sure, it's possible. Theoretically. But that's not the situation."

"How can you know that if you're not seeing other people?"

"I've gone out with a few other people—you know that—but I don't need to date anybody else to know what Nancy means to me."

"What does she mean to you?"

"Wow. We're really getting serious here, aren't we?" I said, taken aback by his directness and by the realization that he had an agenda for this drive.

"I'm worried about you, John."

"Why?"

"Because hearing you talk, I think maybe you're in love with Nancy. Are you?"

"Yes," I said. "Very much so."

"Well, again I ask, aren't you afraid to get so involved with her this soon after Peg?"

"No. Not at all."

"Maybe you should be."

"Why? What's the problem? What am I missing here?"

"I don't know how to say this, son, so I'm simply going to tell you how I feel. And that is that I don't see Nancy as being your kind of girl."

For a moment, I just looked at him, too dumbfounded to speak. Then anger and hurt rose to the surface, demanding expression. "What the hell does that mean, Pop? 'Not your kind of girl.' What's my kind of girl?"

"Don't get upset. I didn't mean to get you upset."

"Well, you did. Now answer my question. What do you mean when you say Nancy's not my kind of girl?"

Again he waited several seconds before answering me, but this time I got the impression he was using the time to summon the strength to say what he wanted to say rather than to find the right words. When he finally began to speak, he spoke slowly and deliberately.

"Nancy's not like Peg, son. She's not like Peg at all. Peg graduated from college. Nancy didn't. Peg was an officer at a major bank. Nancy's a secretary. Peg was sophisticated. Nancy isn't. Peg was always so poised. Nancy isn't. I could go on and on, but don't you see what I'm trying to say? Nancy isn't the same kind of person Peg was. She's completely different from Peg. And I don't understand how you could have loved Peg and married Peg and now be attracted to Nancy. She's a delightful girl, but..." His voice trailed off.

"Jesus Christ! I don't believe you're talking to me like this," I practically shouted. I stared at him, waiting to see if he had anything else to say, and then I turned away, shaking my head in disbelief.

"You know, you're right," I said after several seconds of silence. "Nancy isn't at all like Peg. She didn't graduate from college. She is just a secretary. She's not sophisticated. And when she's around you and Mom, she's not—what did you call it? 'Poised.' That's it. She's not 'poised' around people who make her feel uncomfortable and awkward. So you're right. She is totally different from Peg. But I'll tell you something. There's a warmth to Nancy, an ability to love, totally, that you've never seen, and I love her for that. More than you can imagine. And she loves me and makes me forget what I've lost. What's so wrong with that?"

"Nothing," my father replied. "I didn't mean to imply there was." He paused. "Does Peg's mother know you're dating Nancy?"

"Yeah, she knows."

"How did she find out?"

"I told her one night when she was at your house to see the kids. Before I moved back home. I told her I was going out that Saturday night, and she said that was a good thing for me to do because I was still a 'young man' or something like that. I was surprised she took it so well, but then I wondered if maybe she thought I was going out with one of the guys. That's when I told her I was going out with Nancy."

"How did she react?"

"She got real quiet—didn't say anything other than 'I see'—and went to bed a few minutes later."

"Why did you tell her? You must've known it would tear her to shreds."

"I had to tell her. If I didn't, I'd be acting like I was ashamed of going out with Nancy."

"Did she ever mention Nancy again?"

"No. Never."

"Let me ask you this. What do your friends think of your relationship with Nancy?"

"Why do you ask?" I replied defensively.

"Well, I don't hear you talk about any of them anymore like you used to, other than Beth and Dave occasionally, and I can't help wondering if there's a connection."

"You really have a way of getting to the nub of things, don't you?"

"Not really. But like I said, I'm worried about you. That's why I'm asking these questions."

I sighed and again wondered if I should answer honestly.

"To tell the truth," I said, "I think they're all pretty turned off by the whole situation. I haven't asked anyone what they think about us, and no one other than Beth has volunteered an opinion; but in their own way, some subtly, others not so subtly, they've each made it pretty clear they don't approve of us. And who can blame them? I mean, come on. I know how it looks—my getting involved with Nancy so soon after Peg died—and if positions were reversed, I'd be totally pissed off at someone for doing what I'm doing. But I didn't plan any of this. I didn't plan Peg's death. I didn't plan on taking Nancy out. That just happened. And I sure as hell didn't plan on falling in love with her. I don't know how any of this happened. But it has, and I can't change that. So if my friends have a problem with Nancy and me, or if anyone else does, for that matter, it's just too damn bad. I've played by the rules all my life, Pop. You know that. But sometimes rules get broken."

"That's true," my father agreed, "but sometimes people get broken too."

"Yeah, they do. I'm one of them. And all I'm trying to do, if the world will let me, is put myself back together again."

"I'll say no more," my father said, as he slowed and then stopped at a stop sign. "I just hope you know what you're doing."

"Me too, Pop. Me too."

A left turn and the gatehouse appeared a few hundred yards ahead of us. Our drive through Center Island was over, and so was our first and last conversation about Nancy.

Eighty-five

August 3rd, 1981, was Jennie's fourth birthday. Now a birthday for any little girl is a big day, but a little girl's first birthday without her mother is somewhat off the charts in terms of everyday experience and something I felt ill equipped to handle. But after much discussion on the phone one Tuesday night two weeks before Jennie's birthday, my mother and I decided the best thing to do would be to have a party for Jennie as if nothing had changed and to have it at my house rather than at my parents' house in order to give Jen as much a sense of normalcy as possible.

We also decided that, weather permitting, we'd have cocktails and dinner in the back yard and would open Jennie's presents out there as well. The picnic table could seat six, and I had four lawn chairs and four folding snack tables, which would give us seating capacity for ten, not counting John in his high chair. That would be enough for my mother and father, Maureen Reilly, two of Peg's sisters—Erin and Kathleen—Dave and Beth, Nancy, me and, of course, Jennie. I'd have to scare up one more chair and snack table for Loretta, but otherwise we'd be fine.

We debated whether or not to invite the rest of the family or any of Jennie's friends, but resolved we should limit the party to ten so we could seat everyone and easily move everything indoors if the weather decided not to cooperate. Ten people, we reasoned, would make the party small enough to be manageable and yet large enough to be special for Jennie. I would grill hamburgers and hot dogs, and my mother would bring her

German potato salad, macaroni salad and the bittersweet chocolate cake that was Jennie's favorite.

Having established the location, the guests and the menu, I was ready to move on to another topic. My mother, however, was not.

"Are you inviting Nancy to the party?" she asked.

"I already have," I replied.

"Is she going to come?"

"Of course she's coming. Why wouldn't she? And why are you asking?" I added, sensing we were on the verge of having one of those in-depth, no longer appropriate parent-child conversations.

"Well, I was just thinking about Maureen Reilly and how she's going to feel."

"She knows I'm dating Nancy," I said, as if that solved everything.

"I know, but I think seeing Nancy in her daughter's house will upset her. Maybe I'm wrong, but I'd give this some more thought if I were you."

"Well, I appreciate the concern, but it's a little late for that. We discussed this July 4th weekend. Don't you remember? We were all sitting out on the pool deck, and Nancy told you I wanted her to come to the party, but she didn't think she should. You asked why, and she said she thought her being there would be difficult for the Reillys, Maureen in particular. And we all said she was silly for worrying—that we were certain Maureen would understand her being there. Do you remember that conversation?"

"Of course I do. I've just been having some second thoughts."

"Well, that may be, but I've spent the last two weeks trying to convince Nancy to come, and she finally said she would. She still thinks things are going to be awkward, but she knows Jennie wants her there, and she knows I want her there, so she's coming. Against her better judgment, I might add. But now that I've convinced her to come, there's no way I can ask her not to, Mom. No way."

"I understand. I didn't mean to make you angry. I'm just concerned."

"I'm not angry, and to be perfectly honest, down deep I don't know if I'm doing the right thing either. I don't want to do anything that'll hurt

Maureen or get her upset, but more is involved here than Maureen's feelings. Jennie knows I invited Nancy, and she knows Nancy said yes, and she wants Nancy to come. Plus the fact that I want Nancy to come. Call me silly, but I don't want to be at my daughter's birthday party alone. I'd like Nancy with me. So I'll consider myself forewarned, but I'm not going to uninvite Nancy to Jennie's party. Because she belongs there. Okay?"

"It's okay with me. It's your party."

I gave a little sarcastic snort into the receiver. "Thanks, Mom. Look, I gotta go. I'll talk to you tomorrow night."

"All right. But will you give what I said some thought?"

"No, Mom, I won't. Nancy's coming to Jennie's party. Period."

I waited for a response. None came.

"Say hello to Pop for me, will you?"

"I will. And I still love you."

Another snort, meant to convey amusement more than anything else. "I'm glad to hear that. I love you too. Good night."

I stood next to the wall phone in the kitchen, turning over in my mind what my mother had said, wondering if I had laid the groundwork for some sort of disaster on Jennie's birthday.

I asked myself, *What am I supposed to do? Tell Nancy she can't come because we think Maureen Reilly might get upset after all?* I stared at the floor. *I can't do that.*

I looked up at the ceiling. *At the same time, if Mom's right and Maureen does get upset, she could ruin the whole party—which would hurt Jennie.*

I rubbed my eyes with both hands, frustrated, angry. *Jesus Christ! Why does everything have to be so goddamned complicated?*

But in an instant the confusion disappeared, replaced with resolve.

"It's not complicated," I said out loud to myself, in complete denial of the reality facing me. "Nancy's coming to the party because she belongs there, and Maureen will understand that. That's all there is to it."

Happily confident that all was now under control, I turned off the lights in the kitchen and went to bed.

Eighty-six

August 3rd was a typical August day for Long Island, hot and humid but thankfully sunny. I left the office at two forty-five so I'd have time to change clothes and set up the grill and lawn chairs before anyone arrived for Jennie's party. But when I pulled into the driveway around three-fifteen, I saw that Maureen and Erin Reilly had already arrived. Erin was watching Jennie chase a butterfly across the backyard lawn, and Maureen was sitting on one of the picnic table benches with John on her lap. I parked in front of the garage and got out of the car.

"Hi. How are you?" I said as I walked across the lawn toward Maureen.

"We're fine," Maureen replied curtly.

"I didn't expect to see you guys here so early."

"Kathleen wanted to beat the rush hour traffic, so we left Bergen-field around noon and got here a little after one-thirty."

"Well, that's great. And how are you doing, sweetheart?" I said, calling to Jennie.

"I'm fine, Daddy," Jennie replied as she ran to give me a hug. "Today's my birthday."

"I know, and in a little while we're going to have a party just for you. With hamburgers and hot dogs and birthday cake and presents and all sorts of stuff."

Jennie hugged me tightly for a few seconds and then stood back, her hands clasped tightly in front of her, beaming with anticipation.

337

"But first," I said, "Daddy's got to get out of his suit and into some shorts. Then he's got to set up the grill and some chairs so people will have a place to sit. So you play here with Grandma and Aunt Erin while I go inside and change. All right?"

Jennie nodded and ran across the lawn to Erin.

"And how are you doing, little guy?" I asked, tickling John under his chin.

"He's doing fine," Maureen answered while John squirmed on her lap, trying to grab her glasses. "Aren't you, fella?"

My son's attention for the moment on a pair of eyeglasses and not on his father, I stood up and started to walk back to the car. "I'll see you in a few minutes, Maureen," I said over my shoulder. "I've got to get out of this suit before I melt."

I took my briefcase out of the car and went into the kitchen through the back door. As usual, Loretta was standing at the kitchen sink as I came in, washing what I assumed to be the lunch dishes. She turned toward me on hearing the screen door open.

"Hello, Mr. Herbert. How was your day?"

"It was good, Loretta, but short. Come to think of it, maybe that's why it was good." I put my briefcase down by the pantry doors and picked up the mail on the end of the kitchen counter. "Where's Kathleen?" I asked, focusing on a handwritten envelope without a return address but postmarked in Richmond, Virginia.

"Miss Reilly?" Loretta said.

"Yes. The other daughter."

"Oh, she already left, Mr. Herbert. Some time ago."

"She what?" I forgot about the envelope from Virginia.

"She left, Mr. Herbert. She went home. Over an hour ago."

"Why? I thought she was coming to Jennie's party."

Loretta turned back to the dishes in the sink, visibly upset.

"Am I missing something, Loretta? Wasn't she supposed to come to Jennie's party?"

Loretta continued to wash the dishes for another moment or two. Then she put down the dishrag, wiped her hands on her apron and turned toward me. "Yes, she was, Mr. Herbert," Loretta replied.

"So why isn't she here? Why has she gone home?"

"She went home right after I told her Nancy was coming to Jennie's party, Mr. Herbert. She didn't say anything to me. She just went outside and talked to Mrs. Reilly for a minute. Then she brought Mrs. Reilly's suitcase inside, got into her car and drove off."

I stood in the pantry hall, the mail still in my hand, and looked outside, through the screen door, first at Maureen and then at Erin and Jennie, who were hovering over something in one of the flower beds.

"I'm sorry, Mr. Herbert. I didn't mean to make any trouble for you or for Jennie or for Nancy. Miss Reilly just asked me who was coming to Jennie's party, and I told her."

I turned away from the scene in the backyard and faced Loretta. "I know that, Loretta. You didn't do anything wrong. You just answered a question. But Kathleen's obviously making a statement about Nancy."

I wondered what I should do, but I couldn't think of anything.

"Well…so be it," I said finally, as much to myself as to Loretta. "If Kathleen doesn't want to be in the same room with Nancy, she doesn't have to be. She can stay away forever as far as I'm concerned."

"Yes, Mr. Herbert," Loretta quietly agreed.

I picked up my briefcase and tried to smile at her. "Loretta, we have a little girl out there who's really looking forward to her fourth birthday party, and I don't know about you, but I'll be damned if anyone's going to get in the way of that. What do you say?"

"Yes, Mr. Herbert," Loretta replied, nodding in dutiful agreement.

"Great. I'll see you in a few minutes after I change my clothes. And Loretta?"

"Yes, Mr. Herbert?"

"Forget about Kathleen. It doesn't matter because she doesn't matter."

I went out into the front hall and started to go upstairs to change.

Maybe Mom was right, I thought as I climbed the stairs. *Maybe Nancy's being here is going to be too much for some people to take.*

I reached the top of the stairs and crossed the hall to my bedroom.

"Tough shit," I said out loud as I opened the bedroom door. "Tough shit."

Eighty-seven

When I went back outside after changing my clothes, I found Erin and Jennie sitting at the picnic table with Maureen and John, Jennie feverishly coloring in one of her coloring books, John still happily camped on Maureen's lap. I walked past them on my way to get the grill and considered bringing up Kathleen's departure, but decided that probably wasn't very smart.

The grill hadn't been used since last summer and was covered with grime, so I wiped it down with wet paper towels to restore it to a reasonable level of cleanliness. I then brought the lawn chairs and snack tables out from the garage. Like the grill, they hadn't been used since last summer and were dusty and full of cobwebs. Realizing they were beyond the reach of wet paper towels, I uncoiled the hose and proceeded to wash away a year's worth of neglect, regretting that I hadn't done all this over the weekend.

By the time I finished, it was almost five o'clock and time to pick up Nancy at the Huntington railroad station. She had said she was going to leave work early so she could catch the four-ten out of Penn Station, which got her into Huntington at five-sixteen, so I had just enough time to put away the hose, wash up and drive to the station. As I was coiling the hose, I wondered what, if anything, I should say to Maureen about where I was going. If I told her I was going to pick up Nancy, I left myself open to a response that might not be good for Jennie to hear. But if I said nothing, I could avoid that possibility, at least for now, and by the time I got back, my parents and the Claytons would be at the house, which hopefully would encourage Maureen to keep her opinions to herself. I decided to say nothing.

I went inside to wash my hands and face, then got into my car and began to back out of the driveway. As I pulled past the picnic table, Jennie looked up from her crayoning with a look of confusion and concern.

"Where are you going, Daddy?" she called out.

"I'll see you in a few minutes, sweetheart."

"But where are you going?" she pressed.

Suddenly I wondered what I'd been thinking. How could I have been so stupid as to think I could drive past Jennie without telling her where I was going? I was caught.

"I'm going to pick up Nancy, Jen. At the train station. I'll be right back."

Her curiosity satisfied, Jennie turned back to her coloring book. Maureen and Erin looked up at me, but neither of them made a comment. I closed the car window and continued to back down the driveway. I felt like maybe, just maybe, I had dodged a bullet.

I arrived at the station just as the eastbound five-sixteen was pulling in on the south track. I parked in a spot where Nancy could see my car, and within seconds of my arrival, hundreds of tired-looking men and women started to spill onto the north platform and into the parking area from the pedestrian bridge that crossed over the tracks. I saw Nancy standing on the curb at the base of the pedestrian bridge, looking out over the swarm of waiting cars. I gave the horn two quick toots to get her attention, and she turned in my direction, as did fifty or sixty other people. As soon as she saw me, she began to make her way over to the car. I met her at the passenger side, gave her a quick kiss and opened the door for her. She put a shopping bag on the floor behind her seat and got in.

"How are you?" I asked when I was back in the car.

"Hot."

"No air conditioning on the train again?"

"No, there was air conditioning. Just too many people inside and too hot outside to make much of a difference."

"I'm sorry. Other than that, how was your day?" I looked into my side view mirror and prepared to pull away from the curb.

"It was good. But can we sit here for a minute while I put on some fresh makeup and try to cool off?"

"Sure. Although you look pretty good to me. Hot and sticky maybe, but good."

Nancy shot me a look as she pulled down the visor on her side and flipped up the mirror cover. "Is Jennie excited about her party?"

"She sure is."

"Is everybody there already?"

"Not when I left. Just Maureen and Erin Reilly. My folks were supposed to come around five-fifteen, and Beth and Dave said they'd try to arrive by five-thirty."

Nancy finished applying the last of her lipstick, rolled her lips together a few times and then blotted them on a piece of facial tissue. "Wasn't Kathleen supposed to come too?" she asked.

I looked at Nancy for several seconds, weighing whether to tell her the truth or to make up some story to explain Kathleen's absence. I decided to tell her the truth. I hadn't lied to her yet in the eleven months we'd known one another, and I wasn't about to start now.

"She was," I said, "but she went home."

"Went home? What for?"

I looked out the windshield at the cars leaving the station and at the ones arriving for the next train. "Kathleen asked Loretta who was coming to Jennie's party. When Loretta told her you were coming, Kathleen went outside and talked to Maureen for a minute. Then she brought Maureen's suitcase inside and went home."

"Oh my God," Nancy said. Now she too was looking straight ahead out the windshield. "I told you I shouldn't have come," she said. "I knew it was a bad idea when you invited me, and now look what's happened. I don't belong here, John. Not at your house. Not with the Reillys. Not now. Oh, shit!"

I reached across the seat and gently turned her face towards me. "First of all," I said softly, "calm down."

Nancy nodded in agreement at first, but then shook her head from side to side in exasperation and mild panic.

"Calm down," I repeated.

Nancy inhaled, held her breath and then released it.

"And second," I continued, "you belong here as much as anyone. You've seen how Jennie's latched onto you the last few months. You know she's becoming attached to you. She wants you here. Believe me. And I want you here. Nothing else matters, Nan. Nothing."

"I'm scared, John. I was uncomfortable enough meeting Maureen Reilly for the first time without this happening. But now…" Her voice trailed off, and she turned away from me. "How am I supposed to meet this woman knowing her daughter refuses to be in the same room with me?"

"You just be you. That's all you do. If Maureen Reilly has a problem with you, that's too damn bad. The important thing is we're together, and you're here for Jennie's party. I'll be with you every second. I told you I'd protect you, and I will. I promise."

Eighty-eight

By the time Nancy and I arrived, my folks and the Claytons were already in the backyard with Maureen and Erin. My father had parked in the driveway, so instead of driving around the back of the house to the garage, I parked behind him. We got out of the car, and as Nancy tried to smooth out her skirt, I reached behind the passenger seat to retrieve her shopping bag, which contained Jennie's present. When Nancy was satisfied that she was as wrinkle-free as she was going to be, I took her hand, and we walked down the driveway to the back yard.

As we came around the corner of the house, I saw my parents talking with Beth and Erin, Maureen in one of the lawn chairs with John, and Dave playing tag with Jennie.

My mother saw us first. "Here they are," she called out to no one in particular and everyone in general. "We thought you two had gotten lost."

"Nancy's train was a few minutes late," I lied.

"Hello, Nancy," my mother said. "How are you?"

"I'm fine, Mrs. Herbert. And you?"

"Hi, Nan," my father interrupted, extending his hand. "Good to see you."

"Hello," Beth chimed in cheerily before Nancy could respond.

"Hi, Beth. How are you?"

Now it was my turn to interrupt. "Nan, let me make a couple of introductions. This is Erin Reilly, Peg's youngest sister."

"Hi, Nancy," Erin replied, extending her hand. "It's nice to meet you."

"It's nice to meet you, Erin."

"And this is Maureen Reilly," I continued, gently pulling Nancy away from Erin and over to Maureen, "Peg's mom."

"Hello, Mrs. Reilly," Nancy said, quite warmly, I thought.

"Hello," Maureen responded flatly. She made eye contact with Nancy for a second or two and then turned her attention back to John, while Nancy and I stood awkwardly in front of her. "Forgive me for not getting up," Maureen added finally, "but I have this big beautiful boy on my lap, don't I, little fella?"

Nancy and I forced a smile and were about to turn away when Jennie came running across the lawn, arms spread to give Nancy a hug. "Nancy! Nancy! You came to my party!"

"Hi, Jennie. How are you?" Nancy replied, getting down on one knee to receive her hug. "Happy birthday! Are you really four years old?"

"I am," Jennie confirmed, disengaging from the hug and nodding seriously. "Did you bring me a present?"

"You know you're not supposed to ask that, Jennie," I reminded her.

"I sure did," Nancy replied, ignoring my reprimand, "and I think you're going to love it."

"Can I open it now?"

"Well, maybe we should leave that up to Daddy."

"Can I, Daddy? Please!"

"Nancy just got here, honey. Give her a chance to sit down and cool off. Then we'll open presents, okay?"

Before Jennie could answer, Dave came from behind her, scooped her up in his arms, and in the midst of her squealing extended his hand to Nancy.

"Hi, Nan. Good to see you."

"Hi, Dave. Good to see you too. Looks like you've got your hands full."

"Only until I put this squealing piggy into a garbage can. Then I'm going to grab a drink."

"No, Uncle Dave," cried Jennie, now upside down and over his shoulder. "No! Put me down!"

"Hey, pal," Dave said to me as he started to walk towards the garbage cans. "How're you doing?"

"Doing okay, buddy, and I'll join you in that drink after you get rid of your load there."

With the introductions over and the potentially worst part of the evening behind us, Nancy and I went over to the picnic table to get something to drink. My father had already poured white wines for Beth and my mother and had just finished making a rum and Coke for Erin.

"Nancy, what can I get for you?" he asked as he handed Erin her drink.

"I'll take a scotch, Bill. On the rocks, please."

"I'll take an ice water, Bill," Maureen said, almost simultaneously.

"I'm sorry," Nancy said, immediately flustered. "I thought you were talking to me."

"I was," my father replied. "Just let me get Maureen her ice water, and then I'll get you your scotch."

"I got it, Pop," I said, seeing that Nancy was now both embarrassed and nervous. I reached across him for the bottle of J & B. "You take care of the ice water, and I'll take care of Nancy."

I poured some scotch into two rocks glasses, filled each to the top with ice and handed one to Nancy.

"Well, that was awkward, wasn't it?" Nancy whispered as she took a sip of her drink.

"Don't be silly," I said. "It was nothing. Don't even think about it."

Nancy smiled, but I could tell she was unconvinced.

At that moment we were standing at the end of the picnic table, me facing Nancy, Nancy with her back to Maureen Reilly. My mother, Beth and Erin were chatting, and my father was pouring a bourbon for Dave. Seeing that we were alone and unobserved, I reached out to Nancy and stroked her arm. But as I did, I saw Maureen looking at us and at my hand on Nancy's bare skin. Her eyes were like burning coals.

In an instant I became aware of all that she had seen in the last few minutes. She had seen Jennie run over to Nancy when we arrived. She had seen the way Jennie hugged Nancy, and she had seen the joy on Jennie's face. And now she was seeing me with Nancy, communicating more with my eyes and my touch than with words. Maureen Reilly was not a happy woman, and I understood why. Nancy Charlton was here, her daughter was not, and her daughter's husband and little girl were making the transition from what had been to what could be.

"Why don't we all grab a chair and see if anybody brought Jennie something for her birthday?" I suggested in an attempt to dispel the tension that had appeared out of nowhere.

"Sounds good to me," my father agreed.

"I'm ready," Dave said, "but maybe Jennie's tired and wants to go to bed."

"No, Uncle Dave. I'm not tired. I'm not tired at all!" Jennie protested, and as if to emphasize her position on the matter, the birthday girl promptly abandoned her playmate and ran over to where the rest of us were assembling on the grass.

Jennie opened her presents from Maureen and Erin first, then Dave and Beth's, and then one from Loretta. When it was Nancy's turn to give Jennie her present, Jennie stood in front of her, hands clasped tightly together, rigid with anticipation. Nancy reached into the shopping bag, pulled out a large wrapped package and handed it to Jennie.

"Now be very careful when you open it," she warned, "because what's inside is very breakable."

Jennie nodded and placed the package on the grass so she could open it sitting down. She undid the bow, pulled off the ribbon and tore away the paper. Then she slid her fingers under the top flap of the box and gave the flap a serious tug so she could see what was inside.

"It's beautiful," she cried out." It's beautiful!" She leaped up and gave Nancy a hug.

"What did you get, Jennie?" my mother asked.

"A piggy bank! A great big pink piggy bank!"

"Let me help you get it out of the box," Nancy said as she got up from her chair and knelt down next to Jennie. "You hold onto the box, and I'll take the pig out."

Jennie did as she was told, and a second later Nancy presented her with a truly beautiful piggy bank—glazed ceramic, deep pink, with a warm smile painted on the face. And big—fifteen inches long, six or seven inches wide and at least nine inches high. Jennie loved it.

After Jennie had opened her presents from my parents and me, I lit the grill to get the charcoal ready for our barbecue, and we ate shortly after seven. When dinner was over, my mother brought out dessert—a four-inch-high bittersweet chocolate cake with five candles, one for good luck—and we sang "Happy Birthday" as she placed the cake in front of Jennie.

"Time to make a wish, sweetheart," I said, forgetting that Jennie had never done this before.

"Why do I need to make a wish, Daddy?"

"Everybody does on their birthday."

"Why?"

"Well… if you make a wish on your birthday and blow out all the candles in one breath, and if you don't tell anyone what you wished for, your wish is supposed to come true."

"What should I wish for?"

I thought of Peg.

"Daddy?"

Jennie's voice brought me back from where my thoughts had taken me. "You can wish for something you don't have but would like to have," I said finally, "or you can wish for something nice for someone else."

Jennie nodded and stared at the candles, deep in thought, and then she closed her eyes.

I looked at her from across the table, her eyes closed tightly, the light of the candles reflecting off her face, and I wondered what she was wishing for. Was she wishing that her mother were here? Was she wishing her mother would come back to her? Or was she just wishing for something not among tonight's presents? But before I could guess at a probable answer, Jennie opened her eyes and, with a powerful sweeping blow, blew out all her candles.

The evening came to an unexpectedly quick close moments later, just after we had finished cutting the cake, when Erin got up from the table and announced that she needed to call a taxi to take her to the train station. She wanted to catch an eight twenty-five train into New York, she said, so she could catch the last bus out to New Jersey. We finished our cake, stood to say our good-byes, and within minutes everyone had gone their separate ways—Erin to the curb to wait for her cab, Beth and Dave across the street to their house, Jennie, John, Loretta and my mother inside—leaving my father, Maureen, Nancy and me standing on the lawn in uncomfortable silence.

"I'm going inside to see if your wife needs help putting the children to bed," Maureen said to my father.

"Tell her I'll be in in a minute, would you?" he replied.

Maureen nodded and walked towards the back door.

"It was nice meeting you, Mrs. Reilly," Nancy said to Maureen's back.

"It was nice meeting you too," Maureen answered, several seconds too late and without turning around. She went up the back steps, opened the screen door and was gone.

"Well, Nance, it's been fun," my father said, ignoring Maureen's abrupt departure. "And your pig was certainly the hit of the evening."

We said good night, and Nancy and I walked down the driveway to my car.

"That wasn't too bad, was it?" I asked as I pulled my door closed.

"Could have been better," Nancy answered sadly. "But I guess it could have been worse."

I put the key into the ignition and looked over at her. She was deep in thought.

"What are you thinking?" I asked.

"I'm thinking you haven't heard the last from Maureen Reilly."

Eighty-nine

The ringing didn't stop. It just went on and on, penetrating deeper and deeper into my brain. "What's that noise?" I wondered groggily. "Why doesn't it stop? Please... make it stop."

Finally, I opened the eye that wasn't buried in the pillow. I looked across the bed and located the source of the incessant ringing on the night table—my alarm clock, set for seven o'clock four and a half hours ago and now dutifully bringing me back from the world of darkness to the world of light.

I stretched out an arm, dropped a heavy hand on the off button and tried to summon the energy to get out of bed. I had taken Nancy back to her apartment after Jennie's party, and I hadn't gotten home until two-thirty. Now I was faced with the unwelcome prospect of getting through the day on barely four and a half hours of sleep.

I rolled over onto my back and saw sunlight streaming in around the edges of the window shades. I sighed. At least the day was sunny. I lay on my back for another minute, then threw back the sheet and the coverlet. I swung my legs over the side of the bed. The alarm clock now showed five minutes after seven. I sat on the edge of the bed and reflected for a moment how time just keeps moving. We may not be ready to take advantage of it and put it to use, but it doesn't care. It just keeps moving and expects us to either fall in step with it or let it go on without us. Until it disappears.

On that cheery note, I put on my bathrobe and walked across the upstairs landing to the bathroom. I showered, shaved, brushed my teeth and combed my hair, and then went back to my bedroom to get dressed. I had a meeting at nine-thirty with our advertising agency, so I decided to wear one of my better suits, a gray pinstripe, with a light blue shirt and maroon tie. I put on some cologne, filled my pockets with my handkerchief, comb, wallet, keys, pen and pencil, put my jacket over my arm and opened my bedroom door. I was as ready as I could be to face the coming day.

As I came out of my bedroom, I was suddenly aware of someone else on the landing. With a start, I realized Maureen Reilly was standing at the top of the steps next to the railing, partially blocking access to the stairs, arms folded across her chest.

"Whoa. You scared me for a minute," I said, exhaling deeply. "I didn't expect to see you. Good morning."

For a second she said nothing. Then she took two steps forward, bringing her to within two feet of me. Sensing something was wrong, I stopped and waited for her to speak.

"I want to talk to you," she hissed in a loud whisper.

I was taken aback both by the tone of her voice and by her almost threatening body language.

"Sure," I replied, "but do we have to talk here, or can we talk downstairs while I grab a cup of coffee?"

"I want to talk to you here because I don't want Jennie or John to hear what I have to say."

I took a deep breath and tried to keep my irritation from showing. "Okay. We'll talk here. What's up?"

Her eyes bore into mine, and her mouth worked silently as she prepared to speak. Finally words came. "Don't you ever, ever, bring that woman into my daughter's house again," she said. "Do you hear me?"

"What are you talking about?" I stammered.

"You know what I'm talking about," she spat. "You know damn well what I'm talking about. I don't care what you do with that woman anywhere else, but you will not bring her into my daughter's house ever again. Do you understand me?"

I stood perfectly still and stared at her, trying to absorb what she had just said. But as I did, I felt a darkness come over me, almost as if someone were pouring thick black oil over my head. And as the darkness enveloped me, I began to think the most frightening thoughts I had ever thought in my life. I found myself literally taking the physical measure of Maureen Reilly, realizing as if for the first time how small and frail she was, knowing that in an instant I could drop my jacket to the floor, grab her by the neck with both hands, lift her over the railing and drop her to the floor below. I found myself measuring the distance between her and me, calculating how quickly and from what direction I would have to strike in order to ensure that I could get to her in one sweeping motion before she could avoid me.

Then as quickly as the darkness had appeared, it began to recede, leaving me seething with rage, gulping for air. "Who the hell do you think you are to talk to me like that?" I screamed when I was finally able to speak.

My response had no effect on her. She stood where she was, immobile, eyes blazing with hatred.

"Let me tell you something, Maureen," I continued, taking a half step towards her, shaking uncontrollably. "I love 'that woman,' as you call her, and I'll bring her to my house—note I said *my* house—any goddamn time I please. And let me tell you something else while I'm at it. I loved Peg more than anything else in this world, and I respected her in every way I could while she was alive. But she's dead, and there's nothing you or I can do about that other than get over it as best we can and move on. Oh, one more thing. For the record, this house used to be our house. Peg's and mine. Not just Peg's. But now… it's mine. Just mine. Do you understand that?"

I stepped around her and went down the stairs two at a time, leaving her on the landing, ignorant of how close she had come to violence.

I walked into the kitchen from the center hall and found Loretta standing between Jennie and John, Jennie at the dinette table, John in his high chair. She had a hand on each of their heads, smoothing their hair, calming their fear, and she was facing me, prepared, it seemed, to protect her little charges from their father if necessary. It was obvious they had heard everything.

I walked over to Jennie and gave her a kiss on the cheek. Then I turned to John, who was looking up at me wide-eyed, mouth open, and gave him a kiss on the forehead.

"Good-bye, guys," I said in a voice hoarse from shouting and from anger. "I'll see you tonight."

Neither child made a sound.

I looked at Loretta. "I'm sorry," I mumbled. She didn't reply.

I turned away from the three of them and went out the back door.

I was unable to think clearly for the first twenty minutes of my drive to the office, but as my head cleared, I remembered the thought I had had one winter night almost six months ago. About the swimmer who looks back at the shore he's left behind and is surprised and frightened to see how far away it is.

My relationship with my parents had become painfully strained because of my relationship with Nancy, and except for Dave, all of my friends were gone. And now any connection with Peg's mother had been irreparably damaged, if not destroyed.

The shore was very far away indeed, I realized sadly.

Ninety

The house was empty and quiet Sunday afternoon, November 1st, the children still with my parents and Loretta not yet back from her day off in Brooklyn. I had been trying to reach Nancy all day. I dialed her number for what must have been the tenth time and decided to count how many times her phone rang. On the twenty-first ring, I gave up. I looked at the clock. It was five after five.

I'd started calling her shortly after nine, well before she would have been out doing her errands, and I hadn't gotten an answer then. I knew she wasn't visiting her parents because her car wasn't in their driveway or in front of their house, and she would have let me know if she were coming to Huntington. So I knew some of the places she wasn't, but I didn't know where she was. All I knew for certain was either she wasn't home or she wasn't answering her phone.

I sat at my desk and stared at the neatly piled, squared stacks of unopened mail, bills waiting to be paid and paid bills waiting to be filed. I picked up an envelope with a return address I didn't recognize. I found my letter opener, partially covered by the pile of unopened mail, and slid it under the flap. I had the envelope half open before I realized I didn't care what was inside. All I cared about was being able to talk to Nancy. I put the half-opened envelope back on its pile, squared it with the others and looked at the clock again. It was seven after five.

This is ridiculous, I thought, exasperated. *I can't be obsessive like this. If I reach her, I reach her. If I don't, I don't. That's all there is to it.*

I leaned back in my chair and looked out the window into the back yard. Although it was almost dark, the sky at the horizon still glowed a brilliant orange and was streaked with dark bands of cloud, precursors to the rain predicted for Monday. Most of the leaves were off the trees, and they now covered the lawn and flowerbeds like a thick brown blanket. The yard looked abandoned and uninviting, and the sight of the picnic table and benches and lawn chairs all covered with leaves and pine needles made me feel lonelier than I already was.

I turned away from the window. In spite of my words of self-encouragement a few seconds ago, I was uneasy. I had the same feeling I always had at night when I was alone, but worse this afternoon because I couldn't reach Nancy, and because I thought I might know why.

"I know what I'll do," I said out loud. "I'll take a shower, get dressed and give Nancy one more call. Then, if I still can't reach her, I'll drive over to her apartment and make sure she's all right."

I pushed back my chair and went upstairs. By ten minutes of six I was back at my desk. I sat down and dialed Nancy's number. The uneasiness I'd felt earlier had by now turned into a sharp sense of urgency. She had to answer the phone this time. She had to.

Her phone rang. Once. Twice. Five times. Ten times. I couldn't hang up. She would answer. I knew she would. But her phone kept ringing. Twelve times. Fifteen times. And then, Nancy's voice.

"Hello?"

"My God," I said with a sigh of relief. "Where have you been? I've been calling you all day. I thought maybe something happened to you. Are you all right?"

"I'm okay."

"Where were you?"

"Here."

"In your apartment?"

"Yes."

"Why didn't you answer the phone then? I've been worried sick."

I waited a moment for a response before repeating my question. "Why didn't you answer the phone, Nan? You must've known it was me calling."

After what seemed like an eternity, I heard her exhale sharply into the receiver. "I didn't answer the phone because I knew it was you, and I didn't want to talk to you."

"Why? What have I done?"

"Oh God, John. How can you ask me that after last night?"

"Look, I know you were upset, and I don't blame you, but why wouldn't you want to talk to me?"

"The truth is, John, I'm not even sure I ever want to see you again."

I closed my eyes as a wave of fear started to roll over me. "Was last night that terrible?" I asked.

"Yes, it was."

I tried not to let the fear overtake me, but my eyes began to flood with tears.

"I can't take any more hurt, John. I've done my best to listen to you, to console you, to be there for you. I've done everything I know how to do to make you happy. To give you your life back. To make you love me enough to be happy again. But I've failed. Last night proved that to me. And I can't live with that kind of failure. If I do, it'll destroy me."

"What are you saying? That we're through? That it's over between us?"

Now Nancy was crying too. "I don't know. What I do know is I've spent more than a year of my life with you. But last night, for the first time, I felt like maybe all I've done is waste a year of my life with you."

"How can you say that?"

"John, listen to me. Last night was supposed to be a fun evening. We were going to take the kids out trick-or-treating, drop them off at your parents' and then go out for dinner. Remember? But when I get to your house—at five o'clock just like we planned, so we can take Jennie and John out before it gets too late—who's already there? Your parents. I tried not to get upset—even though you and I were going to take the kids out alone—because I know how much your folks love the kids, but then I sit in the kitchen like a bump on a log while your mother gets Jennie and John into their Halloween costumes. She doesn't ask me to help. In fact, in some way I can't put my finger on, she makes it clear to me she wants to dress the kids herself. So I sit there while you and your father talk about God knows what. Watching. Waiting. Wishing I could sink into a crack in the floor instead of feeling as out of place as I did. Hold on. I need a Kleenex."

I could hear her blowing her nose. "You still there?" she asked a moment later.

"I'm still here."

"Then we go out trick-or-treating. The six of us. You hold Jennie's hand. Your mother and father hold John's hands. And I follow from behind. John, you have no idea how left out that made me feel."

"Nan, I'm sorry. I…"

"Wait. I'm not to the worst part yet. Not even close. So I trundle along behind the five of you, and then we come back to the house. Your folks haven't talked to me since I arrived, so I think maybe they'll stay for a few minutes. But no. They take the kids, still in their Halloween costumes, and they head for home. I tell myself, well, that makes sense, I guess. It's late, the kids haven't had dinner, and your folks want to get them home before they get too hungry or cranky.

"Now you and I are alone. Trick-or-treating was disappointing, but we still have the rest of the evening to look forward to. I go to the bathroom, and when I come out, what do I see? I see you, sitting at the dinette table, your head in your hands. Crying. I ask what's the matter, and you say you're crying because Peg wasn't there to see how cute the kids looked in their costumes. And then, then…" Nancy's words were cut off by a sob. "Then you tell me how messed up your life is, and how you don't know where to turn.

"My God, John. Do you realize how that makes me feel? After I've been there for you whenever you needed me for the last fourteen months? I've been 'where you turn.' I've been the person you've turned to. I never expected you to forget Peg. I never expected you to stop loving her. But I did expect that one day I'd be able to make your life good again.

I did expect that one day, one day, you'd love me enough to feel good about being alive. But you don't love me that much. That's why I left last night. And that's why I say I've failed. So yeah, I'm through. Through with you. Through with your pain. If I haven't been able to make a difference in your life after all these months, after all we've done together, then I'll never be able to. Never. And if I can't make a difference in your life, then I'm wasting my time and my life. And I won't do that."

I knew I had to say something, but my mind wouldn't go into gear. I couldn't formulate words, let alone thoughts. Yet I knew I had to, or Nancy would hang up, and I would lose her forever.

"Nan, listen to me," I said. "Please. For just a few minutes. That's all I ask. Listen to me, and don't hang up. Okay?"

Nancy didn't reply, but I decided to interpret the silence as a yes, albeit maybe only a temporary one.

"First, I'm sorry I made you feel left out and unimportant to me and the kids last night, because nothing could be further from the truth. I just don't realize sometimes how what I do or say affects you. But please, please know I didn't mean to hurt you. I would never do anything to hurt you. You have to know that."

"It doesn't matter. You did hurt me, and it's not the first time, either," Nancy interjected.

"I know. But all I can say is forgive me, be patient with me, and tell me when I hurt you. As far as crying over Peg is concerned, I wasn't crying last night because I missed Peg; I was crying because she wasn't there to see her little girl and her little boy all dressed up for Halloween. I know that sounds stupid, Nan, but they looked so cute, and all I could think of was that Peg missed out on the chance to see them. Just like she's going to miss out on seeing them open presents Christmas morning or hunt for Easter eggs or open their birthday presents, or putting them to bed at night or waking them up in the morning. She won't see or do any of those things, and last night that thought struck me really hard, and I cried. For Peg. Not for me.

"But you need to know, Nan, that there are still times when the memory of Peg washes over me like a wave. And when that happens, when the wave hits, it brings me to my knees. That doesn't mean I don't love you; it only means I still love Peg and still miss her."

"I understand," Nancy replied, "and I know sometimes the memories are more than you can handle. But I don't want to be a witness to that anymore, John. When we first started dating, I could watch you cry, and I could listen to how wonderful your life was with Peg and how much you missed her. But things have changed. Now I'm in love with you. Now when I see you crying because you lost Peg, I feel like a fool. Like you're using me. And I can't live with that. I love you too much to hear you tell me you love another woman—even if she's dead—or to hear you tell me how terrible your life is without her. Can you understand that?"

"Yes, I can," I said softly.

Neither of us spoke for almost a minute.

"Can I see you tonight?" I asked when I could bear the silence no longer.

"No."

"Please, Nan. Don't say no. Nan? Don't leave me, Nan. Tell me when I screw up—what I need to do to be better—but don't leave me.

"Nan? Are you there?"

"I'm here," Nancy answered with a heavy sigh.

"Can I come over? Can I see you tonight?"

"Yes," she said finally, sniffling into the phone, her voice so low I could barely hear her. "Just give me a chance to shower and change. I've been crying all day, and I'm a mess."

I closed my eyes in wordless thanksgiving before answering her. "I'll see you in a little while."

I hung up the phone, leaned back in my chair and thought about how close I had come to losing my second chance.

Ninety-one

Dinner was over, and the two of them stood side by side at the kitchen sink Thursday night, December 17th, Shirley up to her wrists in hot soapy water, Nancy waiting, towel in hand, for the next pot to dry. The kitchen was cozy and warm, and the only sounds in the house were the murmur of the television in the family room as Nancy's father watched the evening news and the clanking of pots in the sink as Shirley scrubbed them.

"So tell me again what your plans are for Christmas," Shirley said as she rinsed the suds off a pot and handed it to Nancy.

"I already told you, Mom," Nancy replied tiredly. "I'm going to help John put up his tree on Christmas Eve after the kids are in bed and spend the night at his house. I'll watch the kids open their presents Christmas morning, and then I'll come over here to spend the rest of the day with you and Dad while John takes the kids over to his parents' house to celebrate Christmas with them."

"Why's he waiting until Christmas Eve to put up his tree?" Shirley asked. "Why doesn't he do it now? Why is he waiting until the last minute?"

"Because Jennie and John think Santa brings the tree. John has to put the tree up Christmas Eve after they go to bed."

"John's too little to know the difference. He's only two."

"Jennie isn't too little to know the difference. She's four."

"Well, it seems silly to me."

Nancy bent down to put a pot in the cupboard next to the sink. Shirley handed her the last pot to dry and began to wipe off the counter.

"Where are you going to sleep?" Shirley asked, as she pushed the last few remaining crumbs into the sink with her sponge.

"When? Tonight?"

"No, not tonight. Christmas Eve. You'll have little children with you, you know."

"I know that, Mom. John and I have already discussed that."

"And?"

"Jesus, Mom. If you must know, I'm going to sleep on the couch in his living room."

"I'm sorry, Nan. I know that's none of my business, but the last few months… seems like all I do is worry about you. And John."

"And John?"

"You know your father and I think he's wonderful, but…"

"But what?" Nancy asked. She sat down at the kitchen table behind Shirley.

"I'm scared, Nan. Scared of what will happen to you if things don't work out between you and John. You're so involved. Too involved, if you ask me."

"Which I didn't."

Shirley turned away from the sink to face Nancy, wringing her hands in the dish towel Nancy had left on the counter top. Her face reflected the torment she felt inside.

"I know you didn't," Shirley said quietly. "But when I hear you're going to spend Christmas Eve with John—decorating his tree for his kids—and you're going to be with him Christmas morning when the kids wake up and open their presents, all I can think of is that husbands and wives, mothers and fathers, do that. Not a couple who are just dating. And I can't help but wonder what happens to you if something goes wrong between you two."

Shirley turned back towards the sink and resumed wiping the counter top she had just finished wiping a few moments before. "Do you think John is going to ask you to marry him someday?" Shirley asked, the sponge in her hand going back and forth over the same spot.

Nancy pondered the question for several seconds, knowing the answer she wanted to give, but couldn't.

"I don't know, Mom," she said finally. "He might. He might not."

This outward acknowledgement of her inner uncertainty was at this moment suddenly more than Nancy could handle. She needed to escape.

"I gotta go, Mom," she announced, and she stood up from the table. "It's after ten, and I'm tired. I'll call you tomorrow from work. Okay?"

She quickly took her coat out of the hall closet and looked into the family room at her father, now asleep in his chair.

"Say good night to Dad for me when he wakes up, will you?"

Shirley nodded, and through the beam of light from the kitchen window she watched her daughter hurry down the driveway to her car.

Ninety-two

The clock on my mantel showed five minutes after one, but as far as Nancy and I were concerned, it was still Christmas Eve, and Christmas morning would not arrive until we woke up a few hours from now.

"Beautiful tree, isn't it?" I asked, sitting on the edge of the sofa, my hands around a bottle of Budweiser.

Nancy leaned forward and slipped her arm under and around mine. "Sure is," she agreed. "I think it's probably the most beautiful Christmas tree I've ever seen. Certainly the most beautiful one I ever helped decorate," she added with a laugh.

I touched my bottle to hers and tipped it towards her in a toast. "To you. For all your help tonight. I could never have gotten this done without you. Thank you."

Nancy touched her bottle to mine, and we settled back into the sofa, side by side, to admire the results of our labor over the past four and a half hours.

The tree was almost ten feet tall when I bought it, which meant I had to take a foot off the top and six inches off the bottom to stand it up in my living room. Almost perfectly shaped, the tree was at least seven feet in diameter at the base and now stood in the corner of the living room adorned with red, blue, green, silver and gold balls of all different sizes. Each ball reflected the light from hundreds of multi-colored tree lights, as did thousands of pieces of silver tinsel as they moved back and forth ever so slightly in unseen air currents.

"I hope Jennie and John like it," Nancy said.

"They'll love it. Believe me. They'll absolutely love it."

"Did you ever wonder when you were a kid," Nancy asked, "how Santa Claus was able to set up your tree and millions of other trees and bring your toys and millions of other toys and set up train sets and doll houses all over the world, all in one night?"

"Not when I was as young as Jennie. When I got a little older, though —old enough to be suspicious—then I wondered. I asked my mother how it was possible, and her answer was perfect."

"What did she say?"

"She said, 'that's the magic of Christmas.' And the funny thing is, I still believe in the magic of Christmas. To me... Christmas has always been a really special time of year. A time when dreams come true. No matter how impossible they may seem. Silly, I guess, but that's the feeling I always get this time of year."

I took a sip of my beer. "I remember as a little boy always wanting some special thing for Christmas—a certain truck or a pair of cowboy pistols or a train set; wanting whatever it was so badly I couldn't imagine life after Christmas without it. And almost always... oh hell, what am I saying?... always, that special thing would be under the tree Christmas morning. Santa always came through." I shrugged. "I guess that's why I feel Christmas is a time when dreams come true."

"But dreams don't always come true at Christmas, do they?" Nancy said quietly.

"No, they don't. But they do sometimes."

Nancy stared at the tree, her thoughts somewhere far away.

Ninety-three

Nancy stared at the half empty coffee mug in front of her. Shirley stared at Nancy from across the kitchen table. Nancy had arrived shortly before noon to spend Christmas day with her parents, but as soon as she had come in the back door, Shirley had known something was wrong. She had poured a cup of coffee for Nancy and herself, but now, having run out of small talk, the two of them sat in silence.

"What's wrong, Nan?" Shirley finally asked, unable to avoid the obvious any longer.

"Nothing's wrong, Mom," Nancy replied, without looking up.

"I think something is wrong. What's the matter?"

Nancy raised her head and looked across the table at Shirley. "John didn't ask me to marry him," she said flatly.

"I kind of assumed that."

"I promised myself I wouldn't get my hopes up. And I was okay… until he gave me my Christmas present."

"What happened?"

Nancy shivered even though the kitchen was warm. "We were sitting on his sofa last night looking at the tree, and he was saying that Christmas was a time when dreams come true. They don't always come true, I said, and he said, 'no, they don't, but they do sometimes.' I was wondering what he meant by that, if he meant what I hoped he meant, when he got up and went over to the tree… and came back with this beautifully wrapped little box with a big red bow on it and gave it to me with that smile of his. 'Merry Christmas,' was all he said. And at that moment, I knew he was going to ask me to marry him. I just knew it. I knew he had guessed my Christmas wish, and he was going to make it happen. Anyway, my hands were shaking so badly I almost couldn't undo the ribbon, but I did, and when I got the paper off, sure enough, it was a ring box."

Nancy's eyes filled with tears. "So I open the box, and what do I see? An engagement ring? No! I see a peridot! 'Your birthstone,' he says. As if I didn't know."

Nancy shook her head sadly and wiped at her tears with her fingertips. "It is beautiful," she continued, "but it's not an engagement ring. And he didn't ask me to marry him, and now I'm wondering if he ever will."

"Nan, I'm sorry," Shirley said, reaching across the table to take one of Nancy's hands in hers. "I wish I knew what to say, but I don't."

"There is nothing to say, Mom," Nancy replied with a deep sigh. "John and I have been going out for almost a year and a half. We see each other three, four times a week, every week. We talk on the phone every night we're not together. You know the kind of relationship we have. So I have to think that when a man and a woman have been as... intimate... as John and I have been, and then the man gives the woman a ring—on Christmas Eve of all nights—and the ring's not an engagement ring... he's telling her something. John must've known I'd think an engagement ring was in that box, so given there wasn't, I've got to assume he was making a statement—telling me this is as far as we go. And if I'm right... well, I can't stay with him anymore."

"What are you saying?"

"I'm saying even though I love John and want him in my life forever, I can't stand the pain of being so close to him and yet so far away. I'm going to leave him. That's what I'm saying."

"You don't mean that."

"I do. And you know what? You were right. You told me there were rules we all had to follow. Rules you just didn't break. But I didn't listen. I thought John and I were special. I thought we were different. I thought we could break the rules, and everything would be okay. But everything isn't okay. John's not going to marry me. Either because he's embarrassed by how his parents and his friends have reacted to us, or because he's ashamed himself at the way we've behaved."

"What are you going to do?"

"I'm supposed to go over to John's tomorrow night for dinner, and I will. But soon… very soon… I'm going to tell him it's over."

Shirley said nothing. She had no advice to offer. Her daughter was no longer a child. She was a woman who knew her own mind. And heart.

Ninety-four

"There you are," I said. I handed Nancy a J & B on the rocks. "Merry Day-After-Christmas."

We touched glasses and took a sip of our drinks. Nancy was sitting on the sofa; I was standing next to her. Both of us were looking at the tree we had so painstakingly decorated two nights before.

I turned away from the tree and looked at Nancy and marveled again at how beautiful she was. She was wearing jeans tonight, the dressy kind, and an oversized maroon turtleneck sweater. She had taken off her shoes while I was in the kitchen making our drinks, and now her feet were tucked underneath her on the sofa. She looked deliciously huggable.

I sat down and pulled her towards me. I kissed her neck, and as always, the smell of soap, shampoo and perfume washed over me. I waited for some sort of reaction, but she sat perfectly still and stared straight ahead at the tree.

"Are you okay?" I asked.

"I'm fine," Nancy answered with a quick smile but without looking at me. "Who's that singing on this record?"

"Willie Nelson," I replied uneasily.

"He's good. I like him."

"I thought you would. That's why I put him on."

Nancy continued to stare at the tree.

"Are you sure you're okay? Because you don't seem like you are."

"How do I seem?" she asked, finally facing me.

"I don't know. Aloof. Tense. Worried. Unhappy."

"Tense, worried, unhappy and… what was the other thing?"

"Aloof."

"Right. Why would I be tense, worried, unhappy and aloof?"

"I don't have a clue. We had a wonderful Christmas Eve together and a wonderful Christmas morning together. As far as I know, you had a good Christmas day with your folks and a good day today. So I have no idea why you seem the way you do, but you do."

The expression on her face was one of pain and sadness. I thought I detected a little anger too, muted but there nevertheless. We looked at one another, each of us trying to take a reading of the other, neither of us finding any answers.

A barely audible hiss of the phonograph needle sliding across a soundless track signaled the next song. A few seconds later, the sound of an acoustic guitar being finger-picked filled the living room, followed by Willie's one-in-a-million voice singing "Someone to Watch over Me."

"I love that song," I said when the track was over. "I don't know if you were listening to the words, but… they really sum up how I feel."

Nancy gave no indication she heard me. She was clearly distressed over something.

"Well, I don't know why you're not feeling happy," I said, "but hopefully I can change that."

I leaned forward and reached under the sofa. When my fingers found what I was looking for, I straightened up and handed Nancy a small box wrapped in gold embossed paper and dwarfed by a large silk silver bow. She looked at the box, expressionless for several seconds before taking it, and when she did, she did so reluctantly, almost as if she were afraid to.

"I thought you already gave me my Christmas present," Nancy said, her voice low and rough as if her throat had closed mid-sentence.

"I did."

"Then… what's this?"

"Open it," I said softly.

With trembling fingers, she carefully undid the bow loop by loop, and then she undid each of the folds of the paper. When the box was finally unwrapped, she looked at it for a long time. Then she started to cry.

Blinking back tears, she opened the lid and saw the round top of a black velvet ring box. She lifted the velvet box from the outer cardboard box, tears streaming down her cheeks onto her hands, her jeans and the sofa. When the little velvet box was finally in her hand, she gently raised its round top and saw a brilliantly sparkling diamond, its facets catching the light from the Christmas tree and reflecting that light into her eyes from a hundred different angles.

"It's beautiful," she whispered, looking first at the ring, then at me, then back at the ring. "It's absolutely beautiful."

"Will you marry me, Nancy?" I asked.

"Yes, yes, yes, yes," she gasped, and she threw herself forward and covered my face with kisses.

When she finally stopped, she took several deep breaths in an attempt to calm herself and wiped the tears from her eyes. As she did, I took the ring box from her hand, lifted the ring from it and slipped it onto her finger. She turned her hand first in one direction, then in the other, and started to cry again.

"I just realized it's a perfect fit," she exclaimed in surprise a moment later, "and so was the peridot."

"Of course."

"How did you know my ring size?"

"I slid your opal onto my pinkie one night a couple of months ago when you weren't looking and made note of how far up my finger it went. Not that tough," I added teasingly.

"A couple of months ago?"

I nodded.

Nancy looked at me, bewildered. "Why did you wait until tonight to give me this?" she asked. "And why did you give me the peridot on Christmas Eve?"

"Did you think I'd propose to you Christmas Eve?"

"Not really, but when I saw the ring box…" Nancy swallowed hard, "I thought an engagement ring was inside."

"Well, there's your answer."

"I don't understand."

I looked into those deep green eyes. "So many people get engaged on Christmas Eve. I thought I should ask you on a night that would be unique to us. That would be ours alone."

"But then why the peridot Christmas Eve? Why two rings?"

"Well… to be honest, the peridot was an afterthought. I saw it while I was looking for your engagement ring. I knew that was your birthstone, I hadn't gotten your Christmas present yet, and the peridot was beautiful. So I decided to buy it for you for Christmas."

"But didn't you realize what I would think when I saw a ring box on Christmas Eve? And then what I would think when it wasn't an engagement ring?" Nancy asked incredulously.

"What did you think?" I asked, beginning to feel less than sharp.

"I thought you had decided not to marry me, and this was your way of telling me."

I shook my head in anger at myself for not realizing something so obvious. "Nan… for months I've had no doubt in my mind that I was going to ask you to marry me. The only question was when. And then I decided I'd ask you during the Christmas holidays. Remember, I'm the guy who believes dreams come true on Christmas. My dreams, that is. Anyway, I didn't want to ask you on Christmas Eve or Christmas Day, so I picked today. But if I had thought for one minute that you would think I wasn't going to propose to you… I would've given you your ring the day I bought it."

Nancy looked at me for a long time before speaking. "You are so dumb," she said finally. "So, so dumb."

"I know I am. But were you surprised?"

"Totally."

"Are you happy?"

"Happier than I've ever been in my life."

Nancy wrapped her arms around my neck and kissed me. "I love you," she said. "I have from the moment I first saw you..."

Ninety-five

The snow is falling heavily now, and it's almost dark. Far across the open expanse of the cemetery, almost at the horizon, I can see a long line of cars, their headlights casting eerie beams through the falling snow as commuters slowly wend their way home. I've told Peg everything. Everything except the most important thing, which is really the reason I came here today. I shiver again and stamp my feet to get feeling back into my toes.

"I've asked Nancy to marry me, Peg." I pause, searching for the right words. "I feel unbelievably good about it, and I hope you will too.

"I know by some people's measure Nancy and I met too soon after you died, and now we're getting married too soon, and I know in some people's opinion she's the wrong person; but in my heart, Peg, I know they're wrong.

"I hope you know my falling in love with Nancy doesn't mean I didn't love you. To the contrary, I need you to know my falling in love with Nancy was possible only because I discovered with you how beautiful love can be.

"Marriage won't be easy for us, Peg. For lots of reasons. For one, the folks don't accept Nancy. You know how my father loved you; there's no way Nancy will ever claim a piece of his heart. And as far as Mom's concerned, her daughter's dead. For another, your mother and I had some pretty harsh words the morning after Jennie's birthday party, and we barely talk to one another now. Your sisters haven't said anything to me about that morning, but I know they're siding with your mother. All of which doesn't bode particularly well for my relationship with your side of the family. And last, all of our friends have turned away from me. Not that I blame them, I guess. They couldn't accept my getting involved with Nancy so soon after you died, so they moved on. Everyone except Dave.

"But the good news is Jennie loves Nancy. The day after I asked Nancy to marry me, I told Jennie what I had done and told her she was going to have a new mommy. Well, she clasped her hands together in front of her chest, scrunched her shoulders and jumped up and down for what must have been twenty minutes, the happiest I've seen her in a long, long time. She even asked me if she could call Nancy 'Mommy,' and I told her she could. I hope you don't mind.

"Then she asked me if she could call Nancy on the phone, so I dialed Nancy's number for her, and when Nancy answered, I told her Jennie wanted to talk to her. I gave Jennie the phone, and the first words out of her mouth were 'Hello, Mommy.' Can you believe that? She talked to Nancy for about fifteen minutes, and I think she used the word 'Mommy' at the beginning and end of every sentence. She was so happy to be able to, I guess.

"John's obviously too young to know what's happening, but Nancy thinks he's really special, so he's going be okay too.

"You never met Nancy, but I know you would have liked her. She's different from you in a lot of ways, Peg, but she's like you in that she's honest right to the core; and she's smart, and she knows what's important and what isn't.

"And she loves me. Totally and without reservation. And I love her.

"I'd be lying, Peg, if I said I didn't miss you. And I'd be lying if I said I didn't still love you. But I can't live without the kind of love you and I once shared, Peg, and I think I've found that with Nancy. Who would have thought I'd be that lucky a second time?"

I look at the frozen landscape around me. The wind rattles the bare branches of a nearby tree.

"Well... I should start to think about going home. But like I said, there were so many things I've wanted to talk to you about, and of course

I wanted to tell you about Nancy. And I feel you telling me it's okay. Thanks, sweetheart. Watch over us."

Epilogue

Ninety-six

I take a sip of my scotch and soda. My glass is almost empty, and the extra ice cubes I asked for have melted. I consider going out to the bar for a fresh drink, but I don't. I'm comfortable where I am in that hard-to-find, harder-to-stay-in zone of having had just the right amount to drink when one is able to see—and appreciate—things normally taken for granted.

Today—Saturday, August 5th, 2006—is John's wedding day. A little over three hours ago, he married Nikki Taich, the love of his life since his freshman year in college.

Only fourteen of us are here. Nancy and I, of course; Jennie and her husband of six years, Nathan; Will, our nineteen year-old son, and Amanda, our fifteen year-old daughter; Nancy's brother Don and his wife Mary; five close friends, two from Pennsylvania and three from Long Island; and Father Byrum, the rector of our church in Huntington.

No one from my side of the family is here. They weren't invited. The last time any of them spoke to Nancy or me was in 2002, at my father's funeral, and the time before that was at my mother's funeral in 1999. After twenty-four years of marriage, we think we've given them enough time to accept Nancy and have decided to move on without them.

The Reillys aren't here either, but that was John's decision. Maureen Reilly died in 2001, and three birthdays and three Christmases have now come and gone without Jennie or John receiving either a phone call or a card from Erin, Megan or Kathleen. Strange given that Maureen Reilly sued us not once but twice to make certain that she and her daughters would always be able to have contact with Peg's children.

The music is pounding, and the dance floor is filled with wildly gyrating young men and women. Our table for the moment is empty except for Father Byrum and me.

"You have much to be thankful for, John," Father Byrum says, his soft voice breaking into my reverie. "You and Nancy have raised four beautiful, wonderful children."

"Thank you, Father," I reply. "I don't know how much we owe to luck as opposed to skill, but you're right. We do have four wonderful kids."

I turn away from Father Byrum and scan the dance floor. One by one the kids come into view out of the writhing mass of bodies. First Jennie—still my little girl even though she turned twenty-nine this past Thursday—with her beautiful, lustrous, thick brown hair, her wonderfully warm and ready smile, and her seemingly endless capacity to love. Then John—good-looking, big, powerful, a rock, loyal to the core, and full of quiet, steadfast love for his family. Then Will—tall, handsome, sensitive, frighteningly intelligent, imbued with love for the beauty and power of words, and more like his dad than either of us care to admit. And last but not least, Amanda—tall, willowy and already stunning with her long flowing blond hair, sharp-tongued, quick-witted and still an unknown as to what she will become—but with such great promise.

Father Byrum is right, I think, nodding in silent agreement. *We have four wonderful children.*

A soft hand curves around the back of my neck. "Hey, good-lookin'." Fingers glide through the hair that curls over my shirt collar. "Wanna dance?"

A song by Norah Jones is playing now. My kind of music. I look up over my shoulder at Nancy standing next to me, looking very glamorous in her sleek, black strapless gown. I smile and look at our children out on the dance floor one more time before pushing back my chair.

"I missed you," I say as I take Nancy's hand and lead her into the midst of swaying couples.

She slides into my arms and rests her cheek against my neck. Her body melts into mine, and I close my eyes.

God, she smells good.

Acknowledgments

First, I would like to thank longtime friends Mike and Monique Stief, who over dinner one night in Düsseldorf, Germany, led me to believe, first by their questions, then by their tears on hearing my answers, that maybe, just maybe, my story would be all I hoped.

Second, sincere thanks to first reader Mickey Clement, author of *The Irish Princess* and *Twelve Shades of Crimson*, for her wonderfully encouraging comments after reading my story and for her valuable input on how to present my book to agents and publishers.

Third, I would like to thank our eldest daughter, Jennie, for her help in putting the finished manuscript into the format demanded by agents and publishers. I can type, but computer-savvy I am not. Thanks to Jennie, no one ever knew.

Fourth, I thank John Lewis, my publisher and president of Oakley Publishing, for seeing the beauty of my story and wanting to publish my book.

Last, but certainly not least, I would like to thank Nancy, my wife of twenty-six years. Nancy told me many times I had a way with words; then one night in Antigua she told me I should write a book. When I said I had nothing to write about, Nancy suggested I write about my life. When I said no one would want to read about a life as ordinary as mine, she suggested I write about Peg and us. Ever my most honest critic, Nancy said my first draft was terrible; then she proceeded to tell me what it needed. She pored over the next draft and the next and the next, each time pushing me to write better—even when I wanted to stop. Good enough was never good enough; she wanted my best. Without her encouragement, patience, faith in me and unconditional love for me, *Rules Get Broken* would never have been written. Thank you, Nan, for all that you did and all that you are.